SOCIAL PATTERNS
IN PRE-CLASSIC MESOAMERICA

SOCIAL PATTERNS
IN PRE-CLASSIC MESOAMERICA

A Symposium at Dumbarton Oaks
9 and 10 October 1993

David C. Grove and Rosemary A. Joyce, *Editors*

Dumbarton Oaks Research Library and Collection
Washington, D.C.

Library of Congress Cataloging-in-Publication Data

Social patterns in pre-classic Mesoamerica : a symposium at Dumbarton Oaks, 9 and 10
    October 1993 / David C. Grove and Rosemary A. Joyce, editors.
        p.   cm.
    Includes index.
    ISBN 0-88402-252-8
    1. Olmecs—Congresses. 2. Mexico—Antiquities—Congresses. I. Grove, David C.
II. Joyce, Rosemary A., 1956- . III. Dumbarton Oaks.
F1219.8.056S6   1998
972' .01—dc21
                                                                98-25729
                                                                CIP

Contents

Contents

Preface

MORE THAN A QUARTER-CENTURY separates the first Pre-Columbian conference at Dumbarton Oaks, on the Olmec, and the 1993 symposium from which this present volume evolved. Comparing the earlier, slim volume from the 1967 conference and this later, larger one, the advances in our understanding of early Mesoamerica are notable, not only in terms of more detailed examinations but also in the number of fine scholars at work.

The Olmec volume was produced at a time when broad brush strokes were still filling in the outline of the nature and dimensions of Olmec culture. It concentrated on large sites, particularly, La Venta and San Lorenzo, looked at regional patterns relating to the Olmec heartland, and addressed such basic questions as the relationship of Olmec and Maya art and the Olmec were-jaguar motif.

This volume, edited by Rosemary A. Joyce and David C. Grove, like its predecessor is both a summation of work that has been carried out over a long period of time and a signpost pointing the way for future studies. In it, we can see the reflection not only of more than two decades' research on early Mesoamerica, but also the theoretical influences of the past twenty-five years. Issues regarding gender, social identity, and landscape archaeology are present, as are the analysis of mortuary practices, questions of social hierarchy, and conjunctive studies of art and society that are in the best tradition of scholarship at Dumbarton Oaks.

Another Dumbarton Oaks publication, in 1981, *The Olmec and Their Neighbors: Essays in Memory of Matthew W. Stirling*, expressed the efflorescence of Olmec studies in the great richness and detail that became possible in the relatively brief period between its publication and the first Olmec conference. Now, we have reached yet another stage in understanding the Pre-Classic. The authors of the chapters in this volume have framed their discussions of early cultures to address broad questions regarding the Pre-Classic throughout a great portion of Mesoamerica. In doing this, they have concentrated on issues of social patterns that represent a new phase and a new view of the issues at stake. And while the debate on the Olmec as the "mother culture" may not be settled, in some quarters, the approach expressed here offers a particularly valuable way of examining the past that directly contributes to discussions of the origins of social complexity in Mesoamerica, Latin America, and beyond. It has only been through the careful and sometimes tedious and difficult research of scholars in both the old and new volumes, over many years, that we have been able to reach such a point in our analyses.

Considerable labor also has gone into the production of this book, which was begun under the guidance of my predecessor as director of Pre-Columbian Studies, Elizabeth H. Boone. It should also be noted that Richard A. Diehl was acting director of Pre-Columbian Studies in 1993, when the conference took place. My thanks to Professors Boone and Diehl and Grove and Joyce for the opportunity to work with this wonderful project that marks a significant milestone in our study of the Pre-Columbian world.

Jeffrey Quilter
Dumbarton Oaks

Asking New Questions about the Mesoamerican Pre-Classic

ROSEMARY A. JOYCE
UNIVERSITY OF CALIFORNIA, BERKELEY

DAVID C. GROVE
UNIVERSITY OF ILLINOIS, URBANA–CHAMPAIGN

B ETWEEN THE INITIAL RECOGNITION THAT THE elaborate art style known from Gulf Coast sites such as La Venta, Tres Zapotes, and San Lorenzo was early in the sequence of Mesoamerican cultures, and the Dumbarton Oaks symposium for which these papers were prepared, research on the Pre-Classic period was in many ways preoccupied with the problem of defining "Olmec." To some extent, this situation reflected the real distinctiveness of features that have come loosely to be labeled Olmec in the development of Mesoamerican societies. More than for any later period, Mesoamerica's Pre-Classic sites were characterized by unprecedented developments, including the development of monumental architecture and public art, whose creation was credited to Olmec people or Olmec influence. Also initially fueling concern with defining Olmec was the patchy nature of the archaeological record of the Pre-Classic. Few sites had been investigated in any detail, and those studies tended to focus on the more monumental features that first attracted attention.

The necessity to understand the changes that took place during the Pre-Classic and the paucity of good contextual data to address this task helped foster the creation of models that stressed common features at the expense of differences, and gave a singular active role in cultural evolution to the presumed originators of Olmec art. With an expansion of projects producing primary data about Pre-Classic life in many areas of Mesoamerica, the integrity of a pan-Mesoamerican Olmec culture and the significance of Olmec influence became points of considerable contention. Debate about the definition of Olmec art, style, and culture, and the role that any of these had in the general developments of the Pre-Classic, was amply reflected in the different points of view expressed by contributors to *The Olmec and Their Neighbors* (Benson 1981) and *Regional Perspectives on the Olmec* (Sharer and Grove 1989).

The papers included in these volumes incorporated data from extensive field projects in the Basin of Mexico, Morelos, Oaxaca, and Chiapas. These projects complemented Gulf Coast research centered initially on La Venta and Tres Zapotes and later on San Lorenzo. The results of these research projects provided a reasonable level of chronological control as well as contextual information for a variety of kinds of activities. They also fostered specialized analyses to address questions of exchange directly. Remaining disagreements about the nature and significance of the Olmec in Pre-Classic Mesoamerica aired in these volumes seem unlikely to be settled by more fieldwork or new analyses of existing data, as they reflect basic differences in the interpretation of the same evidence.

Our purpose in organizing the conference for which the papers in this volume were prepared was to go beyond the terms set by the existing Olmec debate and ask new questions about the Pre-Classic. We begin with the assumption that repeated behaviors should be recognizable in the now abundant and well-documented material remains from good contexts in Pre-Classic sites. We use the contextual data for repetitive behavior as evidence for exploring the meaning objects and places accrued through their use in social life. We argue that patterns in the archaeological record can be understood as material traces of (among other things) the marking of social boundaries, the development of distinct social identities, and the enactment of ceremony. This volume begins to explore the social mechanisms of the radical transformations underlying emerging social stratification that characterized the Mesoamerican Pre-Classic.

THE PRE-CLASSIC REVOLUTION

More than any period of time that followed, the Mesoamerican Pre-Classic witnessed the development of unprecedented features in site form, artifact inventory, and use of materials. Every later Mesoamerican society developed within a framework that was laid in the Pre-Classic. The material features that we see archaeologically as typical of Mesoamerica took their essential form during this period. By the end of the Pre-Classic, monumental architecture in the form of large pyramidal structures was a general feature of the Mesoamerican landscape. The centers visually marked by these monumental buildings were further distinguished by symbolic elaboration embodied in the ornamentation of architecture and in the creation of large-scale freestanding monuments that marked out spaces. Similar media were used to surround the centers with a symbolically rich landscape. Within the centers and hinterlands that thus took form, differences in the scale and elaboration of residences, in the forms and materials of craft products used in daily life and ceremony, and in the tasks carried out by different people formed the basis for defining social identities that continued to typify complex society throughout the remainder of Mesoamerica's Pre-Hispanic history.

We asked participants in the symposium to address aspects of these developments using data specific to particular areas, in order to illuminate processes that might have more general significance for the Pre-Classic as a whole. The phenomena in which we are interested vary in scale. At the most intimate level, the origins of social complexity must be sought in shifts in social relations within and between households. Even in supposedly egalitarian societies, there are sharp disparities in the respect and authority accorded different people. Such factors as age and experience, skill and knowledge, may become recognized bases for certain individuals to be accorded special value and recognition. While the resolution of the archaeological record seldom allows us to identify and follow the individual, we can examine the arenas where differences between individuals are institutionalized and look for the material media through which differences in identity are given imperishable symbolic form.

At a slightly wider scale, the construction of architecture of unprecedented size and form can arguably be taken as an indication of community-level efforts. While it is always possible to suggest that a complex public work could have been carried out by a small number of people working for a long period of time, archaeological data suggest that much of the public construction that we see in Pre-Classic Mesoamerica was accomplished over fairly short periods of time. Regardless of the number of people involved and the length of time required, building these features depended on people undertaking a wholly new kind of activity. Once constructed, monumental buildings changed forever the form of the place and the spatial habits of those dwelling there. These new constructions became part of specialized settings for ceremony and features of reference for everyday movement. They established a difference between places that was part of a deliberate creation of a new social landscape.

The newly differentiated people involved in habitual action within the freshly transformed landscapes of the Pre-Classic were ultimately engaged at a very wide scale in interactions we see archaeologically in the contemporaneous spread of materials and symbolic media from Mexico to Honduras and El Salvador. Through the creation of the networks that linked distant Pre-Classic communities, Mesoamerica itself took recognizable form. The papers in this volume do engage with wider issues of the nature of Pre-Classic Mesoamerica, which have generally been seen as aspects of the Olmec problem. But they do so by first examining the local-level, and even household-level, forces that fueled the formation of long-distance links.

CHANGING ASPECTS OF PRE-CLASSIC SOCIAL IDENTITY

The small-scale setting of probable remains of domestic life is the critical place, the preexisting context for the beginnings of all the transformations that occur during the Pre-Classic period. Residential sites were the location of activities through which social groups reproduced themselves, materially through subsistence and craft production and socially through ceremonies marking social boundaries and transitions. Behavioral contrasts between the inhabitants of different residential groups resulted in variation in, among other things, burial form and contents, evidence of craft production, and use of symbolism. Through such behavioral contrasts and the relative value accorded some kinds of activities, distinct social identities, including those between elites and commoners, took form.

The papers that open this volume all concern this scale of Pre-Classic societies. Drawing on burial data, Rosemary A. Joyce explores variation in aspects of mortuary ritual. She finds that distinctions are more evident between clusters of burials than between individual burials, emphasizing the investment of the social group in the ceremonies that resulted in burial assemblages. Taking the social group responsible for clusters of burials as a corporate participant in competitive and cooperative social relations, Joyce identifies three aspects of burials as potentially indicative of social group interests. First, there are clear differences in the degree to which different groups engaged in mortuary practices that resulted in the burial of resources including pottery vessels, figurines and musical instruments, costume ornaments, and stone and bone tools. It appears that, even in the absence of wide gulfs in wealth and status that can be identified after the emergence of elites, there were already sharp divisions in the ability or motivation of different social groups to engage in competitive displays.

Among those groups that did engage in elaborate burial displays, two notable features can be isolated, both with implications for wider Pre-Classic concerns. The inclusion of tools and raw materials for different kinds of productive activities in burials draws attention to the probable importance of craft production organized at the small-scale social group level in the emergence of social stratification. The singling out of some burials through costumes incorporating exotic materials that have the most standardized form of any burial goods known from Pre-Classic Mesoamerica makes clear that social groups engaged in competitive displays were forming external alliances to mobilize resources from outside the local social system.

Structured burial data like those used by Joyce are one of the more abundant sources for study of repetitive behavior in small-scale social settings of Pre-Classic societies. Norman Hammond contributes an updating of the chapter summarizing burials and caches from the landmark publication of the archaeology of Cuello (Hammond 1991; see Robin and Hammond 1991 for the original version, and Robin 1989 for details of this analysis). Cuello has been a crucial site in the continuing debate about the integration of the Early and Middle Pre-Classic Maya Lowlands in the wider Mesoamerican world. At Cuello, Hammond notes evidence of processes of stratification and formalization of ritual parallel to those taking place elsewhere in the late Early Pre-Classic and Middle Pre-Classic Mesoamerican world.

The inhabitants of Cuello initially buried their dead in what appear to be household compound clusters, with all ages and sexes represented. Hammond describes the earliest burials as having some of the least standardized burial goods of any period, consistent with the general impression for contemporary Mesoamerica of significant individualization and differentiation between house compounds in ritual practices. But at the same time, Hammond describes a range of practices comparable to those Joyce notes in her examination of burials from contemporary Tlatilco. While apparently abstaining from the use of the specific symbolism that spreads across Mesoamerica in the Early and Middle Pre-Classic, the lowland Maya society represented at Cuello already accepted pan-Mesoamerican standards of value and participated in the long-distance exchange and craft patronage necessary to supply early Mesoamerican luxuries. Indeed, Hammond suggests that some of the jade items in these burials were products of exchange with centers fully participating in the use of pan-Mesoamerican symbolism in the Gulf Coast. By the beginning of the Late Pre-Classic period, both the use of space and burial practices signaled a formalization of ritual and the emergence of a segment of society distinguished by the use of human remains as burial inclusions.

Joyce Marcus explores two aspects of social differentiation in Pre-Classic Oaxaca: segregation in ritual between men and women, and the shared veneration of ancestors by men and women of different segments of the population. Marcus identifies ten specialized buildings in Early Pre-Classic Oaxaca which she interprets as sites where men commemorated their individually named and recalled ancestors. She draws attention to the singling out of some males for burial in a distinctive seated position, a format also noted by Hammond for the males who were the center of mass burials accompanying the construction of monumental architecture in Late Pre-Classic Cuello. Marcus identifies seated male burials as probable foci of ancestor veneration. Her argument that these ancestors were preferentially venerated by men draws on previous discussions of the distribution in burials in Oaxaca of vessels with complex iconography that she identifies with Lightning and Earth (Marcus 1989; Flannery and Marcus 1994). She notes that in Oaxaca such vessels were never deposited with adult females, and burials containing them were spatially segregated in different areas. These observations imply the existence of two spatially fixed and differentiated groups in which males shared the prerogative of displaying the symbols of an important supernatural.

Remarkably, throughout the burial material considered by Joyce, Hammond, and Marcus, there is a decided balance between features that are strictly local and others that reflect participation in more widespread practices. Marcus notes burials from Copan that share iconography she identifies with Earth and Lightning descent groups in Oaxaca. Others (Porter 1953; Longyear 1969; Healy 1974; Fash 1985, 1991; Joyce 1992, n.d.) have previously noted correspondences between iconography of vessels from Copan and other Honduran sites, and examples from Mexican archaeological sites including San José Mogote and Tlatilco. Joyce (1992, 1996, n.d.) suggests that in Honduras these and other pan-Mesoamerican motifs were used to assert distinctions between different local groups relating to craft patronage and participation in long-distance exchange, rather than a codified division between two descent groups. At Tlatilco, Paul Tolstoy (1989) noted a tendency for such motifs to occur in specific burial clusters, but his evidence suggested an emphasis on the maternal, rather than paternal, line. While pottery vessels, figurines, and costume are incorporated in burials across Pre-Classic Mesoamerica, burials are simultaneously distinguished by use of local objects in patterns that lack broad distribution. The strongest shared pattern is the use of certain materials, especially greenstone and shell, for ornaments. Pre-Classic burials reflect subtle social differentiation within the small-scale setting of the residential compound mobilizing common practices and standards of value for local ends.

Julia A. Hendon reviews the evidence for common and distinctive patterns in the elaboration of Pre-Classic residential compounds. She emphasizes that analysis of practices whose outcomes can be observed in the material record is ultimately more fruitful than the search for rules of social structure. By emphasizing that group identity is not a given, but needs to be formed and maintained, Hendon draws our attention to one of the implicit social processes of the Pre-Classic: the institutionalization of internal social differentiation between kinship groups. Hendon views the abundant evidence for craft production within the residential setting as an indication of possible competition between residential groups, and between individuals within them, for social distinction, a perspective also extending to participation in ritual within the setting of the residential group (compare Clark and Blake 1994; Clark and Gosser 1995).

Hendon suggests that material from early middens at Uaxactun documents craft production of textiles and shell ornaments. Noting that textile production in later Mesoamerica is virtually universally associated as a specialized practice with female gender, she implicitly identifies the Pre-Classic as the period during which the definition of gender identities may have been formalized. In this regard, the notable disjunction between the prominence of females in Pre-Classic figurine imagery, and their virtual absence in monumental imagery, is brought into sharper relief. Rather than simply reflecting a given reality of sociopolitical organization, in which men had privileged access to positions of power, this disjunction may be a means by which Pre-Classic societies began to create arenas in which women's participation was played down. Hendon, highlighting the probable use of figurines in household-level ritual at Uaxactun, draws attention to the importance of the house compound as an arena of action accessible to both men and women in the Pre-Classic, when separate formal spaces for political and religious ceremony did not already exist.

Marcus interprets the Oaxacan data in a similar fashion, assuming that specialized buildings functioned as lineage shrines for men, while women practiced distinctive ancestor veneration in other locales. Marcus suggests that figurines were made and used by women in house-based veneration of recently deceased, preferentially female, ancestors. Her model is one of several recent analyses of Pre-Classic figurines that view these as media for ritual action and negotiation of social status. Ann Cyphers (1993), like Marcus, identifies a majority of figurines from Chalcatzingo as representations of female subjects, arguing that they symbolize stages in the female life cycle and might have been used in house-based rites of passage. Richard Lesure (1997) identifies a wider range of gender, age, and status differentiations in figurine assemblages from the Pacific Coast, and suggests they reify distinctions between elders who achieved status through ritual and the younger members of their kin groups whose lives they controlled. Joyce (1993, this volume) identifies the Pre-Classic Playa de los Muertos figurines of the Ulua River Valley in Honduras as media for the permanent recording of individual personae enacted through distinctive body ornamentation, particularly of female subjects. While in each area the actual composition of figurine assemblages varies substantially, and consequently models for their social effects are equally varied, production and use of these highly distinctive assemblages in house compounds and in burials are at the same time fairly common aspects of Pre-Classic Mesoamerican traditions.

The production of shell ornaments is the second major craft activity represented at Pre-Classic Uaxactun. This craft activity contributed to differentiation in costume practices like that evident in mortuary data discussed by Hammond, Marcus, and Joyce. Michael Love finds evidence of differential consumption of precisely these kinds of ornaments in conjunction with practices that internally divide the space of sites in Pacific coastal Guatemala. This is not simply a matter of privileged access to, or appropriation of, luxury goods or the products of long-distance exchange and craft production. Rather, as Hendon and Love explicitly argue, the selective use of such materials was a means by which certain individuals actively set themselves apart from others in their communities. Joyce's analysis of practices typical of clusters of burials at Tlatilco extends this analysis to distinctions between groups, not solely between individuals.

The setting of craft activities at Uaxactun within a Pre-Classic household that later features unique buildings, possible stages for ceremony, raises the probability that economic activities within the household were at the heart of the development of social stratification during the Mesoamerican Pre-Classic. Hendon notes that the elaboration of these special-purpose buildings at Uaxactun, and elsewhere in the Maya Lowlands, distinguished them from other quotidian structures in the same groups, providing a distinctive setting for action. Marcus documents equivalent architectural elaboration of otherwise small-scale buildings she calls lineage houses. Hendon and Marcus make the point that households already contained within themselves both means to create distinctions (through limitation of participation in production and ritual) and grounds, including age and sex, for social ranking. At the same time, the spatial setting of the residence offered profound opportunities for the reformulation of the experience of everyday life that, projected to a larger scale, is reflected in the Pre-Classic innovations of monumental architecture and monumental art.

BUILDING THE NEW SOCIAL LANDSCAPE

The small-scale, face-to-face context of the residential compound was necessarily the setting for the development of social distinctions in Pre-Classic Mesoamerica, because it existed before other kinds of marked spatial locations. One of the most disruptive aspects of the social transformations that took place during this period was the elaboration of new forms of architecture—an entirely new pattern of construction of monumental architecture and settings of monumental art creating unprecedented kinds of space in Pre-Classic sites.

Michael Love provides a detailed consideration of the process and effects of the introduction of monumental architecture. He emphasizes the central importance of practices that differentially include and exclude members of society in creating internal social differentiation. He argues that the new constructions evident in Pre-Classic sites created different zones subject to differential access, serving to discriminate between people in ways not possible prior to the existence of those arenas of action. Drawing on data from the Pacific Coast, he documents the beginnings of this process in the elaboration of what appears to be a very large residence which was the setting for more public activity than was typical of other houses. This is followed in the region by the construction of freestanding mounds of monumental scale that Love suggests may have been built as shrines or temples for specific residential groups whose houses encompass the larger structures. By the end of the Pre-Classic, monumental architecture formed new specialized spatial settings including ballcourts and enclosed patios.

Love emphasizes the ways that new monumental construction would have transformed day-to-day experience, ranging from requiring modification of previous patterns of movement through sites to creating differences between those with differential access to the new features. The architectural innovations created new spatial settings that controlled and habituated residents to newly defined, or at least acknowledged, internal social distinctions. Love puts special emphasis on the way that monumental architecture created a center and peripheries. He argues that differences in material culture within households parallel changes at the larger scale, creating an elite distinguished by consumption of stylistically distinctive materials and exotic materials. Hendon echoes some of these themes, arguing that the construction of specialized structures as settings for ritual within the small-scale residential group was in part a competitive response to the construction of other settings for ceremony outside the confines of the house compound. Hammond's description of the correlation between new monumental construction (of a platform, pyramid, and stela complex) at Cuello in the Late Pre-Classic testifies to the same injection of spatial segregation in the intimate confines of residential space. At Cuello this transformation is accompanied by innovations in the scale and form of caches and burials, including the differentiation of some males as subject to privileged burial and other persons as objects for inclusion in graves.

The inextricable connections that Love and Hendon illuminate between transformations within the small-scale, face-to-face context of the household and the large-scale settings that monumental architecture and art newly created are also fundamental to the arguments advanced by Ann Cyphers. Cyphers' work at San Lorenzo has documented the presence of a monument workshop associated with the remains of a residential group. Large-scale and special materials distinguish at least one of the buildings in this group. Cyphers notes the possibility that the workshop was joined to this building by a walled enclosure, creating a segregated physical setting for attached craft specialization.

Cyphers also introduces a discussion of the use of monumental sculpture to mark locations outside the center as of particular significance. She characterizes Loma del Zapote, 3 km from the San Lorenzo plateau, as a hinterland of that center. The monuments whose placement, alteration, and relationships she documents at Loma del Zapote were material media for the incorporation of a wider spatial expanse into a social landscape. As Love argues for the Pacific Coast, through monumental construction and the use of stone sculpture, the scale of social space was broadened and at the same time broken up into different kinds of places. The different possibilities for action posed by the variety of places newly defined through the use of architecture and monuments are at the core of the social differentiation that we recognize as the distinctive product of the Pre-Classic revolution.

Emphasizing the construction in Pre-Classic Maya sites of more formalized house platform groups, and of monumental constructions joined to each other by processional ways, William M. Ringle demonstrates that here, as in the Pacific coastal region discussed by Love, new forms of construction transformed the space within the center into more differentiated settings. Ringle argues that concurrent with the construction of new spatial settings, there is a shift in the location of ritual action from the house compound to the areas of monumental construction and even to the processional ways themselves. The multiplication of different spatial settings within sites would also have increased the grounds for distinctions between the individuals acting within those settings. As Joyce, Hammond, Marcus, Hendon, and Love show, archaeological remains from Pre-Classic households demonstrate the existence of a number of cross-cutting distinctions established in part through the practice of ritual and craft production. The segregation of action in space that created the broader Pre-Classic landscape was accomplished through material changes that began in the households with the construction of distinctive kinds of residential settings.

GIVING MEANING TO THE PRE-CLASSIC LANDSCAPE

Ringle addresses key questions about the meanings that monumental architecture must have had to have engaged the necessary communal labor for construction. He argues that among the Pre-Classic Maya it is not possible to demonstrate the existence, *before* these works were undertaken, of an elite that could have exercised coercive power. He suggests that buildings were seen as fixed points in a flow of energy or spirit through space and time, and had significant value to the people who constructed them as materializations of that flow and the union of space and time it accomplished. He argues that within the "cityscape," processions between different architectural settings were enactments of social relations given sacred sanction through ritual.

The incorporation of a broader landscape in Pre-Classic societies was also clearly accompanied by the impression of meaning on space and on different natural features. Cave sites with Pre-Classic art, such as Oxtotitlan, Guerrero (Grove 1970), extend to an extreme periphery the construction of different kinds of places that Love suggests is made possible by the development of monumental architecture and art. To these cave sites, we can now add the likelihood that water sources were incorporated in Pre-Classic sacred geography. At Laguna Manatí, Ponciano Ortíz and María del Carmen Rodríguez have documented one of the most complex sequences of Pre-Classic ritual yet known at such a marked site on the landscape. The highly structured nature of the deposits at this site suggests the routinization of the ceremonies conducted there. Ann Cyphers suggests that a central theme of monument use at San Lorenzo was the control of water. Ortíz and Rodríguez compare the setting of Laguna Manatí with other Pre-Classic sites placed in relation to natural hills, such as Chalcatzingo's location at the base of Cerro Chalcatzingo. Their argument echoes Ringle's explicit identification, based on later Classic Maya data, of pyramids as built representations of sacred mountains.

David C. Grove takes on the systematic task of providing an analysis of the incorporation of features of a sacred geography into the social world and of replication of these in sacred landscapes. He explores the complex intersections of center and periphery, architecture and natural features at a series of Pre-Classic centers. His argument extends beyond the general propositions of Love, Ringle, and Cyphers to incorporate more specific features of the symbolic and representational content of monumental art used in creating sacred landscapes.

Grove shows that the monuments that occur in different segments of the differentiated spaces created by placements of architecture feature particular themes or groups of themes. A general distinction between monuments with mythic narratives and those with images of rulership is repeatedly associated with the segregation of a political center from its periphery. Distinctive spatial settings in the center are further embellished and given specific inflections of meaning through the distributions of particular kinds of monuments. Grove's analysis in fact suggests that one of the motivations for the creation of Pre-Classic monumental art may have been the desire by new elites to reinforce limitations on free action in new spaces within sites created by innovations in architecture.

Grove argues that monumental art marked the periphery of individual centers as equivalent to the encompassing natural world, and through depiction of cosmological scenes, as equivalent to the distant past (compare Helms 1979, 1988). This particularly dramatic use of art may be an unusually clear example of the way the limitations of action in new spaces were defined through symbolic means. Marking a spatial periphery as a supernatural location, the monumental art discussed by Grove also advances the claim that only those competent to deal with the supernatural can deal with spatial distance.

CONCLUSION

The impact of the spatial reorganization of Pre-Classic sites through innovations in monumental architecture and art is most evident at the small scale of the household and the medium scale of the political center with its periphery. But the Pre-Classic revolution also involved, for the first time, the definition of an even larger scale that we recognize today as Mesoamerica. For elites with the asserted ability to deal with the supernatural world and ancestors placed symbolically beyond the edge of the individual polity, long-distance connections assumed a great weight. The material display of such connections embodied in portable art with common iconographic themes and in the use of materials such as greenstone and iron ore, especially for distinctive costumes, is evidence for the emergence of this ultimate sphere of interaction in the Mesoamerican Pre-Classic.

The papers in this volume contribute to identifying those factors that ultimately define Mesoamerican civilization as an object of study. We hope that the dimensions of variation they single out—internal differentiations within the face-to-face confines of the household, the division of space through the use of monumental architecture and art, and the marking of different spatial domains through symbolic media—will continue to engage the attention of scholars exploring the distinctive phenomena of the Pre-Classic period.

BIBLIOGRAPHY

BENSON, ELIZABETH P.
1981   *The Olmec and Their Neighbors: Essays in Memory of Matthew W. Stirling.* Dumbarton Oaks, Washington, D.C.

CLARK, JOHN E., AND MICHAEL BLAKE
1994   The Power of Prestige: Competitive Generosity and the Emergence of Rank Societies in Lowland Mesoamerica. In *Factional Competition and Political Development in the New World* (Elizabeth M. Brumfiel and John W. Fox, eds.): 17–30. Cambridge University Press, Cambridge.

CLARK, JOHN E., AND DENNIS GOSSER
1995   Reinventing Mesoamerica's First Pottery. In *The Emergence of Pottery: Technology and Innovation in Ancient Societies* (William Barnett and John Hoopes, eds.): 209–222. Smithsonian Institution Press, Washington, D.C.

CYPHERS GUILLÉN, ANN
1993   Women, Rituals, and Social Dynamics at Ancient Chalcatzingo. *Latin American Antiquity* 4: 209–224.

FASH, WILLIAM L.
1985   La secuencia de ocupación del grupo 9N-8, Las Sepulturas, Copán, y sus implicaciones teóricas. *Yaxkin* 8 (1–2): 135–150. Tegucigalpa.
1991   *Scribes, Warriors and Kings: The City of Copán and the Ancient Maya.* Thames and Hudson, London.

FLANNERY, KENT V., AND JOYCE MARCUS
1994   *Early Formative Pottery of the Valley of Oaxaca.* Prehistory and Human Ecology of the Valley of Oaxaca, vol. 10. Memoirs of the Anthropology Museum 27, University of Michigan. Ann Arbor.

GROVE, DAVID C.
1970   *The Olmec Paintings of Oxtotitlan Cave, Guerrero, Mexico.* Studies in Pre-Columbian Art and Archaeology 6. Dumbarton Oaks, Washington, D.C.

HAMMOND, NORMAN (ED.)
1991   *Cuello: An Early Maya Community in Belize.* Cambridge University Press, Cambridge.

HEALY, PAUL
1974   The Cuyamel Caves: Preclassic Sites in Northeast Honduras. *American Antiquity* 39: 433–437.

HELMS, MARY
1979   *Ancient Panama: Chiefs in Search of Power.* University of Texas Press, Austin.

1988   *Ulysses' Sail: An Ethnographic Odyssey of Power, Knowledge, and Geographical Distance.* Princeton University Press, Princeton.

JOYCE, ROSEMARY
1992   Innovation, Communication, and the Archaeological Record: A Reassessment of Middle Formative Honduras. *Journal of the Steward Anthropological Society* 20 (1–2): 235–256.

1993 Women's Work: Images of Production and Reproduction in Pre-Hispanic Southern Central America. *Current Anthropology* 34: 255–274.

1996 Social Dynamics of Exchange: Changing Patterns in the Honduran Archaeological Record. In *Chieftains, Power, and Trade: Regional Interaction in the Intermediate Area of the Americas* (Carl Henrik Langebaek and Felipe Cardenas-Arroyo, eds.): 31–45. Departamento de Antropología, Universidad de los Andes, Bogotá, Colombia.

n.d. Innovation, Communication, and the Archaeological Record: A Reassessment of Middle Formative Honduras. Paper presented at the annual meeting of the Society for American Archaeology, New Orleans, 1991.

LESURE, RICHARD

1997 Figurines and Social Identities in Early Sedentary Societies of Coastal Chiapas, Mexico, 1550–800 B.C. In *Women in Prehistory: North America and Mesoamerica* (Cheryl Claassen and Rosemary Joyce, eds.): 227–248. University of Pennsylvania Press, Philadelphia.

LONGYEAR, JOHN M., III

1969 The Problem of Olmec Influences in the Pottery of Western Honduras. *Proceedings of Thirty-Eighth International Congress of Americanists* 1: 491–498. Stuttgart and Munich.

MARCUS, JOYCE

1989 Zapotec Chiefdoms and the Nature of Formative Religions. In *Regional Perspectives on the Olmec* (Robert J. Sharer and David C. Grove, eds.): 148–197. Cambridge University Press, Cambridge.

PORTER, MURIEL N.

1953 *Tlatilco and the Preclassic Cultures of the New World.* Viking Fund Publications in Anthropology 19. Wenner-Gren Foundation for Anthropological Research, New York.

ROBIN, CYNTHIA

1989 *Preclassic Maya Burials at Cuello, Belize.* British Archaeological Reports International Series 480. BAR, Oxford.

ROBIN, CYNTHIA, AND NORMAN HAMMOND

1991 Ritual and Ideology: Burial Practices. In *Cuello: An Early Maya Community in Belize* (Norman Hammond, ed.): 204–225. Cambridge University Press, Cambridge.

SHARER, ROBERT J., AND DAVID C. GROVE

1989 *Regional Perspectives on the Olmec.* Cambridge University Press, Cambridge.

TOLSTOY, PAUL

1989 Coapexco and Tlatilco: Sites with Olmec Materials in the Basin of Mexico. In *Regional Perspectives on the Olmec* (Robert J. Sharer and David C. Grove, eds.): 85–121. Cambridge University Press, Cambridge.

Social Dimensions of Pre-Classic Burials

ROSEMARY A. JOYCE

UNIVERSITY OF CALIFORNIA, BERKELEY

B URIALS ARE THE MATERIAL RESIDUE OF specific practices carried out in the past. These highly structured data are our evidence for variation in mortuary ritual, reflecting not only characteristics of the individual interred but also significant dimensions of social relations in past communities. For Pre-Classic Mesoamerica, specific mortuary practices have been shown to vary with other indications of differential social power, or rank (e.g., Tolstoy 1989; Grove and Gillespie 1992; Merry de Morales 1987). Analysis of the social relations evident in mortuary practices is one avenue to begin to understand how social differences were created and endowed with social value through distinctive practices in Pre-Classic societies.

Drawing on selected samples of burials from different regions of Mesoamerica spanning the Early to Middle Pre-Classic, I will pursue two basic questions. First, what kinds of practices are represented, and what are their implications for the scale and nature of social relations shaped through mortuary ritual? Second, how did some practices come to distinguish certain individuals and abstract them from the small-scale social context of the residential group? In addressing these questions, I draw attention to the way mortuary practices in different settings within communities contributed to creating residential and communitywide scales of identity and difference. I single out the inclusion of costume and pottery serving vessels in burials as reflecting individual differentiation on the one hand and group participation in mortuary rituals on the other. Finally, I argue that shifts in scale, accompanied by some standardization of other mortuary practices, are evidence of the emergence of individuals claiming and being credited with wider authority and positions of community importance, a key feature of the Pre-Classic development of social complexity.

I use the term "residential group" throughout to label the people who resided together in the groups of buildings arranged around or adjacent to exterior workspace, the residential compounds that characterize Pre-Classic Mesoamerican sites. While I assume that core members were related through kinship links, I do not assume any particular kind of kinship system, nor that all members of the residential group were kin. My model for social relations in residential groups is the "house societies" defined by Claude Levi-Strauss (1983), further discussed by James Boone (1990: 213–218) and ethnographically illustrated by Susan McKinnon (1991), among others. While the concept has perhaps best been illustrated by ethnographers working in Indonesia and, although not explicitly so labeled, in Oceania (e.g., Weiner 1976; Munn 1986), Levi-Strauss' original formulation was based on societies of the northwest United States and other native American groups and was also applied to African, Japanese, and medieval European societies.

The "house" was defined as "a corporate body holding an estate made up of both material and immaterial wealth, which perpetuates itself through the transmission of its name, its goods, and its titles down a real or imaginary line considered legitimate as long as this continuity can express itself in the language of kinship or of affinity and, most often, of both" (Levi-Strauss 1983: 174). Boone (1990: 215) argues that "houses are ranked both internally and externally by birth order, by anisogamy, and by other indices of differential transmissions of estates, heirlooms, titles, prerogatives, and renown." Hierarchy in house societies is contested, constantly under negotiation through alliances and exchanges, negotiations in which individual status and house status may part ways (McKinnon 1991: 259–276).

For my purposes, key factors in this model are that the "house," a cooperative coresidential economic unit with internal ranking and some centralized decision-making authority, seeks through alliances to improve its situation vis-à-vis other houses, while at the same time members of the house (Clark and Blake's [1994] "aggrandizers") seek to improve their individual standing with whatever resources are available (see Joyce 1996). In using house societies as my model, I am assuming that Pre-Classic Mesoamerica initially had little centralized authority above the level of some such small-scale social group; that the interests of individuals were sometimes advanced with those of their group and sometimes held back by within-group obligations; and that in the negotiations between houses, both house and individual identities were defined.

MORTUARY PRACTICE: ETHNOGRAPHIC OBSERVATIONS

Ethnographic accounts of mortuary rituals usually present deaths as disruptions in existing social relations, and burials as the occasion of efforts designed to heal the breach of society (Bloch and Parry 1982; Hertz 1960; van Gennep 1960). Such attitudes are not universal. An analysis of variation in burial practices between groups of hunter-gatherers (Woodburn 1982) suggests that the perception of danger and the expenditure of effort on burial elaboration are related to the degree to which delayed obligations between people are significant within a specific society. In other words, where members of society count on individuals for future benefits, death represents a loss of predictable cooperation that increases the emotional experience of loss (Kan 1989: 165–177).

This argument should not simply be reduced to a kind of utilitarianism. The elaboration of mortuary ritual in these instances is a special case of the more general reality, described by Nancy Munn (1986), that at death social relations constructed through an individual are dissolved and must be reformed without the person's living presence. Mortuary rites are the highly charged occasion on which the web linking one individual to others, through birth, marriage, and clientage, is displayed and the rent social fabric rewoven, now linked through the dead (compare Weiner 1976: 85–90). The surviving members of society array themselves in relation to the dead and by so doing strengthen bonds to each other (Kan 1989: 125–164).

In some ways the construction of social links through the dead is more permanent than links transacted with the living, whose status and interests change continually throughout life. Mortuary rituals may symbolically mark the dichotomy between fleeting and permanent aspects of society (Bloch 1981, 1982). While symbols adopted are specific to their context, the permanence and scale of burial facilities are commonly counterposed to the decay of all or part of the body as representative of social relations transcending the individual lifespan (Bloch and Parry 1982: 27–38). As Thomas Dillehay (1992: 403–405) has shown for the Mapuche of Chile, burial facilities come to stand for more inclusive social identities as they *lose* their specific association with the individual interred within them. In a general sense, the dead are transformed through mortuary ritual from unique persons to members of social collectivities, such as ancestors, of interest to the living (Bloch 1982; Watson 1982). No longer actively seeking their own advantage, the dead can become a powerful moral force guaranteeing claims of solidarity by the living.

PRE-CLASSIC BURIAL PRACTICES

Mesoamerican burial practices during the Pre-Classic period, even from widely separated communities, share a number of common features. Burials may include figurines, pottery vessels, and less common ceramic artifacts (stamps, rattles, whistles, and masks, among others). The deceased may wear costume ornaments, such as necklaces, bracelets, anklets, and ear ornaments, made of a wide variety of materials but commonly including shell, greenstone, and polished iron ore. Stone tools, especially obsidian blades and polished celts, are often included, and other more perishable tools, such as bone awls and punches, are sometimes detected. Finally, while Pre-Classic burials are commonly located in and around residences, specialized burial sites away from any residence may also be employed. The diversity in the precise practices evident at different sites is sufficient to indicate clearly that similarities are the result of varied expressions of shared cultural heritage within similar social contexts, not of the imposition of centralized ritual.

Pre-Classic burials from Honduras are illustrative of all these features.[1] They were placed within residential compounds, in caves removed from sites, and within nonresidential monumental construction within sites. I have argued that variation in burial location in Pre-Classic Honduras created differences in the visibility of mortuary ritual, and quite likely the scale of participation in ceremonies conducted for specific burials (Joyce 1996, n.d.b). Placement within the residential compound is more private, and participation in mortuary rituals for these individuals could have been restricted, perhaps to members of the residential group of the deceased and others with close social links. In contrast, both cave and mound burial are divorced from the residential compound. Burial in monumental architecture created marked sites that cannot be ignored today, and would have dominated the space of the site and the lives of its inhabitants in myriad ways in the past (compare Love n.d., this volume). The location of burials and consequently of some of the attendant mortuary rituals was thus part of the creation of public spaces transcending the defined boundaries of the household, and presumably of the creation of communities of participants in the activities that took place in these spaces.

Among the contents of Honduran burials were costume ornaments of shell, greenstone, and other polished stone, as well as pottery. Individual beads are of forms common in southeastern Mesoamerica:[2] flat discs, cylinders, animal teeth

---

[1] The burials I discuss came from the sites of Copan, Los Naranjos, Playa de Los Muertos, and the Cuyamel caves. My discussion is based on published reports (Baudez and Becquelin 1973: 17–50, 91–93; Fash 1985; Gordon 1898; Healy 1974; Popenoe 1934; Rue, Freter, and Ballinger 1989; Viel and Cheek 1983) and my own examination of the material from caves of Copan and Playa de los Muertos in the collections of Harvard University's Peabody Museum (Joyce 1996, n.d.b).

[2] This observation is based on a comparison between the large body of well-dated ornaments from Chalchuapa, El Salvador (Sheets 1978) and ornaments from Honduran burials (cited above) and other Pre-Classic contexts at Los Naranjos (Baudez and Becquelin 1973) and Playa de los Muertos (Peabody Museum collections; Strong, Kidder, and Paul 1938).

or claws, skulls, and "duckbills." The number of options for unique bodily adornment using these ornaments was very high, even without consideration of the probable use of perishable materials—feathers, barkcloth, and cotton textiles—and the evident use of painted body (or cloth) markings suggested by ceramic stamps and cylinder seals. The creation of unique appearance is abundantly documented in Pre-Classic Honduran figurines and in the individuality of costumes worn by buried individuals. In 16 burials from Playa de los Muertos, containing 10 strings of beads, no two costumes were alike. Simple "napkin ring" earspools, executed in polished black and brown ceramic and fine greenstone, were the only standardized ornament. Ear ornaments were worn only by adults. Wrist, neck, and waist ornaments vary in numbers and arrangement of beads. Shell was employed in children's costume and greenstone in both adult and juvenile ornaments. The common use of certain materials and forms suggests that shared conceptions of beautiful materials were maintained. While some aspects of categorical social difference (age) are reflected in the nature of body ornaments, costumes themselves were individualized.

I suggest that costume, intimately tied to the body, openly displayed, and subject to social assessment, should be viewed as a medium for the creation of individuality. Munn (1986: 96–97, 101–102) labels as "beautification" the social marking of the body as desirable and the person as "persuasive" to others achieved by the use of skillfully worked body ornaments that set one person off from others. She and other ethnographers (e.g., Howard 1991: 62; Kensinger 1991: 43, 47–48) stress that personal adornment, enhancing individual appearance, supports competition for the positive evaluation of others and the personal influence that grows from such evaluation in face-to-face interaction within small-scale societies. By burying the deceased in costume, Pre-Classic Mesoamerican people perpetuated beautification and its enhancement of individual distinction even at the end of life. If costume was a medium for the creation of individuality, its use in burial may be an index of the necessary breakup of personal identity that Munn argues takes place through mortuary ritual. As she notes, "death itself initiates only a *physical* dissolution of the body . . . death dissolves neither the intersubjective amalgam that constitutes the *bodily person* and forms the ground of each self, nor the intersubjective connections between others built on and condensed within the deceased's person" (Munn 1986: 164; original emphasis).

Residential compound mortuary practices at Playa de los Muertos combine the marking of individual identity through adornment with signs of social relations in the form of ceramic vessels. Burials with costume usually also included pots. Because the vessels included are forms used for food serving, they constitute metonymic or indexical signs[3] for commensality, in essence the enactment of a community. Arnold van Gennep (1960: 164–165) noted that meals on the occasion of funerals "reunite all the surviving members of the group with each other, and sometimes also with the deceased" (see also Munn 1986: 172–178; Kan 1989: 35–38). Pre-Classic mortuary rituals might have actually involved meals uniting the people whose links together were endangered by the death. Whether or not the face-to-face groups that shared food enacted their participation as part of mortuary rites, the practice of including serving vessels in burials independently invokes their social setting, meals. Unlike costume, pots in burials at Playa de los Muertos present more regularities, as their status as marked media of social relations extending beyond the individual would suggest. Bottles and open bowls or cylinders were most common, and no burial with pottery lacked one of these forms.

Seven of 23 vessels are lobed or squash-effigy bottles, each executed slightly differently. Freestanding objects can be a focus for communal value created through beautification (Munn 1986: 20). Adornment of objects makes them subjects of comment and comparative evaluation, creating reputations for the objects, their makers, and their users. The recognition of shared standards for adornment and execution of pottery, and the measurement of each attempt at beautification against those standards, ethnographically demarcate those within a group from those outside it (Hardin 1983). Selection of serving vessel forms for elaboration has been identified as an aspect of aggrandizing behavior in the earliest ceramic complexes of Pre-Classic Mesoamerica (Clark and Blake 1994: 23–28), implying both the existence of shared standards and differential evaluation of execution in this permanent, public medium.

I suggest that costume on the one hand and pottery vessels on the other were employed in mortuary ritual in Pre-Classic Honduras to signal the dissolution of individual personal identity and the breakup and reconstitution of the social relations of which the deceased had been part. Survivors with vested interests in the reconstruction of social networks previously focused on the dead person carried out the mortuary rituals that result in the burials we re-

---

[3] Index and metonymy are special kinds of symbolic relations in which an item invokes a chain of associations. These kinds of signs have also been described as "contiguity tropes" (Friedrich 1991: 34), a class of rhetorical figures that are characterized by such relations. Because contiguity tropes are essentially strings of associations, they are open to analysis in ways that more arbitrary symbols are not (Herzfeld 1992: 83–84). At least one of the entailments of serving vessels, an association that would always have been within the awareness of a viewer, was meals. To the extent that meals united certain groups of people (and not others), meals, and the vessels that were used in them, entailed an association with people with whom a viewer had certain kinds of relationships.

cover archaeologically. The degree to which burials were elaborated would depend on the importance to these survivors of the reinscription of their severed connections, and reflect the social strategies of the house and aggrandizers within it.

At Playa de los Muertos, the burials with the largest number and greatest diversity of items were those of juveniles. Such elaboration of select juvenile burials, seen not only in Honduras but throughout Pre-Classic Mesoamerica (e.g., Drennan 1976: 247–256; Grove and Gillespie 1992: 199; Tolstoy 1989: 115; Robin and Hammond 1991: 224; Hammond, this volume), may reflect the position of these individuals at the intersection of social networks especially valued and particularly endangered, by the death so memorialized. Ethnographically, connections between groups created by marriage are strengthened through the birth and growth of children, with regular reinforcement of obligations and rights in ceremonies marking life stages. The death of a juvenile or infant truncates this developmental process and can endanger links not yet securely fixed. Mortuary ritual could take on the burden that would have been borne by other ceremonies in the life of the person had they survived. Through their involvement in mortuary ritual, groups of survivors displayed their regard for the deceased and attempted to ensure continued positive connections with others through that person.

VARIATION WITHIN THE COMMUNITY

Since mortuary rituals are designed and carried out by social groups, their patterned remains in burials can also be examined as evidence of the habitual practices that simultaneously create commonality and distinction between social groups within a community. I apply this approach to a recently published catalogue of more than two hundred burials from Pre-Classic Tlatilco in Central Mexico which includes site plans demonstrating their spatial clustering (García Moll et al. 1991). A preliminary cluster analysis of these burials identified a tendency for adult female burials to contain more pottery and for nonpottery items to be found in adult male or juvenile burials (Serra and Sugiura 1987). Paul Tolstoy (1989) included information on some of these burials, from what is labeled Temporada IV, in an analysis based on complete information for the equally large Temporada II population from earlier work at the site.

Tolstoy concluded that the Temporada IV burials largely were later than those of Temporada II, and defined indicators of social hierarchy in the burial population as a whole. Iron ore mirrors, necklaces, greenstone, and shell objects were all limited to burials constituting the top rank of this status hierarchy (Tolstoy 1989: 109–112). These items, most of them elements of costume, were also among characteristics distinguishing a statistical cluster of Temporada IV burials, with unspecified spatial associations (Serra and Sugiura 1987). Individuals of mixed age and sex were identified as similar due to shared use of iron ore mirrors, jade belts, jade ear ornaments, and "rock crystal" beads, along with certain elaborate ceramic vessels. Also working from the Temporada IV catalogue, Cameron Wesson (n.d.) found that burials of Tolstoy's top rank exhibited distinctive cranial deformation and little evidence of bone pathologies that would have resulted from greater labor demands and poorer nutrition.

Each of these studies suggests that there were real distinctions between individuals at Tlatilco reflected in their general health, appearance (in the form of both physical modification and use of ornaments), and the elaboration of their burials. Tolstoy (1989) found consistent rankings reflected in the quality and quantity of objects included, the depth and preparation of the grave, and the position of the body. Nonetheless, he concluded that not all of the variability in the burial population could be explained simply as due to the reflection of individual rank. "The nature of these objects and their diverse patterns of occurrence suggest that the denotation of rank was not their exclusive function. . . . Though consistent in the ranking they suggest for individual graves, these indicators do not exhibit uniformly strong associations with one another. This suggests that other important and, in part, hidden factors contribute to their distributions" (Tolstoy 1989: 109–112). I explored the possibility that differences, not between the status of buried individuals, but in practices between residential groups engaged in competitive social relations, might be one of these hidden factors, accounting for other variation in the nature of items included in burials.[4]

---

[4] I created variables for each distinguishable category of object in the Temporada IV catalogue and employed the graphical approaches of exploratory data analysis to evaluate variation on the basis of age or sex. Very few tendencies by age or sex, all mentioned in the text, were discovered. The strength of correlations was tested using the chi square statistic when the expected values in cells of the contingency table allowed, and I identify such instances as "significant" in the text. Cases where expected cell size was too small to allow use of the chi square test, but the actual value of a cell in the contingency table diverged from the expected value by a sufficiently high factor (occurrence twice that expected), are noted in the text as "higher than expected" incidence of a particular association. They represent possible tendencies in the population.

I also systematically evaluated correlations of all pairwise combinations of category variables. Through this process, I was able to identify one set of variables—obsidian, bone punches, and some groundstone, discussed below—with significant levels of association. A weaker association was detected between the incidence of bottles and open vessel forms. The open vessel category is very heterogeneous, and the association of bottles with vases is stronger than that with open vessels as a whole.

As Tolstoy's comments suggest, I found no evidence of strong associations among the entire suite of objects included in burials. Instead, the burial assemblages may better be viewed as composed of components included independently of one another. The presence of any one of these components (e.g., figurines) does not provide clear grounds to expect other components. A hierarchical structure of choice may, however, be discernible. Burials with the rarest components usually also include more common components. Pottery vessels are most common and in many burials are the only objects included. Each component can be viewed as an option added to an initial common content, up to the rarest items: costume worn by the deceased. Viewed as a structure of choice, the composition of Tlatilco burials most directly reflects the practices differently employed by survivors belonging to different residential groups.

The burials excavated in Temporada IV fall into well-defined spatial groups. Within groups, orientations tend to be shared, and in each group two major orientations are found. Tolstoy (1989) argued that burial orientation indicates the presence at the site of two moieties, with both inmarried and native residents placed in what are likely residential compound burial locations.[5] As Tolstoy noted, within each spatial cluster, rich burials tend to share a single orientation, perhaps that of the locally born members of the residential group. In some clusters, there are groups of male, female, and juvenile burials that may suggest the use of distinctive burial sites based on age or sex in some compounds (Fig. 1). As seen elsewhere in Pre-Classic Mesoamerica, and as Tolstoy noted, juveniles on the whole have the richest burials.

Among the components of Tlatilco burials with apparently independent patterns of occurrence in individual burials were the use of red pigment, presence of pottery vessels, inclusion of pottery figurines, incorporation of musical instruments and other rare artifacts, the presence of stone and bone tools and debitage, and the use of costume ornaments. Several of these characteristics are

[5] The presence of features such as bottle-shaped pits in the published profiles from the site support the interpretation of these clusters as subresidential compound burials. Although the clusters define small spaces, they in fact are as large as, or larger than, the houses documented for contemporary Coapexco (Tolstoy 1989: 90–91). The Temporada IV clusters could represent as many as 25 of the largest structures, or at least 15 courtyard groups, of the size represented at Coapexco. The number of burials—a mean of 6.8 in areas approximating structures and 12.8 in areas approximating courtyards—cannot represent an entire population accumulating over a long period of time. Some individuals may have been disposed of elsewhere, and others may have been disturbed and relocated to allow later burials. The presence of secondary burial treatment was noted by the excavators and includes the consolidation of skulls in pits. The interments that are the focus of this analysis thus represent a particular moment in a dynamic sequence of burial and reburial and the treatment accorded only selected persons.

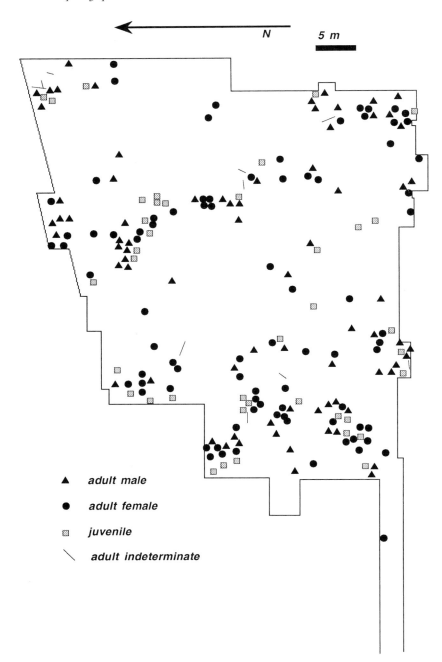

Fig. 1 Adult male, adult female, and unsexed juvenile burials at Tlatilco.

N   **5 m**

bottles with beakers

bottles alone or with bowls

Fig. 2 Bottles and bowls in graves at Tlatilco. The orientation of each burial is indicated
by the enlarged end of the symbol. Burials without bottles or bowls are light gray.

common within the community represented by the Temporada IV burials, while others are spatially restricted and may reflect practices distinctive of specific residential groups.

The most uniform distribution of artifacts across clusters is that of pottery vessels. While a large number of burials lack pots, no well-defined cluster is without some burials containing them. A closer examination of distributions of different forms of vessels reveals some distinctions between clusters that reflect practices differentiating groups within the communitywide pattern of use of pottery serving vessels.[6] Bottles are less generally represented than pottery as a whole, and burials with bottles tend to occur repeatedly in specific clusters (Fig. 2). Within some clusters, bottles were an element in most burials. The presence of tall vases, all of which were found in burials also containing bottles, is another example of apparent diversity in the practices resulting in the incorporation of pottery in burials, with certain clusters repeatedly including bottles and tall vases, and other clusters avoiding the practice entirely, even if they use bottles. Although there are fewer burials with pottery figurines, they also seem to be used widely within the community excavated in Temporada IV. Burials with exceptional numbers of figurines are generally unique in their cluster, but the inclusion of from two to five figurines is a feature repeated in multiple burials in two clusters (Fig. 3).

The inclusion of pottery vessels and figurines in burials is a widespread practice within the community, and these objects are among the most common kinds of burial embellishments. Residential compound-specific patterns are more evident when rarer practices are examined. For example, the use of red pigment in burials is associated with all four of the ranks defined by Tolstoy. It is uncommon, restricted to 32 (out of 213) burials excavated in Temporada IV. Red pigment is slightly more common in female burials than would be expected and is significantly more likely to be used in the burials of young adults (15–30 years of age). The strongest association of red pigment, however, is as a practice typical of certain clusters (Fig. 4). Multiple burials in eight clusters, all concentrated in the southeast edge of the excavated area, employ red pigment. One other cluster used red pigment on half of the burials. Otherwise, red pigment is employed in no more than two burials in any cluster, and is absent from many clusters altogether.

---

[6] Ideally, I would have evaluated the specific decoration of vessels. Inconsistent illustration of vessels and poor resolution of photographs in the catalogue precluded this.

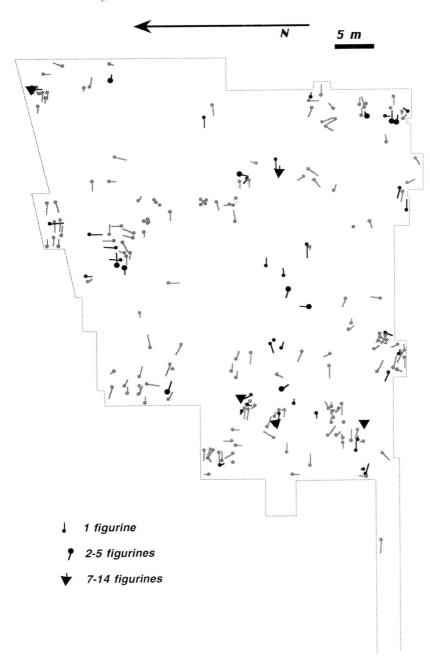

N

5 m

↓   **1 figurine**

♦   **2-5 figurines**

▼   **7-14 figurines**

Fig. 3 Figurines in graves at Tlatilco. The orientation of each burial is indicated by the enlarged end of the symbol. Burials without figurines are light gray.

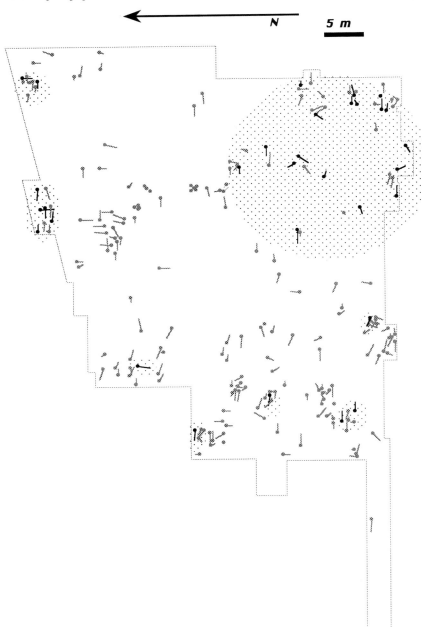

Fig. 4 Red pigment in graves at Tlatilco. The orientation of each burial is indicated by the enlarged end of the symbol.

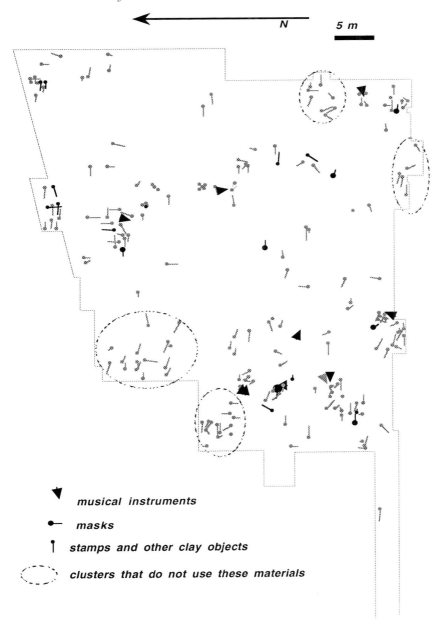

N   5 m

Fig. 5 Musical instruments, masks, stamps, and tokens in graves at Tlatilco. The orientation of each burial is indicated by the enlarged end of the symbol. Burials without musical instruments, stamps, masks, or tokens are light gray.

The inclusion of rare artifacts, clay masks, stamps and tokens,[7] and musical instruments (clay rattles and whistles and shell trumpets) also demonstrates cluster-level patterning. Stamps and miscellaneous tokens are more common than expected in male burials, while musical instruments are more common than expected in female burials. Several clusters of burials lack any of these rare artifacts, even when they are in close proximity to clusters that include them in multiple burials (Fig. 5). Musical instruments are common in clusters in the southwest part of the site; outside this area, they occur at most in a single burial in any cluster.

The distributions of most of the features of burials are independent of each other. The mortuary rituals that resulted in these distributions combined different kinds of actions drawn from a suite of practices common to the community as a whole. The use of pottery vessels in mortuary rites throughout the community may reflect the importance of meals in small-scale social relations between and within groups and the significance of pots as media for symbolism. Differentiation between groups is most obvious in the choice to employ more variable elements of burial preparation, such as red pigment. The inclusion of unusual artifacts, such as musical instruments, in burials introduces the possibility that the use of some or all of these objects also distinguished the residents of the cluster during life.

While the functions of musical instruments, stamps, masks, and tokens are not entirely clear, it is possible that some of them were employed in specialized performances. Flannery (1976) has argued for the interpretation of musical instruments and certain costume elements as evidence of ritual performance in Pre-Classic Oaxaca. If some or all of the rare objects from Tlatilco were employed in the performance of ceremony, the differences between groups in their use might be related to distinctive ritual practice. Clearer implications for action during life can be derived from the various tools included in burials. Among these tools are a wide array of bone and antler punches, needles, and picks, grinding stones, and obsidian debitage.[8]

---

[7] I use the neutral term "token" here to label miscellaneous pottery objects, including small balls, flat rectangular or oval plaques, and other irregular forms. These were described in the catalogue as "fichas" and "objetos." Because, like stamps, tokens are more likely to occur in male burials, I grouped stamps and tokens together in Figure 5.

[8] I reviewed the illustration of each individual object with a common catalogue description, for example, bone or antler "punzon," and regrouped them based on unrecognized formal distinctions. "Punzones" included both tools that were broad relative to their length and others that were long and narrow. A small number had notched ends, and some of the long narrow tools appear to have eyes (needles with eyes were recorded for Temporada II). The long narrow tools and notched end tools are indistinguishable from archaeological

Grinding stone sets (a handstone and platform; see note 8) may have been used in a variety of ways, and the association of two with raw pigment suggests that mineral processing was one task employing these tools. Bone needles and picks are forms appropriate for use in textile or basketry production (for other Pre-Classic instances of evidence for these crafts, see Hendon, this volume, and Marcus 1989: 184). Few burials have either sets of grinding stones or possible weaving picks (Fig. 6). Thus it is striking that burials with grinding stone sets tend to be found in the clusters of the northeast quadrant of the site (including one cluster with 2 examples), while those with bone weaving picks and needles are common in the clusters of the southwest.

In contrast with these less common tools, bone or antler punches that are appropriate for use in lithic production (either to produce blades from prepared cores or for retouch) were present in 25 burials. In 20 of these, obsidian was also included, accounting for 42 percent of the burials with obsidian in the site (where obsidian was present in only 22 percent of the burials). With a single exception (one of a pair of burials isolated away from any cluster), burials with bone punches and obsidian were repeated features of clusters that, in turn, formed three neighborhoods within the site. Sixteen more burials with obsidian, but lacking bone or antler tools, were located in the same three neighborhoods. The clusters in these areas, containing 48 percent of the burials in the site, accounted for 75 percent of the burials with obsidian (Fig. 7).

These clusters also yielded 14 of 17 burials containing single handstones. Four handstones were in burials that had both bone or antler punches and obsidian.[9] A

---

tools identified by comparison with ethnographic sources as weaving picks and needles and were recoded as picks. Similarly, I coded as a set grinding platforms and handstones (described in the catalogue as pestles, manos, metates, mortars, and so on) found together in single burials. I recoded the remaining ground stone artifacts, all handstones (manos, pestles, or hammerstones), separately. Due to the nature of the catalogue, it is not possible to define more precisely what characteristics defined the original variables "mano," "pestle," or "hammerstone." What is clear is that each of these terms was applied to a ground stone item that is of a size to be held in the hand.

[9] A linear regression analysis demonstrated a relatively strong positive association between obsidian and punches ($R^2 = 44.5$). This relationship is strengthened by considering the presence of ground stone ($R^2 = 72.9$), although this is at least in part due to a negative relationship between paired grinding stones and obsidian/punches (that is, the presence of the paired grinding stones generally indicates a high probability of absence of obsidian and punches and vice versa). When a variable tracking only handstones not forming part of sets was evaluated, it actually slightly weakened the regression ($R^2 = 40.7$), despite the evident overlap in spatial distribution between handstones and obsidian and punches. The explanation for this counterintuitive result is that the regression assesses individual burials as cases, whereas the pattern observed is on the level of the cluster and the neighborhood. This example reinforces the utility of treating burial data as the results of community action.

N   5 m

Fig. 6 Weaving tools and grinding stone sets in graves at Tlatilco. The orientation of each burial is indicated by the enlarged end of the symbol. Burials without weaving tools or grinding stone sets are light gray.

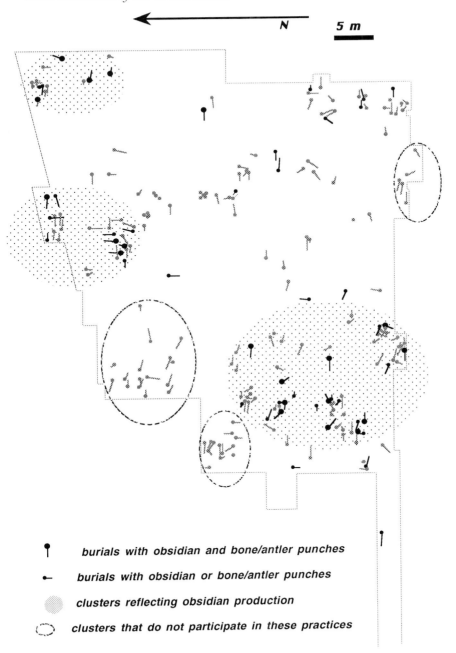

Fig. 7 Clusters with obsidian and obsidian production tools in graves at Tlatilco. The orientation of each burial is indicated by the enlarged end of the symbol. Burials without obsidian or obsidian production tools are light gray.

possible rationale for this association could be the use of handstones in an obsidian industry based on smashing of nodules identified in the same region and time period (Tolstoy 1989: 96; Boksenbaum et al. 1987: 67–68). Such a hammer-and-anvil, or bipolar, industry produces typical debitage, including bipolar cores and large numbers of flakes (Bordaz 1970: 14–15, 19–20; Kuijt and Russell 1993), the predominant form of obsidian in the Temporada IV burials. Ian Kuijt (personal communication, 1993) identified seven of the obsidian flakes illustrated in the Tlatilco catalogue as formally likely to represent bipolar cores, and concurs that the handstones illustrated are consistent with such an industry.[10] The strength of the association of these distinctive by-products with bone or antler tools suggests that the latter were used in retouch of flakes produced by bipolar reduction (compare Bordaz 1970: 16, 19, 27, 80–85). When the distribution of evidence for the bipolar industry was mapped, independently of the presence of products of the rarer core/blade industry, it became clear that the southwestern and north central clusters were particularly distinguished as loci with evidence of this technology (Fig. 8).

Obsidian production was important enough to be featured in the mortuary practices of select clusters at Tlatilco. Two neighborhoods of the site have particularly intense emphasis on obsidian and its production tools and by-products in burials. While the association of obsidian, bone or antler punches, and handstones in certain burials could allow the identification of these as the remains of individuals active in obsidian production, the stronger pattern evident is between clusters as a whole and obsidian production. By including these items in mortuary ritual, the survivors placed one of the activities that marked, not solely the individual, but the group, on display. The preserved evidence for textile production and for manufacturing processes employing sets of handstones is less abundant. Nonetheless, the inclusion of these tools in burials similarly implies not just the activities employing them but also the social recognition of these kinds of labor by the group, as part of the highlighted practices of mortuary ritual.

While I have argued that the wearing of costume is the strongest medium for individuation present in Pre-Classic burials, the distribution of costume ornaments also suggests that an emphasis on costume was more characteristic of certain groups at Tlatilco. Sixteen individuals, including seven adult females

---

[10] The specific objects Kuijt singled out are: probable bipolar core: Burial 46 (4 individuals); Burial 80 (4); Burial 81 (4); Burial 145 (3); classic bipolar core: Burial 53 (3); Burial 82 (1); Burial 121 (5); where the object number in parentheses corresponds to the catalogue. Burial 107 (15) is a probable chert bipolar core.

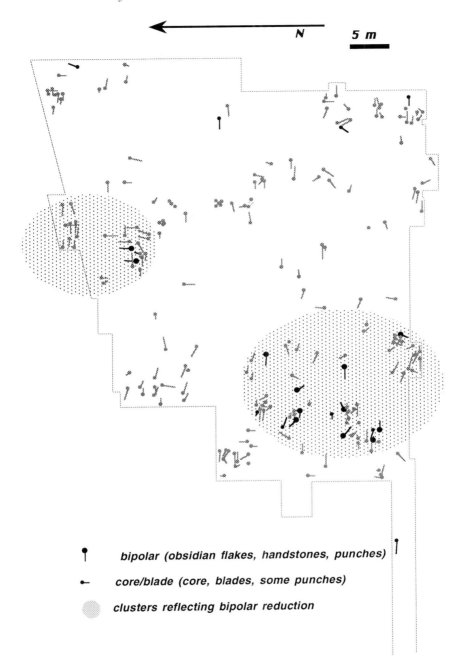

Fig. 8 Distribution of core/blade and bipolar obsidian industries in graves at Tlatilco. The orientation of each burial is indicated by the enlarged end of the symbol. Burials without products of core/blade or bipolar obsidian industries are light gray.

35

and six adult males, were buried wearing costume in the excavated area.[11] Ear ornaments and bead belts were worn only by males. Necklaces are found with females more often than expected. These differences hint at patterns of gender-specific costume elaboration like those evident in later Mesoamerican societies.

Multiple individuals in certain clusters were buried wearing costume (Fig. 9). In clusters with one or more individuals buried wearing costume, the number of other individuals accompanied by costume ornaments not worn at the time of interment was higher than expected. Burials within these clusters were also more likely overall to incorporate exotic, imported material. Fragments of polished iron ore not worn as costume were included in eight burials, seven in the clusters marked by costume elaboration. In contrast, only three of six burials with shell or bone ornaments not worn as costume were found in these clusters.[12]

The cluster-level emphasis on the inclusion of costume ornaments within burials is strong in the same clusters that also included significant numbers of burials with obsidian production tools. Together these two patterns suggest the possibility that slight but perceptible and, more important, publicly marked differentials in the consumption of imported materials existed between residential groups. These patterns could be interpreted as evidence that obsidian-working houses were displaying their wealth during mortuary ceremony.

At the same time that the practice of interring the dead in costume can be seen as a group-level behavior, it also, quite clearly, distinguishes individuals. Four burials—two young adult women, one young adult male, and one older male—wore costumes that included greenstone beads and iron ore pendants. Each of these was unique in its particular cluster. Other costumed individuals in the same clusters wore only shell, bone, or stone ornaments (including greenstone). Thus the presence of an iron ore pendant distinguishes the most elabo-

---

[11] I examined the drawing of each burial to ensure that the ornaments were in proper relative position to have formed part of costume, because the catalogue does not consistently indicate when ornaments were worn. I recorded examples of ear ornaments, necklaces (with/without pendants), bracelets (with/without pendants), necklace with pendant and bracelets, ear ornaments with necklace, bracelet, and anklet, and one belt accompanied by bracelets.

[12] While later Mesoamerican practices would lead to the expectation that greenstone was a prized substance, greenstone beads not used in costume were distributed in the same fashion as shell or bone beads: two of four cases in costume-emphasizing clusters. The single jade beads found in all of these cases may relate not to costume but to the practice of placing jade beads in the mouth of the deceased, common in the Pre-Classic from Cuello (Robin and Hammond 1991) to Oaxaca (Drennan 1976).

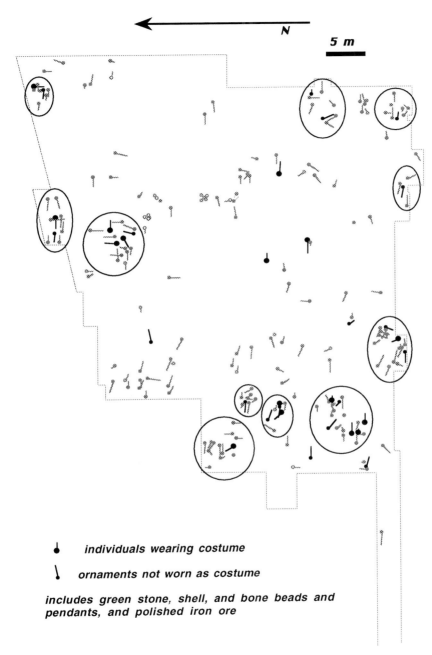

Fig. 9 Distribution of costume and costume ornaments in graves at Tlatilco. The orientation of each burial is indicated by the enlarged end of the symbol. Burials without costume ornaments are light gray.

rately dressed individual in each of the clusters that emphasize costume, consonant with Tolstoy's (1989: 109–112) identification of iron ore mirrors as restricted to the highest rank within the site. As in ethnographic house societies, each group may have had an internal hierarchy symbolized by particular badges of rank. At Tlatilco, we may be seeing the development of codified emblems of status within the shared practice of competitive costume elaboration, or beautification.

CONFORMITY BETWEEN COMMUNITIES

Where Pre-Classic burials divorced from residential compounds are found, costume is the single most consistent element of burial assemblages. My own analyses of burials in nonresidential loci at La Venta (Joyce n.d.a) and Los Naranjos (Joyce n.d.b), Marcia Merry de Morales' (1987) study of the unique burials in mound PC-4 at Chalcatzingo (see also Grove and Gillespie 1992), and John Clark's (n.d.) analysis of burials from Chiapa de Corzo demonstrate shared features of this development. Within sites, there are pronounced regularities in the burials in these locations. In addition, some features of these burials are similar at widely separated sites, suggesting the possibility that individuals involved in these mortuary rites participated in practices that transcended the local sphere.

A unique burial of this kind at the Honduran site of Los Naranjos (Baudez and Becquelin 1973: 49, 91–93), added to a monumental-scale mound in a second construction phase, featured a costumed individual unaccompanied by pottery vessels, otherwise consistent inclusions in elaborate Pre-Classic Honduran burials. On the summit of the platform a single individual was buried wearing a jade collar and double-strand belt, with two enormous earflares placed above the head, perhaps as part of a largely perishable headdress. This costume is comparable to examples from Chalcatzingo and La Venta (Merry de Morales 1987; Joyce n.d.a) that combine a double-strand greenstone belt and wide earflares.

The primary burial at Los Naranjos was accompanied by three other sets of human skeletal elements, one composed of two crania, all placed at the base of the platform along with a greenstone celt and red pigment. The use of greenstone celts and red pigment is also a feature of costumed burials in public architectural contexts at Chalcatzingo and La Venta (Merry de Morales 1987; Joyce n.d.a). More generally, the deposits at Los Naranjos resemble a series of human skeletal elements and arrangements of celts that mark the center line of a contemporary platform at San Isidro, Chiapas (Lowe 1981: 243–252). These caches may incorporate human skeletal remains as features of deposits which mark this as a ritual space, rather than commemorating the individual from whom they were derived. In this respect, they recall Cynthia Robin and Norman Hammond's (1991) characterization of some individuals in Pre-Classic mass burials at Cuello as human grave goods (see also Hammond, this volume), signaling a marked differentiation of such individuals from the individuals for whose burial rites their bodies were appropriated.

The Los Naranjos burial reflects practices distributed widely across Mesoamerica. The formalization of costume and abstraction of the burial from a shared location within the residential compound is correlated with the absence of pottery vessels, signifiers of sociality. In similar contexts at Chalcatzingo and La Venta, standardized sets of pottery were included. David Grove and Susan Gillespie (1992) describe the pairs of small jugs and bowls present in both of the costumed burials in Chalcatzingo PC-4 and in two burials in the elite household, PC-1, and compare them to others at La Venta. The standardization of this inclusion across these two sites and within Chalcatzingo across different burial locations is probably indicative of ritual practices shared by the elite members of Chalcatzingo society and the elite of La Venta, and marks these individuals as different from others interred locally and participants in a practice transcending the local sphere.

The use of earspools and bead belts is characteristic of burials at La Venta, Chalcatzingo, and Los Naranjos, and suggests the possibility that these costume elements were interregionally recognized status badges. They would simultaneously mark the distinction of those wearing the costume from local people not entitled to use these ornaments and the affiliation of those individuals with a wider network of people. As John Clark and Michael Blake (1994: 19) put it, "Effective competition at the community level requires aggrandizers to traffic outside their home communities and establish significant ties to individuals elsewhere, preferably other aggrandizers who also seek outside contacts." Based on an analysis of costume and objects included in burials at La Venta and comparison with depictions of individuals in Pre-Classic art, I have suggested that costumes including bead belts and earspools with pendants were worn by elite males (Joyce n.d.a), the category of persons that Clark and Blake (1994: 30) suggest would have tended to monopolize the aggrandizer positions. But while aggrandizers' efforts are personal, in house societies they reflect prestige on other members of the residential group on whose efforts they rely. At Chalcatzingo and La Venta, the same privileged burial location was shared by other individuals lacking interregionally constant badges. I have argued that some of these individuals may be female members of the elite, sharing the distinction of greenstone costume and the large-scale mortuary ritual that interment in mound architecture implies (Joyce n.d.a). Juveniles of prestigious houses might also be accorded distinguished burial, particularly insofar as they represent the human embodiment of alliances through which competitive houses expand their influence and resources (compare Annette Weiner's description of the gifts of shell ornaments that men involved in *kula* gave to their children; 1976: 129, 180–181).

Children were among the subjects of distinctive practices of burial costuming identified in an analysis of more than 70 burials from Chiapa de Corzo from both mound and nonmound locations (Clark n.d.). More than half of the burials were from a cemetery. All adults, except those that may be human burial goods, were accompanied by objects including pottery vessels and costume ornaments. John Clark defined strata of burials distinguished by elaborate costume and sumptuary goods, and demonstrated the presence of two sets of costume elements restricted to individuals buried in very different locations within the site. In burials placed in mound summits, sometimes including sacrificial victims, individuals wore jade earspools, jade and shell bead necklaces, some with marine shell pectorals, and bracelets, and what are described as greenstone breechcloths, perhaps a variant of the bead belt. Both adults and children shared in this pattern, although children wore incomplete versions of the costume. The presence of shell pectorals distinguished the individuals buried on principal mound summits from all others. Clark relates the individuals with this burial pattern to others from nonmound locations who shared the quantity of elaborate pottery vessels and had bead ornaments with less diverse material but lacked jade earspools.

A contrasting group of burials, never placed in mounds, wore distinctive greenstone tube ear ornaments, some with shell pendants, and carved shell pectoral ornaments with specific distinctive imagery. Within this group, variation was noted between individuals with complete costume and others with just one major ornament. All the juveniles of this group, buried in the cemetery, were without the large shell or jade earplugs or pectoral ornaments, but had at least one jade bead and numerous shell beads. In contrast to the mound burials, these individuals sometimes had utilitarian objects in their graves, including stamps.

Clark interprets the two sets of costume ornaments (which are only schematically summarized here) as badges of a political elite (with access to burial in mounds) and religious specialists (buried elsewhere). Both groups were marked by standardized costumes. Juveniles of each group have incomplete costumes, and Clark suggests that the full costume was a prerogative gained through maturation to adult status. Features of the costumes of the political elite buried in mounds follow some of the standards seen at La Venta, Chalcatzingo, and Los Naranjos, while the shell ear pendants of the possible ritual specialists are specific to the region of Chiapa de Corzo. The association of costume with aspects of personal identity, in this case age, is preserved even as costuming practices are standardized to differentiate corporate groups within the site and link one group to elites elsewhere in Mesoamerica. Differences in the scale of burial facility correlate with apparent participation in widespread networks and with perhaps the most powerful expression of social difference that can be employed, the use of the bodies of others to enhance mortuary rites.

CONCLUSIONS

In Pre-Classic Mesoamerica, residential compound burials preserve the outlines of the creation of personal identity and personal power within the context of group-specific mortuary ritual. Mound burials embody personal identity completely abstracted from the residential group context and its social claims. Along with the movement from burial within residential compounds to burial in the larger architectural settings that create public space in Pre-Classic sites, there is a standardization of costume and, in some sites, restriction of the use of costume ornaments to certain burial sites. Where costume was used within the residential setting, perhaps as a medium to compete for influence by increasing attractiveness, unique costumes were composed from the shared forms and materials of ornaments specific to each society. In contrast, individuals buried in prominent nonresidential locations wear costumes that are standardized within communities and even in some cases between communities.

Burial practices within residential compounds provide the ground against which nonresidential burial practices were distinguished. Some of the distinctions in costume that become standardized, particularly the use of earspools and bead belts, may have already been in place within residential groups at sites like Tlatilco. At Tlatilco, we may see in distinctive burial practices that singled out certain households the competitive processes through which houses sought and gained lasting advantages that allowed their descendants to claim differential status. These practices include the consumption of rare or elaborated materials in mortuary rituals that would have displayed, to members of allied houses, the wealth of the house and its members and their confidence in their ability to replace the goods consigned to the earth. In ethnographic house societies, house treasures and wealth serve to seal alliances that provide the promise of labor necessary to ensure production sufficient to support the house and allow it to expand its influence. The alliances contracted, often through marriage, are regularly reinforced throughout life by exchanges, reciprocal feasting, and shared ritual. In death, the alliances are not dissolved. Rather, the bonds established are reformulated through the dead individual who becomes a permanent link, an ancestor.

The creation of unprecedented forms of social relations characterizes the Pre-Classic. Materially, some of the obvious features associated with these new developments include architecture of extraordinary scale, elaboration of craft items used in display, and pan-regional use of certain materials, symbols, and practices, all drawn into play in burial. Differential use of these materials comes to characterize the elite, but explanations of their Pre-Classic development cannot assume the preexistence of a privileged group. Rather, these features must be viewed as "used or reinvested in forging social alliances," as Kenneth Hirth has argued for Pre-Classic exchange: "Archaeologists must discard the notion that the circulation of primitive valuables through interregional exchange networks was stimulated by a desire to obtain status markers . . . and begin to examine the more specific ways in which primitive valuables are used in the formation of social hierarchy" (Hirth 1992: 23). The very elaboration of Pre-Classic burials, the scale of goods consumed even within villages with relatively modest populations and low levels of status differentiation, such as Tlatilco and Playa de los Muertos, strongly suggest that mortuary ritual was one of the arenas through which status was manipulated, concepts of value formed, and avenues opened for the assertion of legitimate individual distinction in Pre-Classic Mesoamerica.

BIBLIOGRAPHY

BAUDEZ, CLAUDE, AND PIERRE BECQUELIN
  1973   *Archéologie de los Naranjos, Honduras.* Etudes mesoaméricaines 2. Mission
          Archéologique et Ethnologique Française au Mexique, México, D.F.

BLOCH, MAURICE
  1981   Tombs and States. In *Mortality and Immortality: The Anthropology and Archaeology
          of Death* (S. C. Humphreys and Helen King, eds.): 137–147. Academic Press,
          London and New York.
  1982   Death, Women and Power. In *Death and the Regeneration of Life* (Maurice
          Bloch and Jonathan Parry, eds.): 211–230. Cambridge University Press,
          Cambridge.

BLOCH, MAURICE, AND JONATHAN PARRY
  1982   Introduction: Death and the Regeneration of Life. In *Death and the Regeneration
          of Life* (Maurice Bloch and Jonathan Parry, eds.): 1–44. Cambridge University
          Press, Cambridge.

BOKSENBAUM, MARTIN, PAUL TOLSTOY, GARMAN HARBOTTLE, JEROME KIMBERLIN, AND
MARY NIEVENS
  1987   Obsidian Industries and Cultural Evolution in the Basin of Mexico before
          500 B.C. *Journal of Field Archaeology* 14 (1): 65–76.

BOONE, JAMES
  1990   Balinese Twins Times Two: Gender, Birth Order, and "Household" in Indo-
          nesia/Indo-Europe. In *Power and Difference: Gender in Island Southeast Asia*
          (Jane Monnig Atkinson and Shelly Errington, eds.): 209–234. Stanford
          University Press, Stanford.

BORDAZ, JACQUES
  1970   *Tools of the Old and New Stone Age.* Natural History Press, Garden City, N.Y.

CLARK, JOHN E.
  n.d.   A Preclassic Mesoamerican Society: Analysis of Francesca-Phase Burials from
          Chiapa de Corzo, Mexico. Paper provided courtesy of the author, 1983.

CLARK, JOHN E., AND MICHAEL BLAKE
  1994   The Power of Prestige: Competitive Generosity and the Emergence of Rank
          Societies in Lowland Mesoamerica. In *Factional Competition and Political
          Development in the New World* (Elizabeth M. Brumfiel and John W. Fox, eds.):
          17–30. Cambridge University Press, Cambridge.

DILLEHAY, THOMAS
  1992   Keeping Outsiders Out: Public Ceremony, Resource Rights, and Hierarchy
          in Historic and Contemporary Mapuche Society. In *Wealth and Hierarchy in
          the Intermediate Area* (Frederick W. Lange, ed.): 379–422. Dumbarton Oaks,
          Washington, D.C.

DRENNAN, ROBERT D.
  1976   *Fábrica San José and Middle Formative Society in the Valley of Oaxaca.* Prehistory
          and Human Ecology of the Valley of Oaxaca, vol. 4. Memoirs of the Museum
          of Anthropology 8, University of Michigan. Ann Arbor.

FASH, WILLIAM

1985　La secuencia de ocupación del grupo 9N-8, Las Sepulturas, Copán, y sus implicaciones teóricas. *Yaxkin* 8 (1–2): 135–150. Tegucigalpa.

FLANNERY, KENT V.

1976　Contextual Analysis of Ritual Paraphernalia from Formative Oaxaca. In *The Early Mesoamerican Village* (Kent V. Flannery, ed.): 333–345. Academic Press, New York.

FRIEDRICH, PAUL

1991　Polytropy. In *Beyond Metaphor: The Theory of Tropes in Anthropology* (James W. Fernandez, ed.): 17–55. Stanford University Press, Stanford.

GARCÍA MOLL, ROBERTO, DANIEL JUÁREZ COSSÍO, CARMEN PIJOAN AGUADE, MARIA ELENA SALAS CUESTA, AND MARCELA SALAS CUESTA

1991　*Catálogo de entierros de San Luis Tlatilco, México, Temporada IV.* Instituto Nacional de Antropología e Historia, Serie Antropología Física-Arqueología. Mexico.

GORDON, GEORGE BYRON

1898　*Caverns of Copan, Honduras.* Harvard University, Memoirs of the Peabody Museum of American Archaeology and Ethnology 1 (5). Cambridge, Mass.

GROVE, DAVID C., AND SUSAN D. GILLESPIE

1992　Archaeological Indicators of Formative Period Elites: A Perspective from Central Mexico. In *Mesoamerican Elites: An Archaeological Assessment* (Diane Z. Chase and Arlen F. Chase, eds.): 191–205. University of Oklahoma Press, Norman.

HARDIN, MARGARET

1983　The Structure of Tarascan Pottery Painting. In *Structure and Cognition in Art* (Dorothy Washburn, ed.): 8–24. Cambridge University Press, Cambridge.

HEALY, PAUL

1974　The Cuyamel Caves: Preclassic Sites in Northeast Honduras. *American Antiquity* 39: 433–437.

HERTZ, ROBERT

1960　A Contribution to the Study of the Collective Representation of Death. In *Death and the Right Hand.* Cohen and West, London.

HERZFELD, MICHAEL

1992　Metapatterns: Archaeology and the Uses of Evidential Scarcity. In *Representations in Archaeology* (Jean-Claude Gardin and Christopher Peebles, eds.): 66–86. Indiana University Press, Bloomington.

HIRTH, KENNETH

1992　Interregional Exchange as Elite Behavior: An Evolutionary Perspective. In *Mesoamerican Elites: An Archaeological Assessment* (Diane Z. Chase and Arlen F. Chase, eds.): 18–29. University of Oklahoma Press, Norman.

HOWARD, CATHERINE

1991　Fragments of the Heavens: Feathers as Ornaments among the Waiwai. In *Gift of Birds: Featherwork of Native South American Peoples* (Ruben Reina and Ken Kensinger, eds.): 50–69. University Museum of Archaeology and Anthropology, University of Pennsylvania, Philadelphia.

JOYCE, ROSEMARY

1996   Social Dynamics of Exchange: Changing Patterns in the Honduran Archaeological Record. In *Chieftains, Power, and Trade: Regional Interaction in the Intermediate Area of the Americas* (Carl Henrik Langebaek and Felipe Cardenas-Arroyo, eds.): 31–45. Departamento de Antropología, Universidad de los Andes, Bogotá, Colombia.

n.d.a   Gender, Role and Status in Middle Formative Mesoamerica: Implications of Burials from La Venta, Tabasco, Mexico. Revised version of paper presented at the Texas Symposium, "Olmec, Izapa, Maya," 1993.

n.d.b   The Social Construction of Power in Formative Period Honduras. Paper presented at the Annual Meeting of the American Anthropological Association, San Francisco, 1992.

KAN, SERGEI

1989   *Symbolic Immortality: The Tlingit Potlatch of the Nineteenth Century.* Smithsonian Institution Press, Washington, D.C.

KENSINGER, KENNETH

1991   Feathers Make Us Beautiful: The Meaning of Cashinahua Feather Headdresses. In *Gift of Birds: Featherwork of Native South American Peoples* (Ruben Reina and Ken Kensinger, eds.): 40–49. University Museum of Archaeology and Anthropology, University of Pennsylvania, Philadelphia.

KUIJT, IAN, AND K. W. RUSSELL

1993   Tur Imdai Rockshelter, Jordan: Debitage Analysis and Historic Bedouin Lithic Technology. *Journal of Archaeological Science* 20: 667–680.

LEVI-STRAUSS, CLAUDE

1983   *The Way of the Masks* (Sylvia Modelski, trans.). Jonathan Cape, London.

LOVE, MICHAEL

n.d.   Material Culture and Social Practice in Preclassic Pacific Guatemala. Paper presented at the Annual Meeting of the American Anthropological Association, San Francisco, 1992.

LOWE, GARETH

1981   Olmec Horizons Defined in Mound 20, San Isidro, Chiapas. In *The Olmec and Their Neighbors* (Elizabeth P. Benson, ed.): 231–256. Dumbarton Oaks, Washington, D.C.

MARCUS, JOYCE

1989   Zapotec Chiefdoms and the Nature of Formative Religions. In *Regional Perspectives on the Olmec* (Robert J. Sharer and David C. Grove, eds.): 148–197. Cambridge University Press, Cambridge.

McKINNON, SUSAN

1991   *From a Shattered Sun: Hierarchy, Gender, and Alliance in the Tanimbar Islands.* University of Wisconsin Press, Madison.

MERRY DE MORALES, MARCIA

1987   Chalcatzingo's Burials as Indicators of Social Ranking. In *Ancient Chalcatzingo* (David C. Grove, ed.): 95–113. University of Texas Press, Austin.

Munn, Nancy
1986   *The Fame of Gawa*. Duke University Press, Durham, N.C.

Popenoe, Dorothy
1934   Some Excavations at Playa de los Muertos, Ulua River, Honduras. *Maya Research* 1: 62–86.

Robin, Cynthia, and Norman Hammond
1991   Ritual and Ideology: Burial Practices. In *Cuello: An Early Maya Community in Belize* (Norman Hammond, ed.): 204–225. Cambridge University Press, Cambridge.

Rue, David J., AnnCorinne Freter, and Diane A. Ballinger
1989   The Caverns of Copan Revisited: Preclassic Sites in the Sesesmil River Valley, Copan, Honduras. *Journal of Field Archaeology* 16 (4): 395–404.

Serra, Mari Carmen, and Yoko Sugiura
1987   Funerary Rites at Two Historical Moments in Mesoamerica: Middle and Late Formative. In *Studies in the Neolithic and Urban Revolutions: The V. Gordon Childe Colloquium, Mexico, 1986* (Linda Manzanilla, ed.): 345–351. British Archaeological Reports International Series 349. BAR, Oxford.

Sheets, Payson
1978   Artifacts. In *The Prehistory of Chalchuapa, El Salvador*, vol. 2: *Artifacts and Figurines* (Robert J. Sharer, ed.): 2–131. University of Pennsylvania Press, Philadelphia.

Strong, William Duncan, A. V. Kidder II, and A. J. Drexel Paul
1938   *Preliminary Report of the Smithsonian Institution-Harvard University Archaeological Expedition to Northwestern Honduras, 1936*. Smithsonian Institution Miscellaneous Collections 97. Washington, D.C.

Tolstoy, Paul
1989   Coapexco and Tlatilco: Sites with Olmec Materials in the Basin of Mexico. In *Regional Perspectives on the Olmec* (Robert J. Sharer and David C. Grove, eds.): 85–121. Cambridge University Press, Cambridge.

van Gennep, Arnold
1960   *The Rites of Passage* (Monika Vizedom and Gabrielle Caffee, trans.). University of Chicago Press, Chicago.

Viel, Rene, and Charles Cheek
1983   Sepulturas. In *Introducción a la arqueología de Copán, Honduras,* vol. 1 (Claude Baudez, ed.): 551–609. SECTUR, Tegucigalpa.

Watson, James
1982   Of Flesh and Bones: The Management of Death Pollution in Cantonese Society. In *Death and the Regeneration of Life* (Maurice Bloch and Jonathan Parry, eds.): 155–186. Cambridge University Press, Cambridge.

Weiner, Annette
1976   *Women of Value, Men of Renown: New Perspectives in Trobriand Exchange*. University of Texas Press, Austin.

Wesson, Cameron
n.d.   Patterns of Association in Tlatilco Burials. Paper presented at the Midwest Mesoamericanist Meetings, Urbana, Illinois, 1992.

WOODBURN, JAMES

    1982   Social Dimensions of Death in Four African Hunting and Gathering Societies. In *Death and the Regeneration of Life* (Maurice Bloch and Jonathan Parry, eds.): 187–210. Cambridge University Press, Cambridge.

The Genesis of Hierarchy: Mortuary and Offertory Ritual in the Pre-Classic at Cuello, Belize

NORMAN HAMMOND

BOSTON UNIVERSITY

Masses, like individuals, invariably possess elusive traits that no one has seen, that slip though one's fingers—to note them, study them, read, observe, make conjectures, to dedicate one's entire being to their study, to offer the result to humanity as a healthy dish which it has never before tasted, that is the task—the joy of joys!

Modest Mussorgsky, letter to Vladimir Stassov, 1872

RECENT INVESTIGATIONS AT NAKBE, El Mirador, Tikal, Lamanai, Cerros, and other Late Pre-Classic sites of the central and eastern Maya Lowlands have documented the emergence of a complex society in the latter part of the first millennium B.C. manifested in large-scale architecture, elaborate architectural sculpture, and an iconography that suggests a coherent controlling ideology. The cultural tradition thus established continues unbroken for nearly fifteen hundred years, but the development from early farming communities into such proto-urban centers needs further study. As a contribution to this, I here outline briefly some of the evidence for Pre-Classic Maya ceremonial behavior that we have encountered at the small site of Cuello in northern Belize, a community that was probably never of great importance in the Maya world of its day. Cuello has, however, yielded useful evidence on the technology and economy of the Middle and Late Pre-Classic periods, including the identification of manioc and other root crops and the systematic exploitation of dogs for food, and also of funerary and offertory behavior within a slowly aggrandizing architectural matrix which documents the gradual establishment of a local elite.

CUELLO

The site includes a minor ceremonial precinct of two plazas, each with a pyramid ca. 9 m high and a number of long "range" structures, around and south of which is a zone of dispersed settlement covering about 1.6 sq km (Hammond 1991: fig. 2.2). The site as mapped by 1980 comprised some two hundred platforms and structures; the discovery of ground-level dwellings detectable only by excavation led Wilk and Wilhite (1991) to suggest a population of 300–400 in the early Middle Pre-Classic prior to 600 B.C., rising to 2,200–2,600 in the Late Pre-Classic and a peak of 3,400 in the Early Classic period ending ca. A.D. 600.

Further mapping in 1992 added another 52 structures, with density diminishing toward the natural boundary enforced by low-lying terrain to the south; although any postulated higher population requires testing by excavation, an increase of 25 percent over the published estimates would not be unreasonable, to around 500 in the early Middle Pre-Classic and perhaps 3,000 in the Late Pre-Classic; the land to the east remains in dense tropical growth, however, and has not been mapped. The Classic period ceremonial precinct of A.D. 250–900 lies close to the northern limit of settlement, but Platform 34 some 300 m to the south, the apparent core of the Pre-Classic community, can now be seen as centrally located rather than toward the southern end of the community.

Excavations and Chronology

All major excavations so far have been into Platform 34, a broad raised area ca. 80 by 70 m supporting a small pyramid (Str. 35) at the western end; those of 1975–87 are summarized in Hammond (1991), of 1990–93 in Hammond, Clarke, and Robin (1991), Hammond, Clarke, and Estrada Belli (1992), and Hammond, Clarke, and Donaghey (1995) respectively. Test excavations in Platform 34 in 1975 were followed by excavation of 50 sq m to bedrock in 1976 and by further investigations in 1978–80 during which the area was enlarged to include some 3,000 sq m of Late Formative deposits. Within this a "Main Trench" of 300 sq m was dug to either the buried palaeosol or bedrock beneath it. Completion of this area and of an additional trench at the south end of Platform 34 in 1993 has given a cross section of the Pre-Classic deposits at Cuello some 47 m long and 4 m deep.

The ceramic chronology begins with the Swasey complex, which is followed by the Bladen, both within the Swasey ceramic sphere (Kosakowsky 1987; Hammond 1991: figs. 1.2, 3.26–3.33). The Bladen complex and the coeval Bolay complex at neighboring Colha have links with the Xe sphere of the Pasión basin, with the Eb complex at Tikal, and more distantly with the Xox complex of the Salama Valley in Baja Verapaz (Sharer and Sedat 1987). These suggest a span of ca. 900–650 B.C. for Bladen and a date of perhaps 1200–900 B.C. for Swasey (Andrews and Hammond 1990; Housley, Hammond, and Law 1991; Law et al. 1991). The sequence continues after 650 B.C. with the Late Middle Pre-Classic Lopez Mamom and Late Pre-Classic Cocos Chicanel complexes, full members of their respective ceramic spheres, with a Mamom-Chicanel transition generally placed at about 400–300 B.C. (Hammond 1991: figs. 1.2, 3.34–3.44).

I examine first, and briefly, the evidence for Middle Pre-Classic funerary practices in the period 1200–400 B.C., then that for the Late Pre-Classic, and finally the complementary data on Late Pre-Classic caches and other offerings which has resulted from the Cuello research.

Funerary Practices

A total of 162 Pre-Classic individuals were excavated at Cuello, 27 dating to the Swasey and Bladen phases, 1200–650 B.C.; 31 to the Lopez Mamom phase, 650–400 B.C.; and 104 to the Cocos Chicanel phase, 400 B.C.–A.D. 250, comprising the largest present sample of Pre-Classic lowland Maya burials. They are examined here in terms of the format of the grave and burial and in terms of the social, ritual, and ideological mechanisms that may underlie these patterns. Robin (1989: app. A) gives a complete catalogue of data, burial plans, and illustrations of grave goods for burials excavated through 1987; those found in 1990 and 1992 are published in summary in Hammond, Clarke, and Robin (1991) and Hammond, Clarke, and Estrada Belli (1992) respectively, and will be fully published, together with burials excavated in 1993 (Hammond, Clarke, and Donaghey 1995), in a supplement to Robin's monograph.

MIDDLE PRE-CLASSIC BURIALS

Early Middle Pre-Classic: Swasey/Bladen Phases, 1200–650 B.C.

Twenty-seven individuals in 23 graves date to the Early Middle Pre-Classic Swasey and Bladen phases, of which five (19 percent: Burials 62, 159+167, 179+180) are of Swasey date. Seven (26 percent) are definite or probable male adults, ten (37 percent) female adults, two teenagers (7 percent), and eight (30 percent) are children aged six months to ten years.

Most of the Early Middle Pre-Classic interments were in graves cut into house platform floors during initial construction, during use, and at abandonment, indicative of family-type residential burials as Haviland (1985) demonstrated for small Classic period residential groups at Tikal. The earliest burials were not associated with plaster-floored houses, but their clustering suggests that they may have been dug through the earthen floor of a building at ground level. Twenty-two of the twenty-three graves were simple; one grave (Burial 116) is a cist containing a child (Hammond 1991: fig. 10.1).

Extended, flexed, seated, and disarticulated skeletal positions occur, with extended supine burial (nine examples) most common. The earliest Swasey burials (62, 179+180) are extended or slightly flexed, while slightly later Swasey interments (159+167) are tightly flexed and the earliest Bladen burials (176–178) are unusual in being both flexed and supine, with the knees drawn up to the chest. Extended and flexed positions are more common than seated, of which there is only one Middle Pre-Classic example at Cuello (Burial 9). There is no clear relationship between age and sex or context and skeletal position in the sample of Swasey/Bladen individuals.

The Swasey/Bladen grave good assemblage is among the most diversified and least consistent at Cuello, including pottery, a ceramic bird whistle, jade, greenstone, and shell jewelry, bone and chert tools, and ground stone. The presence of jade and greenstone in the burial assemblage by the end of Bladen, ca. 650 B.C., indicates the procurement of long-distance trade items for sumptuary use from as far as 350 km away in the Guatemalan highlands.

Only 7 (26 percent) of the 27 Swasey/Bladen interments had no grave goods, but ceramic and shell objects were the only offerings frequently deposited. The most common occurrence was a medium-to-large-sized bowl inverted over the head. Shell objects were slightly more commonly associated with female adults (6/10; 60 percent) than male adults (3/7; 43 percent); three juvenile burials also contained shell objects, one with some five hundred carefully made discoidal shell beads (which, given the presence of shell-working scrap at this period, may well have been made at Cuello).

Jade was associated with one male (14 percent), three females (30 percent), and four juveniles (50 percent). Two jade objects, associated with adult female burial (114) and child burial (166), are of particular interest. One is a blue jade spangle pendant (Hammond 1991: fig. 9.8n), the other a blue jade mirror-skeuomorph or "clamshell" pendant (Fig. 1; Hammond, Clarke, and Estrada Belli 1992: fig. 5). The geological source for this blue jade is unknown, but, as the former piece resembles blue jade spangle pendants from La Venta, it is possible that it originated as an artifact in the Gulf Coast/Isthmus of Tehuantepec region some 600 km west of Cuello. The latter is similar to jades from Chacsinkin, Yucatan, which Andrews (1986) called "Olmec" before recanting (1987).

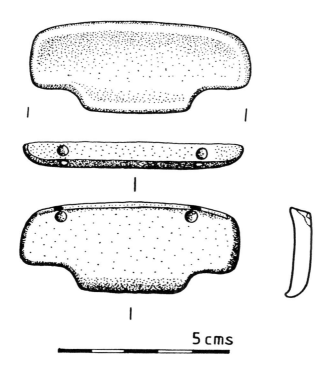

Fig. 1 Blue jade concave pendant of mirror-skeuomorph form from Cuello Burial 166, late Bladen phase, ca. 650 B.C.

Access to both multiple grave goods and long-distance trade items cut across age and sex boundaries. If generalizations on social structure could be based on so few individuals, the distribution of grave goods in the Swasey/Bladen phase would suggest some social differentiation not based on age or sex.

Late Middle Pre-Classic: Lopez Mamom Phase, 650–400 B.C.

Thirty individuals in single graves dated to the Late Middle Pre-Classic Lopez Mamom phase, of which 20 (67 percent) were adults (16 males [53 percent], 3 females [10 percent], and one of unknown sex) and 10 (33 percent) were juveniles.

By Lopez times the patio floor was less the locus of domestic activity than previously. Burial 22, of a male middle-to-old adult, located in the center of the patio, may indicate use of the patio area for communal ritual activity in the form of ancestor veneration, a practice more common in the Late Pre-Classic at Cuello. The subsequent patio floor contained no pits associated with domes-

53

tic use: all domestic activity was relegated to ancillary platforms. Patio floor V was cut by one jade cache (F190), though by no burials.

Twenty-eight (93 percent) of the Lopez phase interments were situated in houses or ancillary structures, one in an occupation surface associated with a domestic platform, and one, as noted above, was located in the center of the patio floor. As in the preceding Swasey/Bladen phases, adults of both sexes and juveniles were interred in domestic platforms. The predominant grave type (29/30; 97 percent) in the Lopez phase continued to be simple, with one cist grave, and there seems to have been a preference for extended positions over flexed, with no prevalent orientation.

Most Lopez burials had pottery vessels, and all those with grave goods had some kind of shell ornament: shell beads were associated with males and juveniles, shell bracelets/necklaces were found with males, females, and juveniles, and groups of shell beads with males and females. Other grave goods, chert, hematite, and jade, were less common. Jade beads were found only with males and by the elbows or in combination with shell jewelry. There was greater differentiation in Lopez between individuals with and those without grave goods than in the Swasey/Bladen sample. Seventy percent of the Lopez phase burials had at least three grave goods, and the majority of those with grave goods had three to five items. A high number of grave goods was associated

5 cms

Fig. 2 Bone gorget made from human skull, Cuello Burial 160, Lopez Mamom phase, ca. 500–450 B.C. The technique combines incision, cut-out, and drilling; the drilled pupils of the eyes may have held jade beads, since loose specimens of an appropriate size were found in the grave.

with long-distance trade items; one of the most elaborate, Burial 160, had jade beads, carved bone tubes at the waist, and a bone gorget (Fig. 2; Hammond, Clarke, and Estrada Belli 1992: fig. 6).

There are also some distinctive traits correlated with the location of burials: Burial 1 lacked the skull, possible evidence of decapitation, or retention for veneration; it was interred, with a slab of chert where the head would have been, in the western platform, Str. 317. In Str. 352 above it a decapitated adolescent burial was placed axially, and a juvenile skull burial was placed at the top midpoint of the final pyramid, Str. 35, at the beginning of the Early Classic; thus only mutilated burials are known from the western platform throughout the Pre-Classic and into the Early Classic. All other Middle Pre-Classic platforms contained only complete burials, although no great architectural distinctions are apparent between the western platforms and those on the other sides of the patio. Thus by the end of the Middle Pre-Classic in the fourth century B.C. we see variability in burial format suggestive of social differentiation, and of differential treatment of some dead compatible with sacrificial and offertory burial or with veneration (see McAnany 1995), although the youth of some individuals makes their designation as "ancestors" problematic.

Late Pre-Classic Burials: Cocos Phase, 400 B.C.–A.D. 250

The largest number of burials, 104 individuals comprising 68 percent of the total Cuello sample, date to the Cocos phase (Robin 1989: tables 16–52). The large size of the sample and an excavation strategy exploring all Cocos phase contexts on Platform 34 suggest that it is representative of the population buried on Platform 34 in this period. As Platform 34 was the apparent focus of the Late Pre-Classic ceremonial precinct at Cuello, the burial practices were perhaps most representative of those of the elite segment of the population. Both sexes and all age groups from infancy to old age are represented in the Cocos phase sample, but it is clear that the 4.8:1 ratio of men to women does not represent a normal population distribution.

Contexts. Early in Cocos times the Lopez patio group was buried by limestone rubble more than a meter deep, in a drastic architectural transformation that culminated in the construction of the broad, elevated, open Platform 34 (Hammond and Gerhardt 1990; Hammond n.d.). A sacrificial mass burial (Mass Burial 1: Burials 29–60) of 32 individuals was placed in the center top of the rubble fill (Hammond 1991: figs. 10.4–10.5). Two adult males were the first to be deposited; in their laps and by their feet lay body bundles of nine male adults: the bones must have been at least partly fleshed prior to burial; interpretation of any or all of these men as venerated ancestor interments is, to me, less plausible than the sacrificial alternative. Around this central group were placed 21 more individuals, all (with one possible exception) males, from young adult to old adult; not all of them were necessarily members of the Cuello community, as the capture of victims for sacrifice cannot be discounted. This holocaust marked the construction of Platform 34 and a change in architectural layout from the Middle Pre-Classic patio group to the broad open platform of the Late Pre-Classic.

Successive plaza floors were constructed on Platform 34 in phases VA to XIV, and in phase XI ca. A.D. 100 the plain Stela 1 was erected above the locus of the mass burial. Another sacrificial mass burial (F128: Mass Burial 2, Burials 68–79), containing 12 male individuals, was deposited east of Stela 1 (Hammond 1991: fig. 10.6). Two single primary burials, a double secondary burial, and two body bundles, containing eight secondary interments, make up Mass Burial 2. In both mass burials two individuals are the first to be placed in position, had human body bundles in their laps, and the remainder of the interments were located around the central pair. Not only are the central pair the focus of each mass burial, but they also possess the most grave goods: such patterning suggests that the two individuals were not just the physical focus of the group but also its social focus.

Six other burials seem to have been sacrifices associated with the construction of Platform 34: two were decapitated adults, one male and one female (?), lying parallel to each other but on opposite orientations, their skulls and mandibles standing upright some little way from their natural position (Hammond 1991: fig. 10.7). The others included two young children, one decapitated with a pot over the stump of the neck (Robin 1989: 382–384).

On the western side of the plaza in phases VI–XIV stood a succession of apparently ceremonial buildings of which the earliest, Str. 352, was a raised platform and the later ones stepped pyramids (Strs. 351, 350, 35). An axial burial of a decapitated adolescent (Burial 27) was placed in the final phase of Str. 352, the first western ceremonial structure. This is the only burial in these western structures in the Cocos phase.

Only the buildings on the north side of the Late Pre-Classic plaza are well known: those to the south and east were badly eroded, although a triadic layout embracing Str. 352 and its pyramidal successors existed. Burials were placed in every Cocos phase residential platform; there were no special funerary structures. As in the Middle Pre-Classic, there was opportunistic placement of domestic burials with continued use of structures, contrasting with the purposeful placement of the two mass burials and two ceremonial platform interments.

It is clear that strikingly different populations were buried in the public plaza area and the residences on the northern edge of the plaza. If one considers only definitely sexed individuals, the ratio of males to females is 28:0, while that of adults to children is 47:0 in the public plaza area; in residential platforms the ratios are 16:10 and 31:11 respectively. Males were selected for public burial, implying their importance in public activity (including sacrifice) in the Cocos phase. Within the residential sector the ratio of men to women to children suggests the same family-type burial grouping seen in the Middle Pre-Classic patio residences; juveniles were about one-third of the buried population in both northern platforms.

Burial format. Fifty-three graves (including the two large mass burial graves) contained the 104 Cocos phase interments. The predominant grave type (42/53; 80 percent) was still simple, although these included single, double, and triple primary and secondary interments, as well as both mass burials. Six cist graves and four crypts were found; two of the latter were plaster crypts. More elaborate types of graves do not seem to be sex-associated; seven were located in residential platforms; no association between grave wealth and grave type is apparent.

The fact that 31 percent (32 individuals) of all Cocos burials were disarticulated reflects the large number of individuals (24) contained in body bundles in the two mass burials; only three examples of completely disarticulated remains were found outside the public plaza locus. Otherwise, the seated position was the most common articulation (43 percent), while 28 percent of individuals were flexed, 17 percent extended, and 12 percent semi-reclining; every cardinal and intercardinal orientation was present, with west (25 percent) the most common. Within the plaza area, 54 percent of burials (7 individuals) were oriented west. The correlation between plaza burials and a predominantly western or toward-the-pyramid orientation may also signify the importance of these burials in public/ceremonial rituals.

Mortuary assemblage. The Cocos phase mortuary assemblage was the most diversified in the Pre-Classic phases at Cuello. Types of grave goods found in the Cocos phase include pottery vessels (one imported), carved bone tubes, jade, greenstone, and shell beads and shell pendants, obsidian blades, a chert tool, two metates, and red ocher sticks. Contact with the eastern Maya Highlands is indicated by an Olocuitla Orange Usulutan tetrapod bowl, dated by Demarest and Sharer (1982) to 400 B.C.–A.D. 100, the only imported vessel found at Cuello (Hammond 1991: fig. 9.5).

In the Middle Pre-Classic the mortuary ceramic assemblage did not differ from that used for domestic purposes; in the Late Pre-Classic also the absence of specifically mortuary ceramics is noted, although burials often included rather large examples of generally used vessel forms (Pyburn and Kosakowsky n.d.), unsurprising given their function of covering the body.

There were a few grave good types unique to mortuary contexts in the Cocos phase, including the Usulutan bowl, an amphora-shaped jar (Hammond 1991: fig. 3.39a), and seven carved bone tubes which could have functioned as handles for feather fans or bloodletting implements (Hammond 1991: figs. 8.35–8.38). All were found in mass burial assemblages, where the body bundles of disarticulated remains might also be considered as "human grave goods." The five tubes with the *pop* motif, together with the cruder examples from burial 160, seem to be the earliest firmly provenanced instances of this symbol of authority in the Maya Lowlands, and suggest that from the late fifth or early fourth century B.C. onward the effective exercise of power was accompanied and advertised by an iconography that developed into a greater Classic complexity.

Seventy-seven percent (n = 61) of the individual Cocos phase interments had grave goods. Sixty-nine percent (n = 55) had at least one ceramic vessel, and 23 percent (n = 19) had some type of shell object. The remaining Cocos phase grave goods were only occasionally found. Within domestic contexts, males (1.05) and females (1.09) had roughly the same mean number of pots per individual, and juveniles had a mean 0.73 pots. Males within public/ceremonial contexts had a higher mean number of pots than either males, females, or juveniles buried in other contexts at Cuello.

Vessel placement includes 64 percent of those thus equipped (n = 35) who had at least one vessel, whole or smashed, inverted over their head. Another vessel position, not found previously, was common in the Late Pre-Classic: 14 individuals (25 percent) had a vessel upright in their lap, suggesting its possible use as a food/beverage container. The vessel-in-lap position was most commonly found with seated burials, perhaps explaining why it was not used until the Late Pre-Classic. The smashing of ceramic vessels was a fairly common Cocos phase custom unrestricted by age, sex, or context.

Fourteen of the 17 long-distance trade items were found with sacrificial burials. Jade was associated with adult male burials insofar as sex can be specified; other greenstone was associated with females and juveniles, suggesting that the Maya could distinguish real jade from "social jade" (Hammond et al. 1977: 61).

Though all ages and sexes had access to long-distance trade items, they were much more commonly associated with public/ceremonial burials of males. In contrast to the Middle Pre-Classic, where access to long-distance trade items was associated with high overall total numbers of grave goods, in the Cocos phase, long-distance trade items were found with individuals possessing no other grave goods, as well as with those possessing many.

The mean number of grave goods per Cocos phase individual is 1.92: almost all the interments fall within two standard deviations of the mean. Only five individuals, those with seven or more grave goods, fall beyond this: all five of these individuals were sacrificial burials, four from the mass burials. Thus, whether the grave goods of these individuals marked individual wealth or the importance of the ritual activity in which they played a part is difficult to say, but certainly "wealth" in terms of total grave goods was concentrated in public/sacrificial burials in Cocos times.

In residential burial contexts, 25 percent (eight individuals) had no grave goods; the mean number of grave goods was 1.30. The same lack of age/sex differentiation in total number of grave goods observed in the Middle Pre-Classic continued into the Late Pre-Classic in residential contexts; but individuals buried in public contexts had significantly more grave goods than those buried in houses.

Sacrifice

In the Late Pre-Classic, human sacrifice may be indicated by the number and condition of those interred in the mass burials and also by four types of disarticulation (n = 14): severed skull, decapitated body, disarticulated complete body, and disarticulated leg bones only. Such burials were most common in public contexts, but three skull burials, perhaps dedicatory, in the northern residential structures indicate that these possibly had a public/ceremonial function sometimes as well as a domestic one.

Individuals packaged into body bundles were unique to the mass burials. Robin and Hammond (1991: 224) suggest that they lost not only their physical identity as individuals but their social identities as well, and can be interpreted as "human grave goods." Although we cannot determine whether mutilation was the cause of death or part of postmortem ritual, such secondary burials are our best evidence for Pre-Classic Maya human sacrifice, although sometimes the context of a primary burial will also indicate it. On the evidence to hand, individual sacrifice was practiced from the Early Middle Formative onward, persisting throughout the Cuello sequence, while mass sacrifice was introduced at the same time as monumental archtectural construction begins to reflect the reality of political power at the beginning of the Late Pre-Classic around 400 b.c.

Offertory Practices: Caches

Thirty-one caches of deliberately deposited artifacts were found at Cuello, all but one definitely of Late Pre-Classic date; the exception (F190) is likely to fall at the very beginning of that period. All pottery vessels included in cache offerings are of the Cocos Chicanel ceramic complex, with the majority belonging to Sierra Red and Society Hall Red, the two dominant ceramic types of the Late Formative. Most are flaring-side bowls, which when paired are set lip-to-lip.

The caches form three main groups: (1) dedicatory offerings for successive plaza floors on top of Platform 34; (2) dedicatory and valedictory offerings for successive buildings on the north side of the plaza; and (3) dedicatory offerings for successive raising and enlargement of the buildings on the west side of the Platform 34 plaza, culminating in the Early Classic pyramid, Str. 35. The main exceptions to this are the earliest offering (F190) of phase IVA, set into the latest patio floor (V), but possibly at the end of its history and actually linked to the infill of the patio and initial raising of Platform 34, with Plaza Floor I as its surface; and the dedicatory cache of Stela 1 (F136), coeval with Plaza Floor VII. Even the exceptional caches, therefore, seem to be associated with construction activity.

Plaza Floor caches. The Plaza Floor caches are varied in their content, but show a certain consistency in the artifacts offered and an increase in the size and number of offerings through time. The earliest caches, associated with Plaza Floor III, consist of a pair of bowls set lip-to-lip (F181) and a concentration of deer (*Odocoileus virginianus*) mandibles with a large tanged chert macroblade "dagger" (F140). The next offering (F30; Hammond 1991: fig. 10.12) is also a concentration of deer mandibles, with upper molars and cranial fragments suggesting that entire heads may have been offered, some two-thirds (20/30 MNI) of them juveniles, associated with Plaza Floor VI. This part of the animal does not carry much meat, so that they are unlikely to be the remnants of a ceremonial meal; the high proportion of juveniles suggests selection. The significance of ritual faunas such as these deer-head offerings has been discussed by Pohl (1983).

Plaza Floor IX has three caches within the area of the Main Trench (F11, 122, 76/15), and eight others probably associated (F6, 12, 28, 47, 58, 60, 76, 83).

F6, the largest cache so far found (Hammond 1991: fig. 10.13), contains 94 bowls in 47 pairs, organized most often in groups of four pairs on a north-south alignment, with a total of 21 jade beads. A north-south orientation predominates where a group is linear: this may be facing the entire group toward (or away from) the pyramid on the west side of Platform 34. On a larger scale, seven of these eleven caches form a north-south line in front of the pyramid (Hammond 1991: fig. 10.16).

North side structure caches. Eight caches were found in the successive subcircular and subrectangular buildings on the north side of the plaza, none earlier than phase VIII. They included single and paired bowls, three of these enclosing a child's skull. One unusual offering consisted of a spindle-shaped limestone hammerstone, a chalcedony flake, and a Colha-type chert tranchet-bit tool.

Pyramid caches. Five caches lie in the succession of buildings on the west side of Platform 34. The earliest (F80; Hammond 1991: fig. 10.17) is associated with Str. 352 at the beginning of Cocos (phases VI–VII). It consists of four unworn chert macroblade "daggers" and two stingray spines, all bundled together as though once wrapped, as well as a worn small dark greenstone ax. All except the ax could have been used in bloodletting. It may be significant that Str. 352 is the first of the succession of west side buildings to be raised to any marked degree, and possibly the first ceremonial rather than residential structure at that locus.

Stela cache. The Late Pre-Classic Stela 1 at Cuello, with an estimated date of A.D. 100, was sealed by Plaza Floor VII; in the pit cut into Plaza Floor VI to receive the stela butt, an offering (F136) of three vessels was made, including a trichrome open bowl, a monochrome red high-necked bowl, and an inverted red bowl with a parrot effigy modeled over it (Hammond 1991: figs. 3.43, 10.19). The stela, one of the earliest in the Maya Lowlands, and its offering are discussed by Hammond (1982).

Discussion

Absent from all these caches are any contents that the vessels might have held, apart from three with child skulls and those with jade beads. The provision of bloodletting equipment in F80 reminds us that bloody paper could have been among these perishable offerings, as well as the foodstuffs often suggested. The parity of content between dedicatory offerings in the west side buildings, which are in form ceremonial, and those on the north side, suggests that the latter also might have had a ritual function, even though they were clearly lived in.

The mass of plaza floor caches shows that reflooring Platform 34 was not just a practical affair, but one accompanied by ceremony and offerings. While F6 with its 94 vessels is among the larger Maya caches known, the vessels themselves and their imperishable contents were, like the grave goods found with the burials, modest in kind. The only vessels that might be seen as made for offertory purposes, being distinct from those found in middens, were those in the cache below Stela 1. Of the few nonceramic offerings, the most unusual are the two collocations of deer mandibles (F30, F140).

The number of caches is low early in the Late Pre-Classic (one to three per phase up to phase X, perhaps four in phase VIII), rising to a maximum of eight in phase XI. This increase in offertory activity coincides with the construction of the first pyramid on the west side of the plaza, with the alignment of Strs. 304–305 on a common front (perhaps forming a triadic group with the pyramid and the south side structures), and with the erection of Stela 1 and then the construction of Str. 302 in the plaza center. The coincidence of stela erection with Mass Burial 2 and the high number of caches suggest that a significant increase in the ritual status of the plaza took place around A.D. 100, and was maintained through subsequent periods of use.

SOCIAL IMPLICATIONS OF PRE-CLASSIC BURIAL PRACTICES AT CUELLO

Throughout the Pre-Classic the inclusion of individuals of both sexes and juveniles in domestic platforms illustrates the family nature of these burials. Domestic burials show no age/sex differentiation of grave "wealth" in terms of type and number of grave goods or their absence. The association of juveniles with as many grave goods as adults could indicate hereditary wealth, or, equally likely, grave goods were personal equipment that did not function as "wealth." The presence of cranial deformation or dental mutilation is not correlated with burial locus or content: it might denote social role, but it does not appear to mark social rank.

Throughout the initial construction, use, reflooring, remodeling, and eventual abandonment or destruction of a building, burials were incorporated into its structural fills and floors, indicating opportunistic sepulture in residential contexts; continued occupation seems to have been the norm, although temporary abandonment is probably archaeologically undetectable. Though some Pre-Classic structures at Cuello lacked burials, none lay completely within the excavation, and unexcavated portions of these structures could hold interments. Although some of the northern buildings have a high density of burials, there is no evidence that they were mausolea; those burials at Cuello not in house platforms seem to have been dedicatory to ceremonial buildings.

Mortuary assemblages were fairly consistent throughout the sequence, internally and in relation to refuse assemblages (Pyburn and Kosakowsky n.d.); although some pottery types are known only from burials, there is no indication that they were made only for sepulture, and where there was apparent selection, as for especially large dishes and bowls in some Cocos burials, there was also a clear practical function of protecting the corpse. Throughout the Pre-Classic at Cuello, ceramic vessels and shell objects, predominantly beads, were the most common grave goods. Jade was used from the end of the Bladen phase, and although obsidian occurred in refuse contexts at Cuello from Bladen onward, it was not part of the mortuary assemblage until the Cocos phase. Chert tools were found throughout the Pre-Classic, bone tools only in Bladen burials, ground stone in both the Bladen and Cocos mortuary assemblages, and red ochre in Lopez and Cocos. The low frequency of many objects, rather than true chronological differentiation, probably causes this apparent association with certain time periods.

Throughout the Middle Pre-Classic, males, females, and juveniles were comparably furnished; in the Late Pre-Classic, residential burials continued to be so, but by this time the focus of elaborate burial activity had changed from the domestic/individual locus to the public/communal one. Males predominated there, especially in the two mass burials, with far "wealthier" grave assemblages containing more exotic and unique items than residential burials. Whether this "wealth" represented individual lifetime possessions or the importance of the public burial rite is uncertain. The nonrandom patterning of grave goods in the mass burials suggests that the two central individuals in both mass burials were elaborately interred not just as the foci of these mortuary rites, but also possibly as members of a perceived elite, either that of Cuello or that of the community from which the burial participants were drawn. If the former, the inclusion of the bone tubes with the *pop* motif suggests veneration of a ruling lineage; in either case, differentiation of nobility in death as in life. Such indications of developing social complexity accord with what is becoming known from other Pre-Classic Maya sites, including K'axob, Colha, and Cerros in northern Belize and several much larger sites in Peten including El Mirador and now Nakbe.

Hansen (1992: 184) suggests that the development of Pre-Classic Maya religion followed a Durkheimian model, itself based on Greek and Roman evidence, whereby ancestor worship became established initially with individual family lineages. Then, as the population grew, cults arose which transcended lineage worship and created a broader religious solidarity which underwrote and legitimized the status and actions of a ruling elite. This manifested itself in the enormous social investment in ritual architecture seen early in the Late

Pre-Classic at Nakbe and then El Mirador, Guiro, and Tintal and more distant centers such as Calakmul, Uaxactun, Tikal, Lamanai, and Cerros. The huge sculptures adorning these buildings were of deities, not kings—focus on the ruler as a link between the mundane and supernal worlds came several centuries later. The burial evidence from Cuello suggests that this latter process began with ancestor veneration from around 600 B.C., with recognition of rulership status by 400 B.C. and iconographic representation of rulers elsewhere occurring in the mid-Late Pre-Classic, initially on small objects such as jades but by the second century A.D. on public monuments also.

CONCLUSION

Both offerings and burials at Cuello document a Pre-Classic community developing a ritual life over a period of nearly fifteen hundred years. While there are few hints of stratification in Middle Pre-Classic society, there is some disparity in grave goods which is not clearly age-linked: ascribed status may well have existed before 700 B.C. By 400 B.C., even though the burials still exhibit a high degree of social homogeneity, Mass Burial 1 and the architectural transformation of Platform 34 indicate the existence and use of political power and its iconographic expression in the carved bones with their *pop* motifs. After this date we see the occurrence of public offerings, the beginnings of the elite culture that was to culminate in the Classic period. The cultural sequence at Cuello, the longest continuous Pre-Classic development so far documented in the Maya Area, is distinctively Maya; yet it is also clearly Mesoamerican in all its essentials and reminds us that, although the Maya evolved their own civilization from deep roots, it was never isolated from the larger world of Mesoamerica.

Acknowledgments The burials excavated at Cuello before 1990 have been discussed in detail by Cynthia Robin (1989), and some of the data presented here have been taken from that monograph and from the chapter by Robin and myself in Hammond (1991). All skeletal analyses were by Julie M. Saul and Frank P. Saul. The data on caches were compiled by Juliette Cartwright Gerhardt, although the analysis is my own. The excavations at Cuello were funded by the National Geographic Society (1978–90), the British Museum (1978–87), Cambridge University (1975–87), Rutgers University (1978–87), and Boston University (1990–93). Figures 1 and 2 were drawn by Sheena Howarth.

BIBLIOGRAPHY

ANDREWS, E. WYLLYS, V
1986   Olmec Jades from Chacsinkin, Yucatan, and Maya Ceramics from La Venta,
        Tabasco. In *Research and Reflections in Archaeology and History: Essays in Honor
        of Doris Stone* (E. Wyllys Andrews V, ed.): 11–49. Tulane University, Middle
        American Research Institute, Publication 57. New Orleans.
1987   A Cache of Early Jades from Chacsinkin, Yucatan. *Mexicon* 9: 78–85.

ANDREWS, E. WYLLYS, V, AND NORMAN HAMMOND
1990   Redefinition of the Swasey Phase at Cuello, Belize. *American Antiquity* 54:
        570–584.

DEMAREST, ARTHUR A., AND ROBERT J. SHARER
1982   The Origins and Evolution of Usulutan Ceramics. *American Antiquity* 47:
        810–827.

HAMMOND, NORMAN
1982   A Late Formative Period Stela in the Maya Lowlands. *American Antiquity* 47:
        396–403.
n.d.   Architectural Transformation in the Late Middle Formative at Cuello, Belize.
        In *Reconstructing the Past: Recent Studies in Maya Prehistory* (David M. Pendergast
        and Anthony P. Andrews, eds.). In preparation.

HAMMOND, NORMAN (ED.)
1991   *Cuello: An Early Maya Community in Belize*. Cambridge University Press,
        Cambridge.

HAMMOND, NORMAN, ARNOLD ASPINALL, STUART FEATHER, JOHN HAZELDEN, TREVOR
GAZARD, AND STUART AGRELL
1977   Maya Jade: Source Location and Analysis. In *Exchange Systems in Prehistory*
        (Timothy K. Earle and Jonathan E. Ericson, eds.): 35–67. Academic Press,
        New York.

HAMMOND, NORMAN, AMANDA CLARKE, AND SARA DONAGHEY
1995   The Long Goodbye: Middle Preclassic Maya Archaeology at Cuello, Belize,
        1993. *Latin American Antiquity* 6: 120–128.

HAMMOND, NORMAN, AMANDA CLARKE, AND FRANCISCO ESTRADA BELLI
1992   Middle Preclassic Maya Buildings and Burials at Cuello, Belize. *Antiquity* 66:
        955–964.

HAMMOND, NORMAN, AMANDA CLARKE, AND CYNTHIA ROBIN
1991   Middle Preclassic Buildings and Burials at Cuello, Belize: 1990 Investiga-
        tions. *Latin American Antiquity* 2: 352–363.

HAMMOND, NORMAN, AND JULIETTE CARTWRIGHT GERHARDT
1990   Early Maya Architectural Innovation at Cuello, Belize. *World Archaeology* 21:
        461–481.

HANSEN, RICHARD D.
1992   El proceso cultural de Nakbe y el área del Petén nor-central: las épocas
        tempranas. In *V Simposio de investigaciones arquelógicas en Guatemala, Museo
        Nacional de Arqueología y Etnología, 15–18 de Julio de 1991* (Juan Pedro Laporte,

H. L. Escobedo A., and Sandra Villagrán de Brady, eds.): 81–87. Ministerio de Cultura y Deportes, Instituto de Antropología e Historia, Asociación Tikal, Guatemala City.

HAVILAND, WILLIAM A.
1985   *Excavations in Small Residential Groups of Tikal: Groups 4F-1 and 4F-2.* Tikal Report 19. University Museum Monograph 58. University Museum, University of Pennsylvania, Philadelphia.

HOUSLEY, RUPERT A., NORMAN HAMMOND, AND IAN LAW
1991   AMS Radiocarbon Dating of Preclassic Maya Burials at Cuello, Belize. *American Antiquity* 56: 514–519.

KOSAKOWSKY, LAURA J.
1987   *Prehistoric Maya Pottery at Cuello, Belize.* Anthropological Paper 47. University of Arizona Press, Tucson.

LAW, IAN, RUPERT A. HOUSLEY, NORMAN HAMMOND, AND ROBERT E. M. HEDGES
1991   Cuello: Resolving the Chronology through Direct Dating of Conserved and Low-Collagen Bone by AMS. *Radiocarbon* 33: 303–315.

McANANY, PATRICIA A.
1995   *Living with the Ancestors: Kinship and Kingship in Ancient Maya Society.* University of Texas Press, Austin.

POHL, MARY D.
1983   Maya Ritual Faunas: Vertebrate Remains from Burials, Caches, Caves, and Cenotes in the Maya Lowlands. In *Civilization in the Ancient Americas: Essays in Honor of Gordon R. Willey* (Richard M. Leventhal and Alan L. Kolata, eds.): 55–103. Peabody Museum of Archaeology and Ethnology, Harvard University, Cambridge, Mass., and University of New Mexico Press, Albuquerque.

PYBURN, K. ANNE, AND LAURA J. KOSAKOWSKY
n.d.   *Burial Practices: Description of Ceramic Grave Goods* [at Cuello]. Manuscript on file, Cuello Project Archive, Boston University, 1982.

ROBIN, CYNTHIA
1989   *Preclassic Maya Burials at Cuello, Belize.* British Archaeological Reports International Series 480. BAR, Oxford.

ROBIN, CYNTHIA, AND NORMAN HAMMOND
1991   Ritual and Ideology: Burial Practices. In *Cuello: An Early Maya Community in Belize* (Norman Hammond, ed.): 204–225. Cambridge University Press, Cambridge.

SHARER, ROBERT J., AND DAVID W. SEDAT
1987   *Archaeological Investigations in the Northern Maya Highlands, Guatemala: Interaction and the Development of Maya Civilization.* University Museum Monograph 59. University Museum, University of Pennsylvania, Philadelphia.

WILK, RICHARD R., AND HAROLD L. WILHITE, JR.
1991   The Community of Cuello: Patterns of Household and Settlement Change. In *Cuello: An Early Maya Community in Belize* (Norman Hammond, ed.): 118–133. Cambridge University Press, Cambridge.

Men's and Women's Ritual in Formative Oaxaca

JOYCE MARCUS
UNIVERSITY OF MICHIGAN

Ancient ritual is a fascinating topic, but unfortunately one in which speculation tends to outstrip solid archaeological data. Archaeologists can attempt to reconstruct ancient rituals only under certain conditions. Unless they are able to open broad horizontal exposures, locate a wide range of units (caches, features, burials, dooryards, patios, house floors, and public buildings), excavate such units in their entirety, and piece-plot all artifacts *in situ,* they have to be very lucky to find evidence for ritual. In Oaxaca we have been able to isolate such units in the ground and to subject the data to a wide range of analyses. Even so, I cannot accomplish as much as the editors of this volume would like.

EARLY VILLAGERS IN THE VALLEY OF OAXACA

After thousands of years of a seminomadic lifeway involving hunting, wild plant collecting, and incipient agriculture, the ancient Zapotec of the Valley of Oaxaca finally settled down, establishing themselves in hamlets on the valley floor (Fig. 1).

The oldest known sedentary community, San José Mogote, was founded between 1700 and 1400 B.C. by farmers using pottery and artifacts that define our Espiridión complex (Marcus 1983a: 42–43; Flannery and Marcus 1994: 45–54). This complex is known from one house at the village, and our only Espiridión "ritual" artifact is a miniature ceramic mask of a feline. Apart from suggesting the antiquity of masks and feline motifs in the Mesoamerican highlands, it tells us little.

Villagers of this period planted maize, squash, pumpkins, beans, chile peppers, and avocados, and continued to collect wild plants such as maguey, prickly pear, West Indian cherry, and hackberry. They also hunted deer, rabbits, peccary,

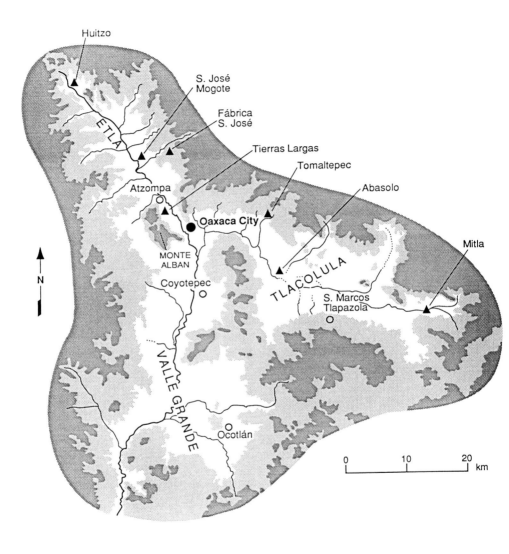

Fig. 1 The Valley of Oaxaca, Mexico, showing Early Formative sites mentioned in the text.

gophers, opossum, raccoons, mud turtles, quail, and doves, and raised domestic dogs for food.

A window into ancient society opens during the Tierras Largas phase, 1400–1150 B.C. During this phase the valley's population grew to an estimated 400 to 600 persons. They lived in 19 hamlets of 1–3 ha each and in one 7 ha village, San José Mogote. Our evidence suggests that this was a time when society was egalitarian and villages were autonomous. It is during the Tierras Largas phase that we can first detect differences between men's and women's ritual.

Building Types

Based on linguistic terms used by the ancient Zapotec to classify their buildings, we might expect to find three different types of structures for the Formative period. The terms for all three structures begin with the word for house, *yoho* (Córdova 1942). The simplest structure was the lean-to or ramada (*yoho yaha* or *yoho yaa*); more permanent was the thatched hut (*yoho quixi* or *yoho coba*); and the most permanent was the lineage or descent group's structure (*yoho tija*).

Of these three types of structures, the house was the most frequently encountered in the early villages of the Valley of Oaxaca. By 1350 B.C. early villages included houses that were 3–4 m wide and 5–6 m long, with walls of wattle-and-daub, pine posts that supported a thatched roof, and a clay floor with a surface of sand. These houses were probably equivalent to the *yoho quixi* or *yoho coba*. The door was usually on one of the long sides, and some houses had a stone threshold (*toayoho*; from *toa,* threshold, and *yoho,* house). Other stones were occasionally used in the foundations of the wattle-and-daub walls. In some houses we recovered silica exoskeletons of reed mats that had been placed on the house floors.

Men's ritual appears to have been conducted at small public buildings which look like forerunners of the *yoho tiya,* or "lineage house," of the later Zapotec. These small public buildings were probably analogous to Men's Houses in societies like those of Melanesia, and they contained no evidence of women's activities or tools. It appears that women's ritual was practiced in and near the home, the *yoho* of later Zapotec society.

This pattern—men's ritual being conducted in the "lineage house" and women's ritual being practiced in the house—continued into the San José phase, 1150–850 B.C. By that time the population of the valley had grown to an estimated 2,000 persons, living in 40 hamlets of 1–5 ha and in one village of 60–70 ha (San José Mogote). During the course of the San José phase, the construction of public buildings and the use of ritual paraphernalia escalated.

Both men's and women's ritual involved ancestors, but there were differences. Women seem to have been more concerned with recent ancestors, especially female ancestors. Men were more concerned with the spirits of remote ancestors, including those of supernatural apical ancestors. Women's ritual involved divining and the manipulation of figurines. Men's ritual involved bloodletting, dancing in costumes, and the use of ritual plants such as tobacco and jimson weed (*Datura* spp.).

By the end of the San José phase, it becomes increasingly difficult to recognize differences between men's and women's ritual because the emergence of hereditary differences in rank gradually began to flood the symbolic system with information on *status* differences. The differences between men's and women's ritual activities thus became masked by an increase in information about the differences between high- and low-status families. It is also the case that smaller communities began to lose their autonomy as they became satellites of larger villages. These larger communities eventually monopolized a great deal of the ritual activity formerly carried out by individual families. This appropriation of ritual by large regional centers ultimately impoverished the ritual inventories of hamlets.

A FRAMEWORK FOR STUDYING RITUAL

In this chapter I will build on three principles expressed years ago in *The Early Mesoamerican Village*: (1) although we cannot directly observe Formative rituals, we can recover the places where they were performed; (2) ritual must be performed over and over, in prescribed ways, to be valid; and (3) such repetitive performances lead to patterning of ritual artifact discard (Flannery 1976). I will further divide ritual into three main components: (I) its content, (II) its loci of performance, and (III) its performers.

I. *Content* refers to the subject matter of the ritual. Among the ethnohistoric Zapotec, the content of many rituals involved invoking the spirits of deceased ancestors and addressing *pée* (the vital force) within powerful components of the cosmos, such as Earth and Sky. Earth was frequently addressed in its active form, *Xoo* or Earthquake. Sky was frequently addressed in its belligerent form, *Cociyo* or Lightning. It is no accident that Earth and Sky became two of the earliest symbols depicted on Oaxaca pottery: Earth/Earthquake versus Sky/Lightning (Marcus 1989: 169–174).

II. *Locus of performance* refers to the place where rites were performed. The house, the graveside, the agricultural field, the mountaintop, and the public building were among the loci used by the ancient Zapotec. For example, sixteenth-century Zapotec farmers made offerings and sacrifices in their fields (*tiquillaya quela*), particularly on the occasion of the harvest (*totinijea*) or when petitioning to Lightning, requesting that he pierce the clouds to send rain to earth (*peni quij cocijo*).

Among the neighbors of the Zapotec (such as the present-day Mixe of Ayutla), offerings are still made to Lightning to secure rain and good crops (Beals 1945, 1973: 92; Lipp 1991). A turkey is killed in the middle of the field just before planting; a round hole is excavated; tortillas and tamales are placed in the hole. Then the blood of the turkey is sprinkled over the tortillas and tamales, and the hole is covered up. A preplanting ceremony conducted at Mixistlán involves burying young dogs, eggs, the blood of chickens, lime, and ashes. At Ayutla, turkey sacrifices and offerings are made in a cave above the town at different times—when the corn tassel first appears, when the first ears are formed, or if an animal is damaging the fields (Beals 1973: 93).

Villagers in Santo Domingo Albarradas, near Mitla, characterize some of their rites as designed "to feed the earth." Thus, during times of drought, four turkeys (two male, two female) are killed so that their blood can soak into the earth (Parsons 1936: 216). This act is part of a pattern among the Zapotec and Mixe, who say they make offerings and sacrifices at planting time "to honor the earth" and "to feed the earth."

Because we have not excavated in agricultural fields or on mountaintops in Oaxaca, we have not found such ritual loci. In addition, such rituals might leave few remains because their key elements are perishable. We have, however, recovered ritual data from houses, gravesides, and public buildings.

III. The *performers* of ritual among the ethnohistoric Zapotec were priests, rulers, and ordinary men and women. During the earliest stages of the Formative, of course, there were no priests or rulers; thus ordinary men and women were the performers of all rituals. During the later stages of the Formative, an elite emerged and (as already mentioned) appropriated many ritual activities formerly conducted by ordinary men and women.

MEN'S RITUAL

One of the loci for ritual during the Tierras Largas and early San José phases was a one-room public building, too small to hold all the members of the community (Fig. 2). These structures were probably used by a subset of the villagers—fully initiated males—who met periodically to petition their ancestors for aid in agricultural production, community events, and perhaps even intervillage raiding.

These early structures, of which we have found about ten, never contain domestic artifacts, figurines, or any tools one might associate with women. They do contain sharp obsidian flakes that could have been used for autosacrifice,

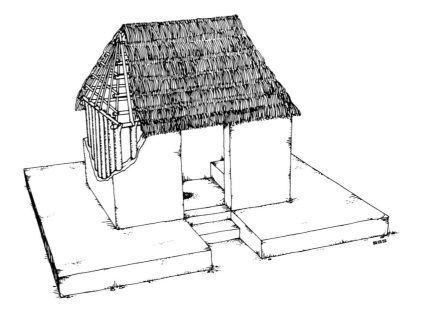

Fig. 2 Example of a Men's House (Structure 6) at San José Mogote.
Drawing by David Reynolds.

and they have lime-filled pits that may be associated with the use of narcotic plants.

These Men's Houses, some with radiocarbon dates as early as 1350 B.C., differed from ordinary residences in a number of ways. First, they were all oriented 8 degrees west of true north, an orientation shared by later public buildings in Oaxaca and other regions of Mesoamerica but not by ordinary houses. It is worth mentioning that these buildings provide our first evidence for such an orientation anywhere in Mesoamerica, antedating buildings of similar orientation at La Venta by more than half a millennium (Marcus 1989: 163). Thus our old notion of ritual influence emanating from the Gulf Coast was premature; both the Valley of Oaxaca and the Pacific Coast of Chiapas seem to have had public architecture at a time when none is known from the Gulf, and the 8 degree orientation was clearly established in the highlands long before we have any evidence for it in Veracruz or Tabasco (Flannery and Marcus 1994: 385–394).

The Tierras Largas phase Men's Houses contained two to three times as many posts as ordinary houses and were given a coat of lime plaster inside and out. The floor was also surfaced with lime plaster, in contrast to the floors of ordinary houses which were of stamped clay covered with a layer of sand. Several of the Men's Houses had a centrally placed, lime-plastered storage pit built into the floor, a feature not encountered in ordinary residences. These pits were filled with powdered lime, possibly stored for later use with ritual plants such as *quèeza* (tobacco) or *nocuanacohui* (*Datura*) or perhaps even for rituals of purification—the Zapotec employ the same word (*teáaya*) for "to purify" and "to whiten with lime" (Marcus and Flannery 1978; Marcus 1989: figs. 8.5 and 8.6 top).

Another place for men's ritual was at graveside. Toward the end of the Tierras Largas phase we see our first examples of seated burials, all middle-aged males (Fig. 3). Given the importance of seated burials in later Mesoamerican societies, we suspect that these are the burials of senior men who had earned a measure of respect in Tierras Largas society. The seated burials are so tightly flexed as to suggest that each was kept as a bundle (Fig. 4). No women were treated in this way, and the majority of male burials were in the extended position (Fig. 5).

During the subsequent San José phase, differential treatment of men becomes more striking. At this time we see the first depictions of Sky/Lightning and Earth/Earthquake carved or incised on the ceramics of the region (Figs. 6–8; see also Flannery and Marcus 1994: 135–286). When such vessels were placed with burials of individuals old enough to have their gender identified, they occur *only* with men. Vessels with Lightning or Earthquake motifs are also found with infants too young to have their gender determined; we assume that these are males, since other infants were buried with miniature versions of the pottery typically found with adult women.

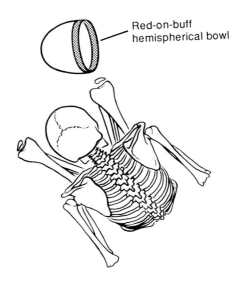

Red-on-buff
hemispherical bowl

Fig. 3 A man over age 40, buried in the seated position, near a Men's House at San José Mogote (Tierras Largas phase).

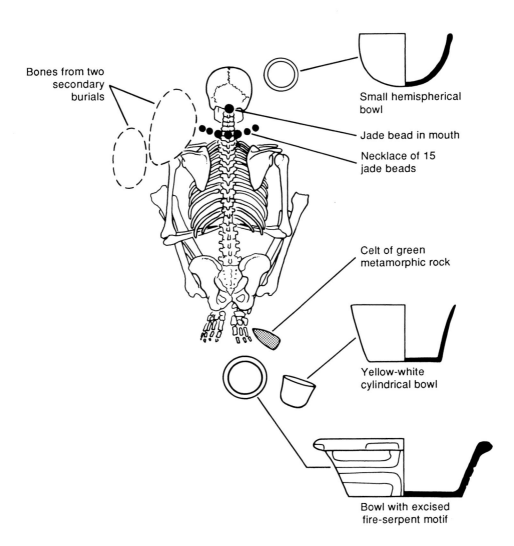

Bones from two secondary burials

Small hemispherical bowl

Jade bead in mouth

Necklace of 15 jade beads

Celt of green metamorphic rock

Yellow-white cylindrical bowl

Bowl with excised fire-serpent motif

Fig. 4 A man 30–40 years old, buried tightly flexed at Tomaltepec in the Valley of Oaxaca. He was accompanied by two secondary burials and a bowl with Sky/Lightning iconography (San José phase).

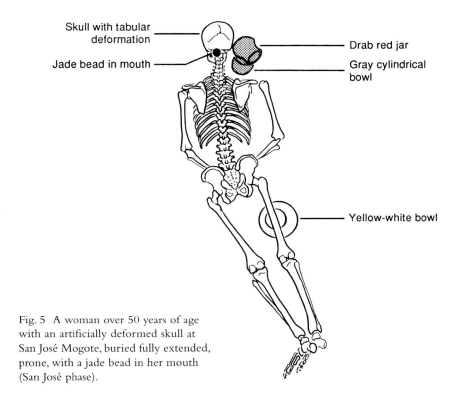

Skull with tabular deformation

Jade bead in mouth

Drab red jar

Gray cylindrical bowl

Yellow-white bowl

Fig. 5 A woman over 50 years of age with an artificially deformed skull at San José Mogote, buried fully extended, prone, with a jade bead in her mouth (San José phase).

Thus motifs of Lightning and Earth seem to have been associated with males from birth, but they were also associated with different residential wards at San José Mogote. Sky/Lightning was associated with Areas A and C, while Earth/Earthquake was associated with Area B (Marcus 1989: table 8.1; Flannery and Marcus 1994: chaps. 14, 16). Hamlets of 1–3 ha were evidently too small to contain members of both descent groups; at such communities only one of the motifs was used.

In Oaxaca, Earth can be depicted as a mask with a feline mouth and a cleft skull, representing a fissure in the earth left by Earthquake; abstract versions are also known (Fig. 6a). Earth is less frequently depicted as a crocodile foot (Fig. 7a). Sky is depicted as Lightning, a "serpent of fire" whose eyebrows are flames (Fig. 8b–e). In the more stylized versions, the face of the serpent is indicated by excised bars, the flame brows by incised sine curves, and his gums by inverted U's (Fig. 8b–c). More complete inventories of these motifs can be found in Flannery and Marcus (1994: chap. 12).

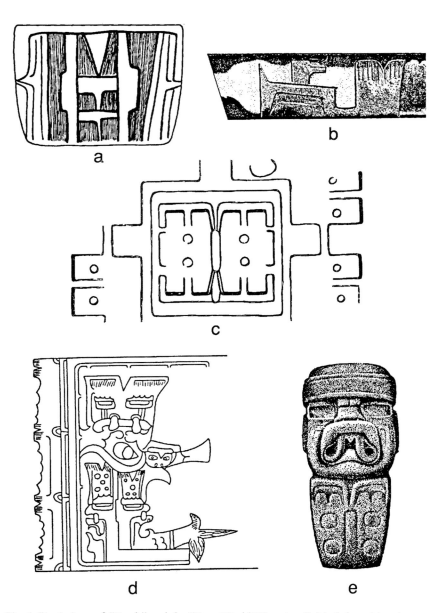

Fig. 6 Depictions of "Earth" and the "Four World Directions": (*a*) cleft-and-bracket version of Earth from Oaxaca vessel (after Flannery and Marcus 1994: 175); (*b*) cleft-and-gum/"shark" motif from Copan vessel (after Fash 1991: fig. 33); (*c*) cleft, tab, and four world directions from vessel at San José Mogote (after Marcus 1989: fig. 8.15); (*d*) were-jaguar, cleft, and Four World Directions from Tlatilco vessel (after Niederberger 1987: fig. 439); (*e*) were-jaguar, cleft, and Four World Direction motif on figurine (after Covarrubias 1957: fig. 32).

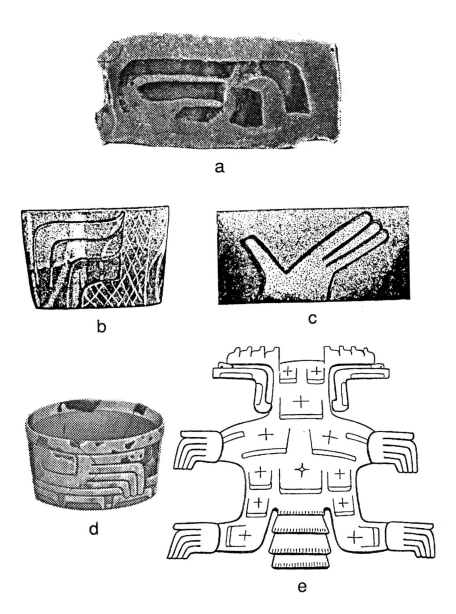

Fig. 7 Depictions of Earth as crocodile's foot: (*a*) impression of roller stamp from San José Mogote (after Flannery and Marcus 1994: 295); (*b–c*) vessels from South Platform, Copan (after Fash 1991: fig. 33); (*d*) ceramic vessel, provenience unknown (after Covarrubias 1957: 78); (*e*) crocodile skin worn by seated male figurine from Atlihuayan, Morelos (after Covarrubias 1957: fig. 21).

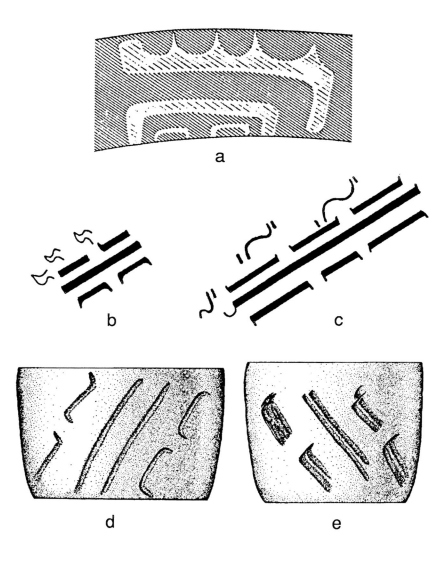

Fig. 8 Depictions of Sky/Lightning on pottery vessels: (*a*) from North Platform, Copan (after Fash 1991: fig. 33); (*b–e*) eyebrow flames, *raspada* bars, and gums of Lightning from Oaxaca (after Flannery and Marcus 1994: 141, 181).

The Earth/Sky Dichotomy in Other Regions

Oaxaca was not the only area of Mesoamerica where early descent groups show this dichotomy between the descendants of Earth and Sky. At Copan, Honduras—far to the south of Oaxaca—burials of the Uir phase (900–400 B.C.) show an analogous dichotomy (see also Joyce, this volume).

At Copan, William Fash (1991, n.d.) has uncovered two cobblestone platforms of the Uir phase, built near each other and formerly supporting pole-and-thatch structures. Below the South Platform were the graves of 15 individuals. Below the North Platform were the graves of another 32.

Ceramic offerings depicting Earth were restricted to the South Platform. At Copan, Earth was represented not by a feline mouth and cleft skull (as in Oaxaca), but via the symbol erroneously called the "paw-wing" motif (Fig. 7b–c). This symbol, as pointed out by Covarrubias (1957) and Grove (1984: 126), is actually the foot of a crocodile (Fig. 7e). This use of a crocodile's foot to stand for the whole crocodile is an example of *pars pro toto* (Fig. 7d). The crocodile's foot is an appropriate representation of Earth for the Maya, because they pictured the earth's surface as a floating crocodile (Thompson 1950: 11, 133; 1970: 216–218). While Oaxaca potters also used the "crocodile foot" motif, their preferred version of Earth was *Xoo*, the Earth's angry state.

Vessels depicting Sky were restricted during the Uir phase to Copan's North Platform. Here the motifs are surprisingly like their Oaxaca counterparts, emphasizing excised (*raspada*) and incised Lightning symbols (Fig. 8a). Even the vessel shapes, which included tall bottles and cylinders, are similar to those of highland Mexican sites such as San José Mogote, Tlatilco, and Tlapacoya (Flannery and Marcus 1994: chap. 12).

Other variables reinforce the Earth/Sky dichotomy at Copan. South Platform graves featured cists or capstones, while North Platform graves did not (Fash 1991: 68–70). Jade was also found much more frequently in the North Platform, that is, with the "descendants of Sky/Lightning."

The use of the Earth/Sky dichotomy at sites as widely separated as San José Mogote and Copan suggests that we may expect more examples of it in the intervening area. We should remember, however, that only the largest and most important sites in each region are likely to have examples of *both* descent groups.

WOMEN'S RITUALS

Although there is no sign of women's tools or activities near our early public buildings, we do find evidence for women's ritual in three places: the house (*yoho quixi* or *yoho coba*); the associated ramada or lean-to (*yoho yaha* or *yoho yaa*); and the surrounding dooryard. These activities are believed to include (1) divination by the casting of beans or maize kernels, and (2) communication with recent ancestors through the use of small solid figurines.

Let us begin with divination, which—by analogy with ethnohistoric descriptions—may have been carried out in special basins in the dooryard of the house. Such basins were waterproofed with a layer of lime plaster, then painted in one of the colors associated with the four Zapotec world directions: red, yellow, white, or black. Two such painted basins were discovered in the yard of a San José phase house, Household C3, at San José Mogote (Fig. 9). East of the house was a red-painted basin, while a yellow-painted basin lay 3 m to the south. The red-painted basin was 1.2 m in diameter and recessed 5 cm into the ground; it had been mud-plastered, given a waterproof coating of lime, then painted red with specular hematite. The yellow-painted basin was similar in every way except color. Whether there were once four basins—each painted a different color and oriented to one of the four world directions—is not known, since exposing the relevant areas of the yard would have required the destruction of a later building (Marcus 1989: fig. 8.20).

We know from sixteenth-century documents that Zapotec diviners sat on a mat and cast maize kernels onto the surface of a water-filled basin, noting whether they fell or floated in groups of 2, 3, 5, or 13. This use of water (*niça*) for casting lots was called *tiniyaaya niça,* and it was used to determine the cause and cure of illnesses affecting household members; to predict whether a particular day was auspicious for planting or marriage; or to assign a name to a newborn child. We suspect that the painted basins of Household C3 may have served for such divination (Fig. 10).

Zapotec women also petitioned their recently deceased ancestors for guidance, often doing so in or near the house where that ancestor had lived. We suspect, on the basis of ethnographic analogy, that small solid figurines— of which we have found hundreds in household context—provided the medium to which the spirits of specific ancestors could return during this petitioning. Women preferred to petition their female ancestors, which may account for the fact that the majority of these figurines are women.

Tierras Largas phase figurines occurred in relatively few styles; more effort was expended depicting elaborate hairdos than facial features. Thus, while the spirit of a specific ancestor was probably thought to inhabit each figurine during the ritual for which it was made, we do not believe that a serious attempt was made to make the face of each figurine resemble that specific person. The hairstyle, the ornaments, and other secondary features were probably considered specific enough.

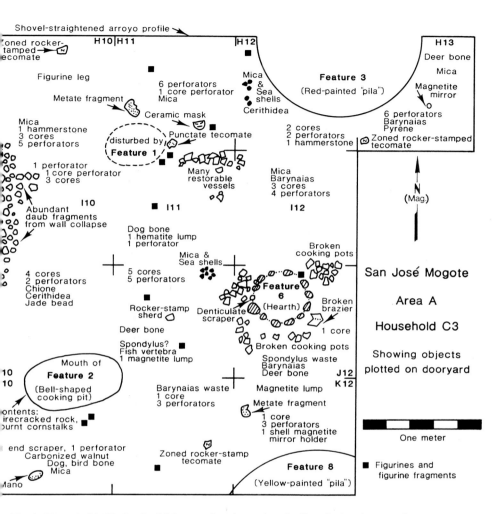

Fig. 9 Household C3, San José Mogote, showing red and yellow basins that may have been used for divination.

This statement also applies to the San José phase, when figurines exploded in number and became more standardized, with stereotyped ways of depicting eyes, noses, and mouths. Scores of figurines from this period look identical in every detail, yet they may have represented different ancestors during a specific ritual. As we will see, groups of figurines were sometimes arranged in ritual scenes during the San José phase.

Fig. 10 Seated on a mat near her house, this Zapotec woman is divining, throwing corn kernels into a water-filled basin to see how many will float and how many will sink. Drawing by John Klausmeyer.

There are many agricultural village societies in which the role of contacting recent ancestors falls to women. In the naming and mourning ceremonies of the Cubeo of northwest Amazonia, specific ancestors are invoked "by name and by specific kinship reference, as the mother or the grandmother of the sib" (Goldman 1963: 191). Some activities associated with invoking the ancestors are secret, while others are not; for the former, the home would be a logical venue. This rule of secrecy often applies to musical instruments, such as the flute and trumpet, as well. These bear the names of ancestors, and when the instruments appear, a specific ceremonial role is assigned to women. For example, in mourning rites the ancestor trumpets sound their notes of grief, and the women respond with their own wailing. "That is, when the Ancients enter the maloca [residence] they naturally establish a relationship with the women of the house" (Goldman 1963: 191).

THE EMERGENCE OF RANK

During the San José phase, our ability to separate men's and women's ritual becomes complicated by the emergence of status differences. These differences affected public buildings, ordinary houses, figurines, and artifact assemblages.

Our data suggest a continuum of status differences in San José Mogote, rather than a division into actual strata as occurred during the era of the Zapotec state. Houses showed a continuum from simple wattle-and-daub structures (like House 13 at San José Mogote) to well-made whitewashed residences with attached ramadas or lean-tos (like Houses 16–17 at the same site) (Flannery and Marcus 1994). The higher a family's status, the greater the likelihood that their house would show evidence of pottery from other regions and of marine shell, mica, jade, and abundant deer bone.

Burials also show a continuum of status, with men and women buried with variable amounts of jade, magnetite, and marine shell. While some individuals might be buried with only one jade bead in the mouth, others had up to three beads and two jade earspools. In a cemetery at Tomaltepec in the Valley of Oaxaca, Michael Whalen (1981) recovered almost 80 San José phase primary and secondary burials. Most primary burials were fully extended face down, but one group of six adult males stood out as different because they were tightly flexed in a kneeling position (Fig. 4). Although representing only 12.7 percent of the cemetery, these six males received 88 percent of the jade beads, 50 percent of the vessels with carved Sky or Lightning motifs, and 66 percent of the stone slab grave coverings in the cemetery.

Finally, both men and women of high status often had their heads artificially deformed. Since this procedure must be done while the individual is a child, the right to deformation must have been inherited rather than achieved.

Differences in Figurines and Burials

Both figurines and burials began to show intriguingly similar evidence for status differences during the San José phase. A limited number of figurines appear in stereotyped positions that seem to reflect *authority*; most of these are adult males, seated, with hands on knees (Fig. 11). A much larger number of figurines, both male and female, appear in positions that would seem to reflect *obeisance* or *subordination*. They are shown with arms folded across their chests and in a fully extended position (Fig. 12). A correspondingly large number of men and women were buried fully extended, face down, with arms folded across their chests. Many fewer burials were seated and tightly flexed (or kneeling and tightly flexed), and all of the latter were adult males (Fig. 13). These tightly flexed males were high-status people who may have been wrapped up as bundles to facilitate later reburial.

Next to a high-status residence (House 17) at San José Mogote we found four figurines forming a ritual scene, buried beneath the floor of a lean-to (called "House 16" in the field). We suspect that this scene depicts a high-status

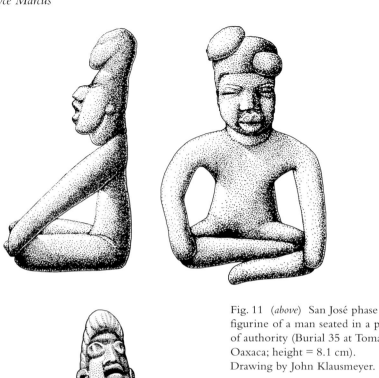

Fig. 11 (*above*) San José phase figurine of a man seated in a position of authority (Burial 35 at Tomaltepec, Oaxaca; height = 8.1 cm). Drawing by John Klausmeyer.

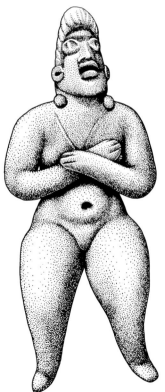

Fig. 12 Figurine of a person in a subordinate "obeisance" posture from House 16, San José Mogote (San José phase). Drawing by John Klausmeyer.

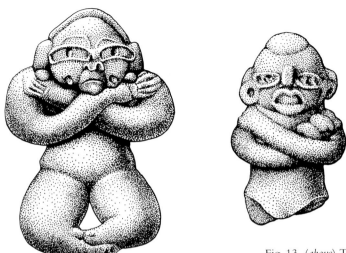

Fig. 13 (*above*) Two male figurines tightly flexed for burial, San José Mogote (San José phase). Drawing by John Klausmeyer.

Fig. 14 Scene of four figurines from House 16, San José Mogote. Drawing by John Klausmeyer.

multiple burial (Fig. 14). Three of the figurines were in the most common burial position of the period—fully extended, arms folded across their chests. While these three individuals lay supine in the scene, the fourth figure—also a male—was seated atop the other three. This arrangement is reminiscent of some chiefly burials from the Coclé site in Panama. For example, Grave 26 from Coclé featured a chiefly male seated atop a layer of 21 fully extended, face-down subordinates (Lothrop 1937: fig. 31). Strengthening this analogy is the fact that at San José Mogote we also find miniature four-legged stools, small ceramic versions of the ones on which Panamanian chiefs were buried. We suspect that our miniature stools were for use with seated figurines.

To the south of the figurine scene, and below the floor of House 17, was a middle-aged woman buried with two jade earspools and three jade beads. (For all we know, she may have been the woman who arranged the figurine scene in the lean-to adjacent to her house.) Her residence contained additional artifacts for use in ritual, including stingray spines (and other fish spines) for bloodletting, ceramic dance masks, and abundant marine shell. There were also vessels imported from the Basin of Mexico and possibly from Morelos (Marcus 1989; Flannery and Marcus 1994).

Since this figurine scene from San José Mogote is somewhat earlier than the famous Middle Formative figurine arrangement from La Venta (Drucker, Heizer, and Squier 1959: fig. 38), it indicates that such scenes were part of a long-standing tradition in Mesoamerica. By Middle Formative times at La Venta, however, the figurines were of jade and serpentine, and the scene was in a public, rather than household, context.

Changes in Public Buildings

The emergence of ranking during the San José phase also affected public buildings. By perhaps 1000 B.C., small buildings like the "lineage houses" or Men's Houses of earlier times had begun to disappear. They had given way to much larger and more spectacular public buildings, often serving more than one community. It is still unclear whether these Formative buildings should be called "temples," but they are certainly more complex than the Men's Houses of the Tierras Largas phase.

For one thing, their construction involved much more labor. The "lineage houses" of the Tierras Largas phase could have been built by a dozen men in a matter of weeks. The largest public buildings of the San José phase sat on platforms requiring tons of earthen fill and hundreds of man-days of labor. By the end of the phase, planoconvex or "bun-shaped" adobes were being produced by the hundreds to construct retaining walls for fill, and many tons of heavy boulders were being brought to the site so that the outer surfaces of the platform could be built of dry-laid stone masonry. Many limestone and travertine boulder stones were brought from communities at least 5 km from San José Mogote, suggesting that these smaller villages were no longer autonomous; they had become satellites of San José Mogote and were contributing manpower and materials to a larger chiefly center.

Structures 1 and 2 at San José Mogote are examples of this more elaborate architecture (Fig. 15). Each structure apparently served as the pyramidal platform for a public building. Both were contoured to a gentle slope coming down from the hill on which most of the later ceremonial architecture of San José Mogote was built. Each platform was different, a rough-and-ready structure adapted to the slope without much concern for bilateral symmetry or straightness of walls. The public buildings atop the platforms had largely eroded away. What remained were a few patches of hard-packed, almost burnished clay floor which indicated where the perishable buildings had been (Flannery and Marcus 1994: 370).

Structure 2 stands a meter high and may once have spanned 18 m. The structure's irregular eastern edge was faced with boulders, some local and some brought in from as far away as Rancho Matadamas and Fábrica San José. Two

Fig. 15 Reconstruction of Structures 1 and 2, San José Mogote.
Drawing by David W. Reynolds.

carved stones, one depicting a feline and the other a raptorial bird, had fallen out of a nearby wall; both display a local, rather than pan-Mesoamerican, style (Marcus 1976a; Flannery and Marcus 1983: fig. 3.7).

The east face of Structure 2 contained our earliest stone stairways. Each was so narrow that only one person at a time could have been accommodated. The North and South Stairways were inset into the wall and consisted of three to seven steps. Despite the informality of these buildings, it is worth noting that stone masonry, stone stairways, adobes, and lime plaster were largely unknown at this time on the Gulf Coast. This fact further reinforces the impression that our earlier notions of Gulf Coast influence were overly enthusiastic (Marcus 1989: 193–194; Flannery and Marcus 1994: chap. 20).

These late San José buildings are clearly more monumental than those of the Tierras Largas and early San José phases. The most likely explanation is that the responsibility of public construction had shifted from small groups of initiated men to a hereditary elite whose sphere of influence transcended the local community. From this point on in our sequence, we see more impressive displays of manpower by the elite and correspondingly less evidence for ordinary men's ritual.

The Disappearance of Women's Ritual

Women's ritual was also affected by the emerging elite monopoly of ritual activity. The small solid figurines that had played so great a role in Early Formative household ritual decreased in number after 700 B.C. and virtually disappeared by 200 B.C.

Simply put, the recent ancestors of ordinary people were no longer as important as they had been at the egalitarian village level. Their place was taken by the well-known Zapotec effigy urn, a venue to which the spirits of the departed elite could return. Invoking the spirits of ancestors continued to be an important component of Zapotec ritual, but now it was mainly noble ancestors who were invoked (Marcus 1983b). Divination continued to be important, but it was eventually conducted by full-time priests. Thus the rise of the Zapotec state partially closed the window through which we had glimpsed ordinary men's and women's social identity.

The Legacy of Earlier Times

With the wisdom of hindsight, we can see traces of the old Formative ritual system surviving in readapted form during the Classic period. Zapotec rulers continued to claim descent from *Cociyo* or Lightning, the most frequently depicted supernatural force in Zapotec art. And *Xoo* or Earthquake, that symbol of Earth in its most animate and belligerent form, became one of the days of the Zapotec 260-day calendar (Marcus 1976b).

In the modern era, with Pre-Columbian elite culture largely peeled away by the Spanish Conquest, we can once again see ordinary Zapotec men and women engaging in ritual. Many still pray to Earth and Lightning, still conduct divination, still make blood sacrifices, still believe that different colors are associated with the four world directions.

Ask a Zapotec farmer in Mitla where the four colors of indigenous corn—white, yellow, black, and red—came from, and he will tell you they were created by Lightning, who put a grain of a different color into four separate sacks so that the Zapotec could have four colors of corn (Parsons 1936: 330). Mitleños will also point to a small lizard called a *chintete* and tell you that if you burn him in a fire, he will be resurrected as Lightning (Parsons 1936: 335–336). It is an amazing survival of man's three-thousand-year relationship with the angriest, most active version of Sky.

DISCUSSION OF OAXACA DATA

Ritual, social identity, and cosmology were related in ancient Oaxaca, but their relationship—and archaeological visibility—changed over time. In the Tierras Largas phase, one's identity seems to have depended on (1) whether one was a man or woman, and (2) whether one was initiated or not. Initiated men met in "lineage houses" to engage in rituals from which women and uninitiated males were probably excluded. Women conducted rituals within and near the household, invoking ancestors and engaging in divination. It is doubtful that any women were excluded from this ritual; indeed, one of the differences between men's and women's ritual is that men's is more competitive and exclusionary. By the early San José phase, some deceased men and boys were identified as descendants of Earth or Sky by their burial vessels, and some women consulted their household's ancestors by arranging figurines of them in ritual scenes beneath the floors of their houses.

With the emergence of chiefly society between 1150 and 850 B.C., social identity began to change. Now one's birth into an elite family was at least as important as one's achievements or degree of initiation. Positions of authority and subordination were revealed both in figurine posture and gesture and in burial position and ritual. The use of sumptuary goods and foreign imports escalated. Elite families took over the construction of public buildings, transforming them from modest Men's Houses into grander temples of regional significance.

At 1100 B.C., to show that a burial was descended from Lightning would have identified the individual as (1) a man and (2) a member of a large descent group. By 200 B.C., to show descent from Lightning was to identify a member of the nobility. At 1100 B.C., men and women had rituals with different *content* and *loci of performance*. By A.D. 300, elite men and women were shown walking together, side by side, in polychrome murals depicting the procession exiting from a royal funeral. The difficulty of documenting social identity—even if we limit ourselves to a single region like the Valley of Oaxaca—is that we are aiming at a target that moves and evolves over time.

The Search for Wider Significance

We have seen that some patterns of men's ritual in early Oaxaca find analogues in men's ritual at early Copan. It is more difficult to find analogues for women's ritual because so few early household units have been excavated elsewhere in Mesoamerica.

My reading of the literature, however, suggests that many practices of Formative women find analogues in village societies elsewhere in the world. In this chapter I will discuss only one of those areas, village China. China is a long way from Mesoamerica, and I am not suggesting that it can serve as a model for the Mesoamerican Formative. Rather, I suggest that we may have, in both areas, independent examples of a widespread pattern in which exclusionary groups of men honor more remote ancestors, while inclusionary groups of women honor more recent ancestors.

During the Neolithic period (5000–3000 B.C.), in the middle Yellow River basin, hundreds of early villages are known. Those that have been extensively excavated (Chiang-chai, Pan-p'o, and Pei-shou-ling) are about 5 ha in area. The pottery at this time displayed incised symbols, interpreted as being comparable to clan emblems used by the later Shang. These emblems are individual characters, often on the black band near the rim of the vessels, and, significantly, many depict fish or other animals. In other words, they may be the Chinese equivalents of the crocodiles, fire-serpents, and were-jaguars associated with men's burials in Mesoamerica.

In later periods in China, animals continued to be important as lineage emblems, playing roles in ritual and in communicating with the Sky, Earth, and the dead (Chang 1980: 209). The Shang-period Chinese (1200–1000 B.C.) depicted animals on bronze vessels, including dragons or snakes. Such depictions were called *wu*, a term that has been translated "animal offerings." According to K. C. Chang (1983: 65):

> to make animal offerings was a concrete means of achieving communication between heaven and earth, the dead and the living. We thus

come to the inevitable conclusion that the animal designs on Shang and Chou bronzes are iconographically meaningful: they are images of the various animals that served as the helpers of shamans and shamanesses in the task of communication between heaven and earth, the spirits and the living.

Significantly, in ancient China we see the ancestors honored at the same three loci we saw in Formative Oaxaca: (1) special Men's Houses called "Ancestral Halls," to which women were denied admission; (2) the home, where all women's ritual was practiced (Freedman 1980: 83–85); and (3) the graveside, where the ancestors were buried with vessels whose animal agent motifs helped communicate with Earth and Sky. The intimacy between the living and the deceased was not broken by death, and their relationship continued to be one of reciprocity.

As in our reconstruction of women's ritual in Formative Oaxaca, the ancestors honored in the house were the recently deceased whose living descendants still occupied the structure. Household ritual did not include ancestors farther removed than four generations, and most were much more closely related. In contrast, the ancestor worship that took place in the Ancestral Hall involved a longer sequence of ancestors, one that could even lead back to the lineage founder.

What integrated these two phases of ancestor worship was the fact that some ancestors, originally buried in the cemetery and honored in the household, could later be lifted out of "household context" to be honored in the Ancestral Hall. Once there, an ancestor's worship became "more impersonal," for in the hall he was endowed with a more remote and less individualized personality. As Freedman (1980: 84) expresses it: "Once an ancestor had been placed in the shrine belonging to a hall he had ceased to be an object of personal devotion and had become part of the ritual centre of a lineage segment."

Freedman's analysis shows us that men's and women's ancestor worship, though it took place in different loci, was in fact part of a multistage program. An individual might be honored for several generations in the home, in a very personal way, by women who knew his individual characteristics. After several generations passed, there would be no one left who actually knew him. At that point he could be transported to the Ancestral Hall to be honored by men for whom he was an impersonal, nonindividualized, more distant member of a larger descent group.

If this situation provides an analogy for Mesoamerica, it may help to explain two phenomena: the deliberate breaking and discarding of small solid figurines around houses and the appearance of seated male bundle burials near Men's Houses. If household veneration of immediate ancestors lasted only a few generations, there would come a time when the small solid figurines of these ancestors would no longer be needed. They could then be broken, or even have their features battered off to keep anyone from using them, as was apparently done with figurines at La Victoria, Guatemala (Coe 1961: 92). Also, if the remains of important men were eventually to be transferred near the Men's House (= Ancestral Hall) after a period of veneration in the home, it would make sense to keep them tightly bundled in the seated position in preparation for that transfer.

Finally, the Chinese data provide evidence for divination practices analogous to the *tiniyaaya niça* we think Zapotec women practiced in shallow water-filled basins. Chinese divination, however, was performed by using the bones of animals. Diviners used either a turtle (usually the plastron, less often the carapace) or the scapula of a cow; the former is known as *plastromancy* and the latter as *scapulimancy*.

Although divination predated the Shang dynasty, it was during the Shang era that we see standardized preparation of such "oracle bones." First, diviners drilled a series of evenly spaced holes on the backs of the bones; then they applied heat to produce cracks. These cracks provided a basis around which diviners or scribes incised the record of divination. Diviners carved out some of the cracks to make them more visible, and many were filled with red or black pigment to make them clearer.

Scholars suspect that only those times when a Shang ruler's predictions proved to be true were deemed worthy of permanent recordkeeping. For example, one oracle bone says: "The ruler, reading the cracks, said 'if a child is born on a *ting* day, that is good; if it is a *keng* day it will be very good.'" Then the actual birth was recorded. Another bone says: "the ruler, reading the cracks, predicts danger." This was followed by verification: "on the 8th day there were arriving clouds . . . and the coming of a rainbow." For the Chinese, those were indeed signs of danger (Keightley 1989).

DISCUSSION AND CONCLUSIONS

Ritual, as interesting a topic as it may be, remains one of the most difficult behaviors to document and interpret archaeologically. Even in the Valley of Oaxaca, where we have thousands of bits of piece-plotted information from a wide variety of contexts, there are gaps that can only be bridged by ethnographic analogy.

At the egalitarian, or autonomous village stage (1400–1150 B.C.), I have divided ritual information into three components: its content, its loci, and its performers.

Women's ritual seems to have been conducted in the house, the adjacent lean-to, and the surrounding dooryard. The recently deceased ancestors—both males and females, but especially females—appear to have been the focus of much of this ritual. Small solid figurines, sometimes arranged in ritual scenes, evidently provided a venue to which the spirits of the ancestors could return; in that venue they were probably consulted, petitioned, and involved in the ongoing affairs of their descendants. Women also made figurines of animals (principally dogs and birds), which may have served the ancestors as "animal agents" like those described for China.

Women may also have been involved in *tiniyaaya niça,* divination by casting maize kernels onto the surface of shallow, water-filled basins. Suitable basins were found in the dooryard of an Early Formative household, painted in two of the colors (red, yellow) associated with the four great world directions. There is no reason to believe any women in the village were excluded from any of the rituals discussed, since they conducted them in their own households.

Men, on the other hand, evidently conducted their ritual in a lime-plastered, astronomically oriented Men's House or "lineage house" apart from their residences. These buildings were so small that only a subgroup of the village's men, presumably "initiates" of some kind, could have entered them. We therefore assume that men's ritual was more exclusionary than women's, with certain men being allowed into ritual society based on achieved status.

Men's Houses had no figurines, no associated shallow basins, no hearths, and no domestic artifacts. They did, however, contain lime-filled pits. This lime may have been for mixing with powdered tobacco, jimson weed, morning glory, or some other ritual plant described in the ethnohistoric record. No such lime-filled pits have been found with any of the ordinary households we have excavated, suggesting that women (and uninitiated men) did not participate in the associated rituals.

Near some of these Men's Houses or "lineage houses" we found seated burials of tightly bundled middle-aged men. Perhaps, therefore, after a period of ritual veneration in the household, certain important men were moved to a position near the Men's House in which they had once practiced rituals. This practice would be analogous to the Chinese tradition (presented earlier by way of comparison) in which some ancestors are honored in the household by women for a few generations, then transferred to the Ancestral Hall. If the Chinese example is relevant, we should look for clues that Formative Mesoamerican ancestors were treated (1) as personalized individuals while honored in the home, but (2) as impersonal and less individualized ancestors when buried near the "lineage house."

After the appearance of inherited rank in the villages of Oaxaca, it becomes increasingly difficult to separate men's and women's ritual, because the archaeological record is flooded with information on differences in rank. One still finds abundant use of small solid figurines, ritual basins, and small Men's Houses well into the San José phase (1150–850 B.C.). One also suspects that men's ritual was exclusionary, since certain men were buried with vessels depicting Earth or Sky, while others were not.

As public buildings grew larger and more elegant, however, and as households began to display stronger and more flamboyant evidence of status paraphernalia, it is clear that a great deal of ritual was being taken away from ordinary villagers by ritual specialists. By 700 B.C., Zapotec society came to be run by elite families with deformed skulls, jade and mother-of-pearl ornaments, luxury drinking vessels, and abundant trade goods. These families participated more heavily in ritual than did families of lower status, and the public buildings at which they performed those rituals were now of regional, rather than local, significance.

BIBLIOGRAPHY

BEALS, RALPH L.

1945 *The Ethnology of the Western Mixe.* University of California, Publications in American Archaeology and Ethnology 42. Berkeley.

1973 *Ethnology of the Western Mixe.* Cooper Square Publishers, New York.

CHANG, K. C.

1980 *Shang Civilization.* Yale University Press, New Haven.

1983 *Art, Myth, and Ritual: The Path to Political Authority in Ancient China.* Harvard University Press, Cambridge, Mass.

COE, MICHAEL D.

1961 *La Victoria: An Early Site on the Pacific Coast of Guatemala.* Harvard University, Papers of the Peabody Museum of Archaeology and Ethnology 53. Cambridge, Mass.

CÓRDOVA, JUAN DE

1942 [1578] V*ocabulario en lengua zapoteca.* Pedro Charte y Antonio Ricardo, Mexico.

COVARRUBIAS, MIGUEL

1957 *Indian Art of Mexico and Central America.* Alfred A. Knopf, New York.

DRUCKER, PHILIP, ROBERT F. HEIZER, AND ROBERT J. SQUIER

1959 *Excavations at La Venta, Tabasco, 1955.* Smithsonian Institution, Bureau of American Ethnology, Bulletin 170. Washington, D.C.

FASH, WILLIAM L.

1991 *Scribes, Warriors and Kings: The City of Copán and the Ancient Maya.* Thames and Hudson, London.

n.d. A Middle Formative Cemetery from Copan, Honduras. Paper presented at the Annual Meeting of the American Anthropological Association, Washington, D.C., 1982.

FLANNERY, KENT V.

1976 Contextual Analysis of Ritual Paraphernalia from Formative Oaxaca. In *The Early Mesoamerican Village* (Kent V. Flannery, ed.): 333–345. Academic Press, New York.

FLANNERY, KENT V., AND JOYCE MARCUS

1983 The Growth of Site Hierarchies in the Valley of Oaxaca, pt. 1. In *The Cloud People: Divergent Evolution of the Zapotec and Mixtec Civilizations* (Kent V. Flannery and Joyce Marcus, eds.): 53–64. Academic Press, New York.

1994 *Early Formative Pottery of the Valley of Oaxaca.* Prehistory and Human Ecology of the Valley of Oaxaca, vol. 10. Memoirs of the Museum of Anthropology 27, University of Michigan. Ann Arbor.

FREEDMAN, MAURICE

1980 *Lineage Organization in Southeastern China.* London School of Economics, Monographs on Social Anthropology 18. Humanities Press, New York.

GOLDMAN, IRVING

1963 *The Cubeo: Indians of the Northwest Amazon.* Illinois Studies in Anthropology 2. University of Illinois Press, Urbana.

GROVE, DAVID C.
  1984   *Chalcatzingo: Excavations on the Olmec Frontier.* Thames and Hudson, London.
KEIGHTLEY, DAVID N.
  1989   *Sources of Shang History.* University of California Press, Berkeley.
LIPP, FRANK J.
  1991   *The Mixe of Oaxaca: Religion, Ritual, and Healing.* University of Texas Press, Austin.
LOTHROP, SAMUEL K.
  1937   *Coclé: An Archaeological Study of Central Panama,* pt. 1. Harvard University, Memoirs of the Peabody Museum of Archaeology and Ethnology 7. Cambridge, Mass.
MARCUS, JOYCE
  1976a   The Iconography of Militarism at Monte Alban and Neighboring Sites in the Valley of Oaxaca. In *The Origins of Religious Art and Iconography in Preclassic Mesoamerica* (H. B. Nicholson, ed.): 123–139. UCLA Latin American Center, Los Angeles.
  1976b   The Origins of Mesoamerican Writing. *Annual Review of Anthropology* 5: 35–67.
  1983a   The Espiridión Complex and the Origins of the Oaxacan Formative. In *The Cloud People: Divergent Evolution of the Zapotec and Mixtec Civilizations* (Kent V. Flannery and Joyce Marcus, eds.): 42–43. Academic Press, New York.
  1983b   Rethinking the Zapotec Urn. In *The Cloud People: Divergent Evolution of the Zapotec and Mixtec Civilizations* (Kent V. Flannery and Joyce Marcus, eds.): 144–148. Academic Press, New York.
  1989   Zapotec Chiefdoms and the Nature of Formative Religions. In *Regional Perspectives on the Olmec* (Robert J. Sharer and David C. Grove, eds.): 148–197. Cambridge University Press, Cambridge.
MARCUS, JOYCE, AND KENT V. FLANNERY
  1978   Ethnoscience of the Sixteenth-Century Valley Zapotec. In *The Nature and Status of Ethnobotany* (Richard I. Ford, ed.): 51–79. University of Michigan, Museum of Anthropology, Anthropological Papers 67. Ann Arbor.
NIEDERBERGER, CHRISTINE
  1987   *Paléopaysages et archéologie pré-urbaine du Bassin de Mexico,* vol. 2. Etudes mesoaméricaines 11. Centre d'Etudes Mexicaines et Centraméricaines, México, D.F.
PARSONS, ELSIE CLEWS
  1936   *Mitla: Town of the Souls.* University of Chicago Press, Chicago.
THOMPSON, J. ERIC S.
  1950   *Maya Hieroglyphic Writing.* Carnegie Institution of Washington, Publication 589. Washington, D.C.
  1970   *Maya History and Religion.* University of Oklahoma Press, Norman.
WHALEN, MICHAEL E.
  1981   *Excavations at Santo Domingo Tomaltepec: Evolution of a Formative Community in the Valley of Oaxaca, Mexico.* Prehistory and Human Ecology of the Valley of Oaxaca, vol. 6. Memoirs of the Museum of Anthropology 12, University of Michigan. Ann Arbor.

Classic (Smith 1950: 18–19, fig. 58c; Valdés 1989). At Río Azul/BA-20, a Chicanel house (Op. 206 Str. 3) lacks a platform but has an overall rectangular shape (Hendon 1989). The earliest occupation at Cerros, although dating only from the beginnings of the Late Pre-Classic period, mirrors that of Middle Pre-Classic Cuello, Uaxactun, Seibal, and Altar de Sacrificios in consisting of perishable houses built on clay platforms without retaining walls, trash pits, burials, and middens. Stone-walled rectangular platforms appear later (Cliff 1986).

MIDDLE TO LATE PRE-CLASSIC RITUAL PRACTICE

Both architectural and artifact data from living areas allow us to consider household-level ritual practice. Figurines, another major part of the artifact inventory from Uaxactun's Pits E-4 and E-18, are one of our best indicators of household-level ritual activity at Middle Pre-Classic Maya sites (Hammond 1991; E. Ricketson 1937: 210–217; O. Ricketson 1937: 139–149; Willey 1965: 393–394; 1973, 1990; see Drennan 1976 for a discussion of the ritual function of figurines). By the end of the Middle Pre-Classic or beginning of the Late Pre-Classic, special ritual structures appear at a number of Maya sites. Some of these structures seem to be antecedent to the Classic period temples and shrines found in residential compounds, while others develop into the monumental architecture of the centers or at any rate occupy the same place and are covered over by later, more clearly public works.

One of the earliest known examples comes from below Platform 34 at Cuello where an early Middle Pre-Classic (Bladen phase) round platform, Str. 324, was built in the center of the patio (Hammond, Gerhardt, and Donaghey 1991; Gerhardt and Hammond 1991: table 5.1). Round platforms without a superstructure constitute one form of ceremonial architecture for the time period. These platforms are sometimes embellished by the addition of a small rectangular or trapezoidal terrace or step. This addition, seen in Strs. E and F of Uaxactun, makes them resemble a "keyhole" (Glass 1965: 52).[5] I excavated another example at the site of Río Azul. A residential zone with significant Pre-Classic occupation known as BA-20 lies northeast of the main center (Adams 1990). Here I excavated Strs. 1 and 2 of Op. 206 (Hendon 1989). While Op. 206 Str. 1 dates from the Early Classic, Str. 2, its predecessor, is Late Pre-Classic in date. At Altun Ha, Str. C-13-3rd (and probably its predecessor, C-13-4th), located in a residential area, also takes this form (Pendergast 1982: 184–187, fig. 97).

---

[5] After some debate as to their function (Ricketson n.d.c: Notebook II, pp. 39–40), Ricketson and A. Ledyard Smith decided to call Strs. E, F, and G "ceremonial platforms" designed for ritual use (Smith 1950: 73; 1973: 27).

Several round platforms have been found in Middle Pre-Classic residential contexts at Cahal Pech (Aimers and Awe n.d.; Powis 1993a). Str. G at Uaxactun, with its two circular platforms linked by a stucco "bar," may also be considered another variant on this pattern. Keyhole-shaped structures continue to be built in the Early Classic at some sites but eventually disappear (Glass 1965: 51–59; Hendon 1989; Powis 1993b).

The keyhole or round ritual platforms do not necessarily differ markedly in form or size from contemporary residences. Nevertheless, several special features set the ceremonial platforms apart. These features include quality of construction, location, lack of a superstructure,[6] and the presence of associated ritual deposits. The circular platform of these ritual structures is generally quite regular in outline and usually plastered (Aimers and Awe n.d.; Hendon 1989; Powis 1993a). At Uaxactun, the plaster surfaces of Strs. E and F are harder and better prepared than those covering the house platforms, to the point of making them difficult to excavate (Ricketson n.d.c: Notebook III, p. 18; Smith 1950: 17). At Río Azul/BA-20, an associated house was built of unplastered cobbles, while the keyhole platform, Str. 2, was not only plastered but painted red on its exterior (Hendon 1989).

Energetic investment, decoration, and lack of a superstructure point to these round platforms as having a different purpose from houses. This purpose has been broadly labeled ritual. But specific features of these platforms suggest something about the nature of the ritual activity associated with them, namely, that the activity was meant to be open to view (Aimers and Awe n.d.) and that its performance did not involve large groups of people. These inferences stem from the height of the platform and its lack of superstructure, which make it like a stage, and from its relatively small size, which limits the number of people the stage could hold.

Although all the keyhole-shaped or round ritual structures discussed here are built in residential areas, they are sometimes marked as special or different from adjacent houses by location as well as by the sorts of formal features discussed above. Strs. E, F, and G provide the most striking example of this. Their location at the edge of the main plaza floor makes them seem peripheral, although this impression may be misleading in that we have a poor understanding of just how many Middle Pre-Classic houses existed and where they were located. Strs. E–G, however, are segregated from the more central part of Group

---

[6] In my 1989 report I suggested that Op. 206 Strs. 1 and 2 had a superstructure, but I have since reconsidered the data and feel that the stuccoed wall lines found represent the remains of a platform.

E where Strs. A, B, and D were located, by a wall. Despite the fact that this wall destroyed part of Str. F and the uncertainty of the stratigraphic connections between floors, it does seem that Strs. E and G, and possibly even F, continued in use after the wall's construction. At the very least, all four platforms remained visible during this phase of Group E (O. Ricketson 1937: 134–136).

Elevation separates the residential and ritual structures at Río Azul/BA-20. Op. 206 Str. 2 is built on higher ground than the house, Str. 3. Since both structures date from the same phase of occupation, this difference in location may reflect a desire to give greater physical prominence to the building where ritual practices related to the creation of a group identity for the residents of the area took place (Hendon 1989). Although we lack data on residences from Zone C at Altun Ha which would be contemporary with Strs. C-13-4th or 3rd, it is possible that the marked spatial separation of Str. C-13 during the Classic period may have first emerged during the Pre-Classic period (Pendergast 1982: 170).

In some cases, these areas continue to be residential rather than public into the Classic period. As noted above, the Río Azul/BA-20 Late Pre-Classic platform is rebuilt and used in the Early Classic period, the peak period of occupation of the site. The Tolok Group at Cahal Pech, a four-structure Late Classic patio group, illustrates even longer use (Powis 1993a). Underlying all four structures of the group are remains of Late Pre-Classic occupation and Middle Pre-Classic floors, walls, and midden deposits surrounding a round platform found below the Late Classic patio floor. The importance of domestic space as the center of group identity may be indicated by the ceremonial use of this platform by the Late Classic household which placed four burials on the Middle Pre-Classic platform. At Altun Ha, both the construction of Str. C-13-3rd and its replacement by a four-sided temple platform were occasions for the deposition of caches and burials (Pendergast 1982: 188–190). The replacement of a round platform by a temple platform is also found in the Zotz Group of Cahal Pech (Aimers and Awe n.d.) and at early Late Pre-Classic Cuello (Gerhardt and Hammond 1991). These examples underscore the continued importance of ritual practice to households, although the change in building shape may indicate that the kinds of rituals carried out changed.

EMERGING SOCIAL DIFFERENTIATION

Ornaments of shell or other materials and deliberate alteration of the body in the form of dental inlays or filed teeth (Hansen 1992; Willey 1973: 28; Tourtellot 1990: table 1) hint that the Middle Pre-Classic Maya shared the Formative Mesoamerican emphasis on personal adornment and alteration of the body that Joyce (following Munn) has called beautification. Beautification, while aimed at differentiating individuals and related to the acquisition of prestige, is not inherently or necessarily productive of hierarchical or permanent differences (Joyce 1996; see also Adams 1975). During this same time period, variation in Maya domestic architecture also appears. Greater size and the use of architectural decoration not only reflect greater access to labor and other resources but also associate the household with the symbolic language of authority. The domestic built environment, rather than the individual body, provides a way for households to differentiate themselves, as a group, from other households. This emphasis on establishing the importance of the group and the means used—energetic investment and manipulation of symbolism—signal the emergence of more permanent hierarchical differences that underlie the consolidation of centralized political authority during the Late Pre-Classic period.

Examples of domestic elaboration come from Cuello, Uaxactun, and Altar de Sacrificios. We have already noted the appearance at Cuello in the Middle Pre-Classic of Str. 315 with a stone superstructure. A comparable shift from clay to stone-walled platforms occurs at Cerros during the Late Pre-Classic period, which Cliff (1986) has suggested may mark the emergence of social differences among residents of the area. More generally, Middle Pre-Classic settlement at Cuello encompasses both raised and ground-level construction which requires different energetic investments. The trend toward greater differences in energetic investment becomes more marked at Cuello in the Late Pre-Classic period. Platform 34, built over the Middle Pre-Classic patio group, serves as the foundation for a number of buildings, most of which have their own individual substructures. Despite the large-scale, even monumental, nature of Platform 34, however, its construction does not mark an immediate shift in the function of the area. In other words, the platform supports houses, outbuildings, and a ritual structure which together form a patio unit. These structures are rebuilt many times but maintain a consistent association between function and location, with the ritual structures on the west side and the residences on the north. At some point in the Late Pre-Classic occupation of Platform 34, its residents introduce boundary walls and use differences in elevation to restrict access to the northern part of the platform. This suggests that during the early Late Pre-Classic the entire area of Platform 34 was, like the Middle Pre-Classic patio it covered, domestic space for the use of a single group or household. The walls and differences in floor height that appear in the late Late Pre-Classic suggest that use of the ritual structure on the west side, now a terraced pyramid supporting a small temple, became more public, or suprahousehold (Gerhardt and Hammond 1991). Wilk and Wilhite (1991) identify several other contemporaneous examples of large platforms supporting a complex of ritual and relatively larger houses and point to similar constructions at Nohmul, Cerros, and Seibal.

Although the data are less complete from Altar de Sacrificios, a similar pattern may be seen (Smith 1972; Willey 1973). The earliest occupation is early Middle Pre-Classic and consists of perishable houses built directly on the ground in association with domestic refuse, food remains, figurines, and burials. In the latter part of the Middle Pre-Classic, the construction of some houses becomes more substantial. Raised platforms, some with stone facings, appear. Evidence from Group B, one of several monumental plazas that make up the civic-ceremonial core of the site in the Classic period, shows a continued elaboration in construction. By the Middle to Late Pre-Classic transition, red-painted plaster and platforms faced with lime-encrusted shells set in mud mortar are built. The size, decoration, and location of the platforms, which surround an open patio, imply a greater control of labor and of the desire for visual display. Although Smith (1972: 118–120) assumes that these structures are ceremonial, Willey (1973: 27–31) points to the occurrence of manos, metates, and mortars to suggest that they may be elite residences rather than public buildings.[7] Like Platform 34 at Cuello, then, Middle to Late Pre-Classic Group B continues to be living space where both quotidian and ritual action takes place but whose inhabitants would seem to belong to an emerging (or consolidating) elite. Public buildings, in the form of tall temple pyramids decorated with paint and molded stucco, replace these elite residences during the Protoclassic to Early Classic period.

---

[7] Smith's interpretation conflates function and social structure. This conflation, common in analyses of Maya architecture, fails to keep separate the use of a structure from the social status of its users. Willey's interpretation, by considering both architectural and artifact information, is more convincing. His analysis also exemplifies the problems in studying deeply buried early deposits at Maya sites. Willey (1973: 29) writes:

> Other ground stone artifacts . . . were also encountered in connection with the San Felix [Middle Pre-Classic] B Group platforms. These are metates, . . . mortars, and . . . mano stones. Here we run into a problem of provenience and association. Are these . . . items *in situ* . . . domestic debris or fill inclusions? The metates and mortars were fragments, as were most of the manos. Our exposures were not large enough to clear sufficient floor areas of these early platforms so that we could be absolutely certain that we were dealing with *in situ* floor finds; however, on balance, and considering the amounts of living detritus found on and around these B Group platform levels, I am of the opinion that these various milling stone implements were probably once in use in B Group buildings. Such an interpretation would see domestic and ceremonial functions carried on within the same immediate precincts and, perhaps, within the same buildings.

These examples help us understand Uaxactun's Group E sequence. The data are more equivocal, but I think they do support a similar transition at Uaxactun, based on my interpretation of the function of Strs. A, B, and D and of the meaning of the replacement in Group E of Str. A by Str. E-VII–Sub. Ricketson could not decide if Strs. A, B, and D remained in use after the construction of Floor II, but he felt that B and D were at least visible. His construction sequence for Group E, however, has Str. E-VII–Sub replacing Str. A (O. Ricketson 1937: fig. 98b–c).[8] Ricketson does not discuss the function of these mounds, although figure 98 shows Strs. B, D, and A forming three sides of a plaza with Str. A looking very much like a temple because of its markedly smaller size and squarer shape. As shown in the figure, Ricketson hypothesized the presence of a fourth structure, labeled C, on the east side of the plaza opposite Str. A, but found no archaeological evidence of such a platform. He appears to have assumed that these early structures would have followed the same four-sided arrangement found in the later, monumental phase of Group E (illustrated in parts d–f of fig. 98).

Although Ricketson does not address the issue of the function of these platforms directly, his construction sequence in figure 98 suggests that he saw Strs. A, B, and D as precursors to the monumental ritual structures of Group E. As the Altar de Sacrificios Group B sequence demonstrates, however, location underneath later monumental architecture does not necessarily mean continuity in function. The replacement of Middle to early Late Pre-Classic houses by large, nonresidential buildings that serve as the Late Pre-Classic nucleus of the emerging civic-ceremonial center, documented at such sites as Cuello, Seibal, and Altar de Sacrificios (and later at Cerros), appears to be part of the transition to a more centralized political structure in the Maya Lowlands (Cliff 1986; Willey 1973, 1990). The differences in building material of these final houses from their predecessors or contemporaries suggest that differences in status were becoming fixed enough to achieve expression in architectural design and materials. Such differences are not as strongly marked as in the Late Classic period, but the way of embodying these differences through the built environment is like the later time period. Returning to Uaxactun, the shape and size of Strs. B and D suggest to me that they were residential platforms of a larger and more permanent construction than others from that time period. Str. A, I would

---

[8] I am ignoring the earlier phase of Str. E-VII found by Valdés, Str. E-VII-1, to make my discussion comparable with Ricketson's. The presence of this earlier phase of Str. E-VII does not affect my argument since it is also monumental in scale. It is, of course, *its* construction which would result in the disappearance of Str. A. Readers may therefore substitute E-VII-1 for E-VII–Sub in the discussion.

suggest, was a ritual structure for the use of the residents of Strs. B and D. Str. A was thus part of household-focused religious practice for a household commanding significantly greater resources than its neighbors. It is only with the appearance of Str. E-VII-Sub (or 1) that we see the appearance of a ritual construction that transcends any particular household and thus the shift in function from residential to public.

At least two different types of ritual structures were built in the Pre-Classic period. To a certain extent, we may discern a trend for the replacement over time of open round or keyhole platforms by perishable temples on top of tall pyramidal substructures. Based on their form, it has been suggested that the round or keyhole platforms served as open stages for the performance of rituals. In contrast, the temples are enclosed small spaces made more remote by being raised above eye level.

A similar shift occurs in the Oaxaca Valley, where cleared areas, bounded by walls but unroofed, are replaced by small single-roomed temples (Drennan 1983a, 1983b; Marcus 1989). Drennan presents an interpretation of this change which applies equally well to the Maya case. He argues that the open areas, found first in the Preceramic period at the site of Gheo-Shih but continuing into the Early Formative at San José Mogote, served as dance floors for community rituals. These open areas are demarcated by boundary walls. At San José Mogote, a row of posts and stone slabs sets the space apart from the houses (Flannery and Marcus 1976). The temples not only restrict the number of participants but also limit the number of onlookers to those people who are actually inside the sacred space of the room. These factors suggest in turn that a different kind of ritual celebration took place.

In the Maya area, we have both temples integrated into the household compound and temples as part of an elite controlled civic/ceremonial core. The decision by Maya households to replace their round platforms by temples which continue to be associated with a specific set of houses, the precursors of the Classic period patio units, occurs in the context of the development of a ritual and administrative center and of more permanent social differences. These two developments may mark a shift not only in the nature of ritual space and the kinds of rituals carried out but also in the degree of integration such rituals achieve. Although ritual action by the ruling elite living at the center may be intended to represent the community as a whole, its increasing spatial and social remoteness may have led households at all levels of society to feel a greater, rather than lesser, need to emphasize their own ritual practices as part of the continuing validation of their identity as a social group and, for the elite, of their social status.

Julia A. Hendon

IDENTIFICATION AND DIFFERENTIATION THROUGH ECONOMIC PRODUCTION AND RITUAL

The activities discussed at the beginning of this chapter as key elements in the creation of household identity in Mesoamerica, gendered economic production and household-level ritual practice, have been shown to have a long history in the Maya area. The data presented here are less complete than those available for the Classic period, especially with respect to the spatial distribution of activities, but they are sufficient to establish the existence of these activities and their residential associations. Economic production, to some extent gendered, and household ritual practice situated in the residential compound represent a basic element of Pre-Hispanic Maya society. The economic and political import of these activities extends far beyond the living space where the production and ritual practice take place. Control of the labor, resources, or products of the economic production represents an important potential source of political power and therefore an area of conflict between different groups. The fact that this production is not detached from its residential location suggests that it remained embedded in the social space and control of the household and was only indirectly available to the centralizing political authority as a source of income and power (see Ball 1993).

Middle Pre-Classic figurines, caches, and burials show that people engaged in ritual behavior in their residential compounds before and during the emergence of formal structures dedicated to such behavior. Like much of Mesoamerica, economic production and ritual practice as activities and as constructors of social identity in the Maya Lowlands precede and develop in tandem with public architecture and monumental art.

Investment in monumental architecture is accompanied, as one moves into the Classic period, by an increased emphasis, in both visual representation and the content of texts, on individual political elites. The iconography of Maya rulership attempts to create a social identity for the ruling elite that monopolizes ritual action, totalizes gender categories, and naturalizes power relations (Joyce 1992). The ruler becomes a central figure uniquely equipped to carry out ritual action (Demarest 1992; Gillespie 1993). Depictions of economic production in other media, such as figurines (Joyce 1993), and the archaeological evidence from residential areas (Hendon 1991, 1992b) create a counterpoint to this identity by highlighting one based on complementary gender roles and the centrality of household-based ritual practice. The effort to monopolize ritual action, and hence the intangible resources controlled through these rituals, may result from the ruler's inability to detach completely control over economic production from subordinate households, a failure that stems in part from the fundamental link in Maya society between productive and ritual action and group social identity.

The decision to devote resources to the construction of keyhole-shaped or round ritual structures reflects the formalization of group ritual practice in the Middle to Late Pre-Classic periods. This change parallels the formalization of religious practice and symbolism by the ruling elite expressed through the architectural and iconographic elaboration of the monumental space of the centers. People living in the surrounding residential compounds effected changes in their ritual practice and made use of some of the same material symbolism, such as plaster and red paint, not in imitation of the center but as a response to the actions of the ruler. Such a response may challenge as much as it supports the ruler's desire to be the central axis of political power. Over time, rituals carried out in the residential compounds, separate from those of the center, grow more, rather than less, important to the maintenance of the social identity of the residential group as its members contend with the economic and social consequences of political centralization.

BIBLIOGRAPHY

ADAMS, RICHARD E. W.
1990   Archaeological Research at the Lowland Maya City of Río Azul. *Latin American Antiquity* 1: 23–41.

ADAMS, RICHARD N.
1975   *Energy and Structure: A Theory of Social Power.* University of Texas Press, Austin.

AIMERS, JIM, AND JAIME AWE
n.d.   Circular Reasons: A Performative Platform at Cahal Pech, Belize. Paper presented at the 58th Annual Meeting of the Society for American Archaeology, St. Louis, April 1993.

ASHMORE, WENDY, AND RICHARD R. WILK
1988   Household and Community in the Mesoamerican Past. In *Household and Community in the Mesoamerican Past* (Richard R. Wilk and Wendy Ashmore, eds.): 1–27. University of New Mexico Press, Albuquerque.

BALL, JOSEPH W.
1993   Pottery, Potters, Palaces, and Polities: Some Socioeconomic and Political Implications of Late Classic Maya Ceramic Industries. *In Lowland Maya Civilization in the Eighth Century A.D.* (Jeremy A. Sabloff and John S. Henderson, eds.): 243–272. Dumbarton Oaks, Washington, D.C.

BLACK, STEPHEN L., AND CHARLES K. SUHLER
1986   The 1984 Río Azul Settlement Survey. In *Río Azul Reports,* no. 2: *The 1984 Season* (Richard E. W. Adams, ed.): 163–192. Center for Archaeological Research, University of Texas, San Antonio.

BOURDIEU, PIERRE
1977   *Outline of a Theory of Practice.* Cambridge University Press, Cambridge.

CLIFF, MAYNARD B.
1986   Excavations in the Late Preclassic Nucleated Village. In *Archaeology at Cerros, Belize, Central America,* vol. 1: *An Interim Report* (Robin A. Robertson and David A. Freidel, eds.): 45–63. Southern Methodist University Press, Dallas.

DEMAREST, ARTHUR A.
1992   Ideology in Ancient Maya Cultural Evolution: The Dynamics of Galactic Polities. In *Ideology and Pre-Columbian Civilizations* (Arthur A. Demarest and Geoffrey Conrad, eds.): 135–157. School of American Research Press, Santa Fe.

DEVEREAUX, LESLIE
1987   Gender Difference and Relations of Inequality in Zinacantan. In *Dealing with Inequality: Analysing Gender Relations in Melanesia and Beyond* (Marilyn Strathern, ed.): 89–111. Cambridge University Press, Cambridge.

DRENNAN, ROBERT D.
1976   Religion and Social Evolution in Formative Mesoamerica. In *The Early Mesoamerican Village* (Kent V. Flannery, ed.): 345–368. Academic Press, New York.
1983a   Ritual and Ceremonial Development at the Early Village Level. In *The Cloud People: Divergent Evolution of the Zapotec and Mixtec Civilizations* (Kent V. Flannery and Joyce Marcus, eds.): 46–50. Academic Press, New York.

1983b Ritual and Ceremonial Development at the Hunter-Gatherer Level. In *The Cloud People: Divergent Evolution of the Zapotec and Mixtec Civilizations* (Kent V. Flannery and Joyce Marcus, eds.): 30–32. Academic Press, New York.

FLANNERY, KENT V., AND JOYCE MARCUS
1976 Evolution of the Public Building in Formative Oaxaca. In *Cultural Change and Continuity: Essays in Honor of James Bennett Griffin* (Charles E. Cleland, ed.): 205–221. Academic Press, New York.

FLANNERY, KENT V., AND MARCUS WINTER
1976 Analyzing Household Activities. In *The Early Mesoamerican Village* (Kent V. Flannery, ed.): 34–47. Academic Press, New York.

FREIDEL, DAVID A.
1986 Introduction. In *Archaeology at Cerros, Belize, Central America,* vol. 1: *An Interim Report* (Robin A. Robertson and David A. Freidel, eds.): xiii–xxiii. Southern Methodist University Press, Dallas.

FREIDEL, DAVID A., AND LINDA SCHELE
1988 Kingship in the Late Preclassic Maya Lowlands: The Instruments and Places of Ritual Power. *American Anthropologist* 90: 547–567.

GARBER, JAMES F.
1989 *Archaeology at Cerros, Belize, Central America,* vol. 2: *The Artifacts* (David A. Freidel, ser. ed.). Southern Methodist University Press, Dallas.

GERHARDT, JULIETTE C., AND NORMAN HAMMOND
1991 The Community of Cuello: The Ceremonial Core. In *Cuello: An Early Maya Community in Belize* (Norman Hammond, ed.): 98–117. Cambridge University Press, Cambridge.

GILLESPIE, SUSAN D.
1993 Power, Pathways, and Appropriations in Mesoamerican Art. In *Imagery and Creativity: Ethnoaesthetics and Art Worlds in the Americas* (Dorothea S. Whitten and Norman E. Whitten, Jr., eds.): 67–107. University of Arizona Press, Tucson.

GLASS, JOHN B.
1965 The BR-1 Mound. In *Prehistoric Maya Settlements in the Belize Valley* (Gordon R. Willey, William R. Bullard, Jr., John B. Glass, and James C. Gifford): 36–90. Harvard University, Papers of the Peabody Museum of Archaeology and Ethnology 54. Cambridge, Mass.

GONLIN, NANCY
1993 *Rural Household Archaeology at Copan, Honduras.* University Microfilms, Ann Arbor.

GROVE, DAVID C.
1987a Other Ceramic and Miscellaneous Artifacts. In *Ancient Chalcatzingo* (David C. Grove, ed.): 271–294. University of Texas Press, Austin.
1987b Raw Materials and Sources. In *Ancient Chalcatzingo* (David C. Grove, ed.): 376–386. University of Texas Press, Austin.

GROVE, DAVID C., AND SUSAN D. GILLESPIE
1992 Ideology and Evolution at the Pre-State Level: Formative Period Mesoamerica. In *Ideology and Pre-Columbian Civilizations* (Arthur A. Demarest and Geoffrey Conrad, eds.): 15–36. School of American Research Press, Santa Fe.

HAMMOND, NORMAN
1991   Ceramic, Bone, Shell, and Ground Stone Artifacts. In *Cuello: An Early Maya Community in Belize* (Norman Hammond, ed.): 176–191. Cambridge University Press, Cambridge.

HAMMOND, NORMAN, JULIETTE C. GERHARDT, AND SARA DONAGHEY
1991   Stratigraphy and Chronology in the Reconstruction of Preclassic Developments at Cuello. In *Cuello: An Early Maya Community in Belize* (Norman Hammond, ed.): 23–55. Cambridge University Press, Cambridge.

HANSEN, RICHARD D.
1992   El proceso cultural de Nakbe y el área del Petén nor-central: las épocas tempranas. In *V Simposio de investigaciones arqueológicas en Guatemala, Museo Nacional de Arqueología y Etnología, 15–18 de Julio de 1991* (Juan Pedro Laporte, H. L. Escobedo A., and Sandra Villagrán de Brady, eds.): 81–87. Ministerio de Cultura y Deportes, Instituto de Antropología e Historia, Asociación Tikal, Guatemala City.

HENDON, JULIA A.
1989   The 1986 Excavations at BA-20. In *Río Azul Reports,* no. 4: *The 1986 Season* (Richard E. W. Adams, ed.): 88–135. Center for Archaeological Research, University of Texas, San Antonio.
1991   Status and Power in Classic Maya Society: An Archeological Study. *American Anthropologist* 93: 894–918.
1992a   Architectural Symbols of the Maya Social Order: Residential Construction and Decoration in the Copan Valley, Honduras. In *Ancient Images, Ancient Thought: The Archaeology of Ideology* (A. Sean Goldsmith et al., eds.): 481–495. Proceedings of the Twenty-Third Annual Conference of the Archaeological Association of the University of Calgary, Calgary.
1992b   Hilado y tejido en la época prehispánica: tecnología y relaciones sociales de la producción textil. In *La indumentaria y el tejido mayas a través del tiempo* (Linda Asturias de Barrios and Dina Fernández García, eds.): 7–16. Museo Ixchel del Traje Indígena de Guatemala, Guatemala City.

JOYCE, ROSEMARY A.
1981   Classic Maya Kinship and Descent: An Alternative Suggestion. *Journal of the Steward Anthropological Society* 13: 45–57.
1992   Dimensiones simbólicas del traje en monumentos clásicos mayas: la construcción del género a través del vestido. In *La indumentaria y el tejido mayas a través del tiempo* (Linda Asturias de Barrios and Dina Fernández García, eds.): 29–38. Museo Ixchel del Traje Indígena de Guatemala, Guatemala City.
1993   Women's Work: Images of Production and Reproduction in Pre-Hispanic Southern Central America. *Current Anthropology* 34: 255–274.
1996   Social Dynamics of Exchange: Changing Patterns in the Honduran Archaeological Record. In *Chieftains, Power, and Trade: Regional Interaction in the Intermediate Area of the Americas* (Carl Henrik Langebaek and Felipe Cardenas-Arroyo, eds.): 31–45. Departamento de Antropología, Universidad de los Andes, Bogotá, Colombia.

KIDDER, ALFRED V.
1947   *Artifacts of Uaxactun, Guatemala.* Carnegie Institution of Washington, Publication 335. Washington, D.C.

KOSAKOWSKY, LAURA, AND NORMAN HAMMOND
1991   Ceramics. In *Cuello: An Early Maya Community in Belize* (Norman Hammond, ed.): 173–176. Cambridge University Press, Cambridge.

LEWENSTEIN, SUZANNE M.
1987   *Stone Tool Use at Cerros: The Ethnoarchaeological and Use-Wear Evidence.* University of Texas Press, Austin.

MARCUS, JOYCE
1989   Zapotec Chiefdoms and the Nature of Formative Religions. In *Regional Perspectives on the Olmec* (Robert J. Sharer and David C. Grove, eds.): 148–197. Cambridge University Press, Cambridge.

McKINNON, SUSAN
1991   *From a Shattered Sun: Hierarchy, Gender, and Alliance in the Tanimbar Islands.* University of Wisconsin Press, Madison.

McSWAIN, REBECCA
1991a   Chert and Chalcedony Tools. In *Cuello: An Early Maya Community in Belize* (Norman Hammond, ed.): 160–173. Cambridge University Press, Cambridge.
1991b   Chert Trade. In *Cuello: An Early Maya Community in Belize* (Norman Hammond, ed.): 192–195. Cambridge University Press, Cambridge.

PENDERGAST, DAVID M.
1982   *Excavations at Altun Ha, Belize, 1964–1970,* vol. 2. Royal Ontario Museum, Toronto.

POWIS, TERRY
1993a   Burning the Champa: 1992 Investigations at the Tokol Group, Cahal Pech, Belize. In *Belize Valley Archaeological Reconnaissance Project: Progress Report of the 1992 Field Season* (Jaime J. Awe, ed.): 97–115. Trent University, Peterborough.
1993b   Special Function Structures within Peripheral Groups in the Belize Valley: An Example from the Bedran Group at Baking Pot. In *Belize Valley Archaeological Reconnaissance Project: Progress Report of the 1992 Field Season* (Jaime J. Awe, ed.): 212–224. Trent University, Peterborough.

PRINDIVILLE, MARY, AND DAVID C. GROVE
1987   The Settlement and Its Architecture. In *Ancient Chalcatzingo* (David C. Grove, ed.): 63–81. University of Texas Press, Austin.

RICKETSON, EDITH BAYLES
1937   *Uaxactun, Guatemala Group E—1926–1931,* pt. 2: *The Artifacts.* Carnegie Institution of Washington, Publication 477. Washington, D.C.

RICKETSON, OLIVER G., JR.
1929   Report of O. G. Ricketson, Jr. on the Excavations at Uaxactun. *Carnegie Institution of Washington Yearbook* 28: 316–322.
1937   *Uaxactun, Guatemala Group E—1926–1931,* pt. 1: *The Excavations.* Carnegie Institution of Washington, Publication 477. Washington, D.C.

n.d.a   Report of Oliver Ricketson on the Excavations at Uaxactun, 1929. Report on the Excavations at the Ruins of Uaxactun for the Carnegie Institution of Washington 1929. Manuscript on file, Archives of the Peabody Museum of Archaeology and Ethnology, Harvard University, Cambridge, Mass.

n.d.b   Report of Oliver G. Ricketson, Jr. on the Excavations at Uaxactun, 1930. Manuscript on file, Archives of the Peabody Museum of Archaeology and Ethnology, Harvard University, Cambridge, Mass.

n.d.c   Unpublished Field Notes for the 1930 Season. Three notebooks and one envelope of drawings on file, Archives of the Peabody Museum of Archaeology and Ethnology, Harvard University, Cambridge, Mass.

ROBERTSON, ROBIN A.

1983   Functional Analysis and Social Process in Ceramics: The Pottery from Cerros, Belize. In *Civilization in the Ancient Americas: Essays in Honor of Gordon R. Willey* (Richard M. Leventhal and Alan L. Kolata, eds.): 105–142. Peabody Museum of Archaeology and Ethnology, Harvard University, Cambridge, Mass., and the University of New Mexico Press, Albuquerque.

ROBIN, CYNTHIA, AND NORMAN HAMMOND

1991   Burial Practices. In *Cuello: An Early Maya Community in Belize* (Norman Hammond, ed.): 204–225. Cambridge University Press, Cambridge.

RUST, WILLIAM F., III

1992   New Ceremonial and Settlement Evidence at La Venta, and Its Relation to Preclassic Maya Cultures. In *New Theories on the Ancient Maya* (Elin C. Danien and Robert J. Sharer, eds.): 123–129. University Museum Monograph 77. University Museum Symposium Series 3, University of Pennsylvania, Philadelphia.

SHAFER, HARRY J., AND THOMAS R. HESTER

1983   Ancient Maya Chert Workshops in Northern Belize, Central America. *American Antiquity* 48: 519–543.

SHARER, ROBERT J.

1994   *The Ancient Maya*, 5th ed. Stanford University Press, Stanford.

SMITH, A. LEDYARD

1950   *Uaxactun, Guatemala: Excavations of 1931–1937.* Carnegie Institution of Washington, Publication 588. Washington, D.C.

1972   *Excavations at Altar de Sacrificios: Architecture, Settlement, Burials, and Caches.* Harvard University, Papers of the Peabody Museum of Archaeology and Ethnology 62 (2). Cambridge, Mass.

1973   *Uaxactun: A Pioneering Excavation in Guatemala.* Addison-Wesley Module in Anthropology 40. Addison-Wesley, Reading, Mass.

SMITH, ROBERT E.

1937   *A Study of Structure A-1 Complex at Uaxactun, Peten, Guatemala.* Contributions to American Archaeology 19. Carnegie Institution of Washington, Publication 456. Washington, D.C.

1955   *Ceramic Sequence at Uaxactun, Guatemala*, 2 vols. Tulane University, Middle American Research Institute, Publication 20. New Orleans.

THOMPSON, PHILIP C.
 1978   *Tekanto in the Eighteenth Century*. University Microfilms, Ann Arbor.

TOURTELLOT, GAIR, III
 1990   Burials: A Cultural Analysis. In *Excavations at Seibal, Department of Peten, Guatemala* (Gordon R. Willey, ed.). Harvard University, Memoirs of the Peabody Museum of Archaeology and Ethnology 17 (2): 81–142. Cambridge, Mass.

VALDÉS, JUAN ANTONIO
 1986   Uaxactún: recientes investigaciones. *Mexicon* 8 (6): 125–128.
 1988   Breve historia de la arquitectura de Uaxactún a la luz de nuevas investigaciones. *Journal de la Société des américanistes* 74: 7–23.
 1989   El Grupo A de Uaxactún: manifestaciones arquitectónicas y dinásticas durante el Clásico Temprano. *Mayab* 5: 30–40.
 1991   Los mascarones preclásicos de Uaxactún: el caso del Grupo H. *Cuadernos de arquitectura mesoamericana* 14: 3–10.

VOGT, EVON Z.
 1969   *Zinacantan: A Maya Community in the Highlands of Chiapas*. Belknap Press, Harvard University Press, Cambridge, Mass.

WAUCHOPE, ROBERT
 1934   *House Mounds of Uaxactun, Guatemala*. Contributions to American Archaeology 7. Carnegie Institution of Washington, Publication 436. Washington, D.C.

WILK, RICHARD R., AND HAROLD L. WILHITE, JR.
 1991   The Community of Cuello: Patterns of Household and Settlement Change. In *Cuello: An Early Maya Community in Belize* (Norman Hammond, ed.): 118–133. Cambridge University Press, Cambridge.

WILLEY, GORDON R.
 1965   Artifacts. In *Prehistoric Maya Settlements in the Belize Valley* (Gordon R. Willey, William R. Bullard, Jr., John B. Glass, and James C. Gifford): 391–522. Harvard University, Papers of the Peabody Museum of Archaeology and Ethnology 54. Cambridge, Mass.
 1973   *The Altar de Sacrificios Excavations: General Summary and Conclusions*. Harvard University, Papers of the Peabody Museum of Archaeology and Ethnology 64 (3). Cambridge, Mass.
 1990   General Summary and Conclusions. In *Excavations at Seibal, Department of Peten, Guatemala* (Gordon R. Willey, ed.). Harvard University, Memoirs of the Peabody Museum of Archaeology and Ethnology 17 (4): 175–276. Cambridge, Mass.

WINTER, MARCUS C.
 1976   The Archeological Household Cluster in the Valley of Oaxaca. In *The Early Mesoamerican Village* (Kent V. Flannery, ed.): 25–31. Academic Press, New York.

Ideology, Material Culture, and Daily Practice in Pre-Classic Mesoamerica: A Pacific Coast Perspective

MICHAEL LOVE

UNIVERSITY OF CALIFORNIA, SANTA BARBARA

THE FIRST AND SECOND MILLENNIA B.C. saw the initial development and subsequent elaboration of social complexity throughout Mesoamerica (Grove 1981). The development of social complexity is marked by a number of features, but chief among these are the emergence of institutions, practices, and beliefs linked to power relationships and the domination of societies by elites (Mann 1986). There is now abundant documentation of such institutions and relationships in Pre-Classic Mesoamerica at the regional, household, and individual levels.

Archaeology has the benefit of viewing change over the long term. We can see the emergence of complexity and civilization in Mesoamerica over the course of a thousand years and select for analysis the salient and enduring relationships. Trajectories of demographic change, economic intensification, environmental relationships, and material culture change all become much more clear with the benefit of long-term perspective. The benefit of such perspective, however, can blind us to the way in which the enduring structures we witness were created and recreated. Social and cultural structures are the emergent properties of daily action, the patterns built from repeated individual actions (Giddens 1979, 1982, 1984). No structure, whether related to social roles and behavior or culturally held ideas, exists outside the way in which it is practiced by individual actors on a daily basis. A theory and model of daily social practice and the transformation of daily routines over time are thus indispensable to understanding change in the past if we are to move beyond simple description and reconstruction.

The structures of prehistoric social practice leave patterned material remains in the archaeological record. The emergence of social complexity in Mesoamerica and elsewhere is marked by the creation of new material forms: the monuments that transform the landscape, new assemblages of pottery and tools that fill houses, the jewelry, clothes, and other accoutrements that decorate and define people as individuals and members of groups. That such changes in material culture should occur in concert with changing social relations is often taken for granted, in that material culture is frequently used to define complexity or is explained by simple functionalist accounts. This chapter attempts to establish broader links between material culture and the various aspects of social complexity. My approach is interpretative and seeks to understand how dominance, ideology, and material culture are linked at the level of daily practice in Pre-Classic Mesoamerica.

I propose to analyze daily practice in ancient Mesoamerica from two perspectives. The first is spatial and investigates the ways in which various aspects of the built environment and material culture reflect and shape the structures of daily routine and social interaction. The second perspective examines the way in which people interacted when they did come together. At both levels I seek to define and interpret the dynamic and recursive relationships among three artificially bracketed realms of prehistoric life: social structure and practice, ideology, and material culture. I then apply and expand the model via an analysis of the Early and Middle Pre-Classic period, ca. 1700–500 B.C. in the Pacific Coast region of Guatemala and Chiapas.

I will not repeat the arguments outlining the general aspects of structuration and daily practice theory, as those are now well established in the general archaeological literature, though not particularly well known in Mesoamerica (Hodder 1991; Johnson 1989; Shanks and Tilley 1988). Some general remarks regarding how ideology and material culture relate to general theories of practice are needed, however, before addressing the particulars of the case study.

PRELIMINARY DISCUSSION

Ideology and Practice

Ideology is cultural. As such, it is understood differently by individual agents and different groups within a society (Giddens 1984; Hodder 1991). Such a view requires that ideology not be equated simply with religion (compare Demarest 1989) or viewed as an immutable core of Mesoamerican culture in all times and places (compare Coe 1981). While religion and "worldview" are important aspects of ideology, a broader concept of ideology must include how social identity and social relations are conceived and realized. As with other types of cultural structures, ideological structures are reproduced via practice.

They must be seen as dynamically linked to social action, especially to the negotiations and contestations inherent in any context of inequality. This must be all the more true in the Mesoamerican Pre-Classic, when large-scale inequality first emerged and must have been strongly contested.

The analysis of ideological change in Pre-Classic Mesoamerica has, until now, focused primarily on ceremonial ritual and the symbolic expression of dominant ideologies, or what James Scott has called "Official Transcripts" (Scott 1990). Such a limited focus is unfortunate on several counts. First, it gives the impression that the dominant ideologies were supported uniformly throughout society and were uncontested. We are then left with either an incomplete functionalist account of what ideology does (e.g., Drennan 1976) or a just-so story that glosses over the most critical issues of social dynamics (e.g., Schele and Freidel 1990). Second, a focus on ceremonial ritual alone ignores the possible tensions between the "Official Transcripts" and other possible "transcripts" reconstructed from economic and social evidence. Finally, a focus on ceremonial ritual alone portrays ideology as static and ignores the ways in which ideology is practiced and transformed in the act of practice.

Ideology is contested through processes of domination and resistance. Neither domination nor resistance generally takes place through an explicit discussion of ideology. Rather, they are carried out through social action in both overt and covert forms (Scott 1990). There are clear needs, both theoretical and pragmatic, to move the analysis of ideology beyond ceremonial ritual and to conceive of how it was practiced on a wider basis. Ideology as practiced dominance has clear behavioral associations. Primary among these are the practices of inclusion and exclusion by which dominant groups control social discourse. Exclusionary practices may seek to control when and where social interaction takes place between members of various social groups. The maintenance of dominance is in part dependent upon promoting social distance between the elite and other groups (Berreman 1982; Love 1991). A primary mechanism of exclusion is to erect physical or symbolic barriers that discourage interaction between groups. Elites seek to limit interaction to times and places of their choosing, where they control both the agenda and the presentation of discourse.

Material Culture

Material culture has been widely recognized by archaeologists, in Mesoamerica and elsewhere, to have a role in the expression of wealth, power, and status of individuals and groups. Mesoamerican archaeologists in particular have done an excellent job of linking the symbolic dimensions of material culture to concepts of religion and worldview (e.g., Ashmore 1991; Schele and Freidel 1990).

Material culture must be seen as more than just symbol, however. The place of material culture in social practice is much more pervasive and encompassing (Hodder 1982a, 1982b, 1991). Pierre Bourdieu speaks of material culture representing a "world of objects . . . which is the product of the application of the same schemes to the most diverse domains, a world in which each thing speaks metaphorically of all the others, a meaning in which practices—and particularly rites—have to reckon at all times, whether to evoke or revoke it" (Bourdieu 1977: 91). The world of objects situates and guides social action. Bourdieu conceives of social practice as consisting in large part of habitual action, in which the various parts of the material world serve as mnemonics that shape but do not determine action. As noted by Moore and Hodder (Moore 1986; Hodder 1991), Bourdieu's concepts of how practical knowledge is applied to the world of objects open a tremendously important avenue for analyzing ideology, social practice, and material culture. Bourdieu's observations can also be expanded and elaborated by drawing additional theoretical strands from geography, as discussed below.

The world of objects, social practice, and ideology stand in a complex recursive relationship in which each at once makes and is made by the others. In such a framework, the production and use of material culture must be seen as forms of social practice that recursively act back upon social structure and ideology. The material world is created by structured practice and ideology, but it also transforms them via the daily actions of reflective agents.

The ways in which ideology and dominance are both expressed and shaped by the material world of objects are illustrated in the sections that follow. After a brief synopsis of the regional prehistory of Pacific Guatemala and Chiapas, these theoretical points are expanded and clarified.

Pacific Guatemala and Chiapas: A Synopsis of Regional Prehistory

My data are drawn from the Pacific Coast and piedmont region that encompasses southwestern Guatemala and Chiapas (Fig. 1). Over the past two decades the corpus of archaeological data for this region has expanded dramatically and forced a reassessment of standard interpretations of how social complexity first developed in Mesoamerica. We now know that this region witnessed the development of social complexity as early as anywhere else in Mesoamerica and that the scale and complexity of its sites and settlement systems match or surpass those of other regions of Mesoamerica throughout the Pre-Classic epoch (Love 1990, 1991, n.d.a).

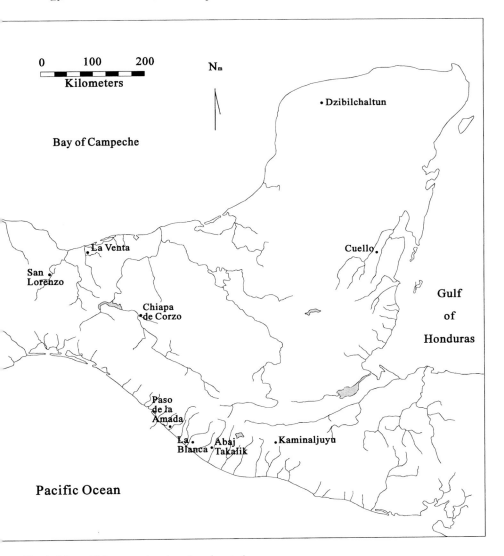

Fig. 1 Map of Mesoamerica showing the study area.

During the Early and Middle Pre-Classic, society in this region was transformed from one with nearly egalitarian social structure to one with much more dramatic social inequality. John Clark and Michael Blake have investigated the initial stages of this transformation in the Mazatan region of Chiapas, especially at the site of Paso de la Amada (Blake 1991; Blake et al. n.d.; Clark 1991; Clark et al. n.d.; Clark, Lesure, and Perez Suarez n.d.). Their data traces the development of social complexity from the beginnings of sedentism in the Barra phase (ca. 1600 B.C.) through the end of the Early Pre-Classic.

A further stage of social elaboration is reached in the Middle Pre-Classic when larger regional centers emerge. In the Río Naranjo region, where I have worked, this stage of development is seen in the emergence of a multitiered regional settlement hierarchy (Love 1990, 1991, n.d.a). Household level data also indicate the emergence of marked social inequality at this time.

Two major regional centers developed in Pacific Guatemala at the beginning of the Middle Pre-Classic. The Río Naranjo region was dominated by the site of La Blanca, whose sphere of influence probably extended from the Río Suchiate and Izapa in the west to the Río Ocosito in the east (Fig. 2). The second major center was Abaj Takalik, located 45 km east of La Blanca in the piedmont region. Information about Abaj Takalik during the Early and Middle Pre-Classic is limited, but the impressive corpus of Olmec sculpture from the site marks it as one of the most important regional centers of the Pacific Coast at this time (Graham 1977, 1979, 1981, 1989; Graham and Benson 1990; Graham, Heizer, and Shook 1978; Orrego Corzo 1990).

The trajectory of increasing complexity continued into the latter half of the Middle Pre-Classic, but in a greatly changed historical setting. La Blanca declined sharply at about 600 B.C. and became a small village. Sometime after that a Maya group arrived at Abaj Takalik and either conquered or displaced the previous inhabitants, as witnessed by the great corpus of early Maya sculpture (Graham, Heizer, and Shook 1978). These events at Abaj Takalik are not well dated, but the expected publication of the ceramic sequence developed by the Guatemalan national project working at the site will clarify the cultural and chronological relationships.

Related in some way to these two major events was the founding and growth of the settlement of Ujuxte. Ujuxte lies on the coastal plain just 12 km east of La Blanca and 40 km southwest of Abaj Takalik. The ceramics of Ujuxte show that it was founded near the end of the Conchas period, at about 600 B.C., just as La Blanca declined (Love n.d.c; Love and Herrera n.d.). Although Ujuxte has a complex settlement history, it appears that most of the site area was occupied soon after 500 B.C. and occupation continued expanding during the Late Pre-Classic.

The social and political paroxysms outlined above were accompanied by equally dramatic changes in material culture. The world of objects that existed at the end of the Middle Pre-Classic differed vastly from that which existed in the Early Pre-Classic. Large centers had monumental architecture arrayed in formal plans. Many had sculpture, such as the Olmec monuments and colossal

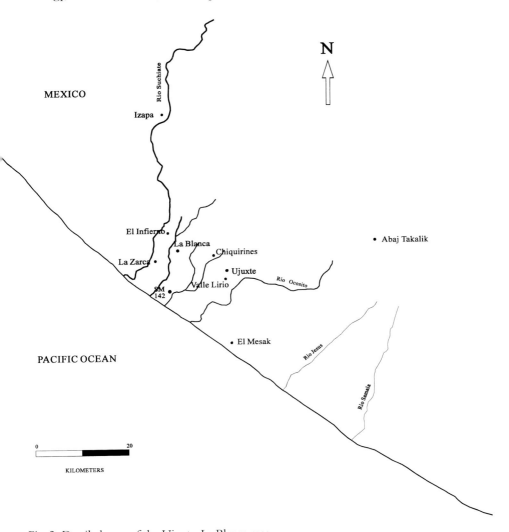

Fig. 2 Detailed map of the Ujuxte-La Blanca area.

heads of Abaj Takalik. The members of some elite households, such as those at
La Blanca, used objects such as jade earspools and necklaces, mica pendants,
elaborately decorated ceramic earspools, and ceramics decorated with an array
of motifs not found in other households. The analysis that follows expands
upon both the theoretical and the descriptive framework already presented in
order to establish these links more concretely.

MACRO-SCALE: SPACE, MONUMENTS, AND REGIONALIZATION

The study of daily social practice in the Mesoamerican past can begin by examining how practices take place in space. A significant accomplishment in social theory during the past ten years has been to link structuration theory as presented by Giddens (1979, 1984, 1985) and Bourdieu (1977), among others, to a theory of space and time. Time-space geography, derived principally from the work of Hagerstrand (1970, 1975), has opened very productive lines of inquiry into how societies are reproduced and transformed by daily routines of action (Giddens 1985; Pred 1985; Soja 1985, 1989).

At the heart of these studies is a concern with how the practical daily activities of life occur in time and space, especially how face-to-face social action, co-presence, occurs. Hagerstrand attempted to study the webs of interaction constructed by an individual over the course of his or her life. He analyzed the trajectories of interaction over the course of a day, a week, a year, and the life of an individual to study spatial constraints on their conduct (Giddens 1984). Both Anthony Giddens and Allan Pred (1985) further develop Hagerstrand's ideas by linking them to theories of structure, agency, power, and social interactionism. Giddens and Pred both stress the importance of socially created space in interaction. Pred defines such space as "place," while Giddens defines it as "locale." To the concept of locale Giddens adds the idea of regionalization, or the zonation of time-space in relation to routinized social practices. Regionalization takes place at almost all locales, as types of social action and interaction become habitually separated in space and time.

Regionalization is vitally important to establishing power and dominance in that disciplinary power is often based upon enforcing co-presence or separation of social actors. For example, the disciplinary power of institutions such as prisons, asylums, and schools is based upon the routinization of certain patterns of co-presence within the prison and separation from the world at large (Foucault 1977; Giddens 1984).

As these theorists argue, we can interpret the organization of space in complex societies as a means by which dominance is practiced and discipline is enforced. Dominance, as seen in early complex societies, may be characterized as the emergence of regionalized social practices (in Giddens' sense) that shape social interaction between members of different groups. Such spatial segregation serves to reproduce social inequality, dominance, and their linked ideological principles by controlling co-presence and interaction, and, more specifically, by zoning locales and the social practices that occur in them. Regionalization enables the categorization of locales and practices, creating oppositions such as core-periphery, town-country, sacred-profane, elite-commoner, frontstage-backstage. Dominance can be reproduced only when such distinctions and practices become routinized, and this can occur only when the material world is transformed to fix these practices actively in space.

The nature of dominance relationships consequently can be studied by linking spatial organization to other evidence for social organization within a society. To return to the case study, we can now link changes in the built environment to altered daily routines and examine how daily routines of social action and interaction were shaped, transformed, and habitualized via alterations to the landscape. In the Pacific Coast, this theme links the history of the built environment to evidence of changing social structure.

BUILDING A SOCIAL WORLD

The earliest sedentary villages of the Pacific Coast region are found during the Barra phase at about 1600 B.C. We have no solid evidence of the spatial organization of society for this period, however. For the succeeding periods some very good data on spatial organization are now available. Surveys show evidence of differences between settlements that reflect the development of regional political institutions and nascent social inequality soon after the beginning of the Locona phase. Within one of the larger settlements, Paso de la Amada, Clark and Blake have evidence of early public architecture dating to the Locona and Ocos phases (ca. 1400–1200 B.C.) from Mound 6, representing one of the earliest building sequences in Mesoamerica (Blake 1991; Blake et al. n.d.).

The best-preserved structure in this sequence is Structure 4, a rectangular building with rounded ends whose preserved clay walls stand nearly a meter tall (Fig. 3). The structure is 22 m in length, 10 m in width, and stands on a platform with about 164 cu m of fill. Structure 4 lies in the middle of the Mound 6 architectural sequence, overlying two earlier floors of similar shape and orientation (Blake et al. n.d.).

The floors of other similarly shaped structures dating to the Early Pre-Classic have been found by Clark and Blake in the Mazatan region. Structure 2 at Aquiles Serdan is also apsidal in shape, but only 6 by 4 m in size. The artifact assemblage is also similar to that of other excavated structures, so that Blake et al. (n.d.) believe that all of these structures are residential. In their opinion, Structure 4 in Mound 6 at Paso de la Amada is most likely the residence of a high-ranking person, possibly a chief. The artifacts of this mound contain a large number of decorated serving vessels, leading Blake and his colleagues to suggest that many of the activities at the location were public and possibly ceremonial.

Fig. 3   Paso de la Amada Structure 4, Mound 6. Photograph courtesy of Michael Blake.

Other possible public constructions dating to the Early Pre-Classic may be located at El Mesak in Retalhuleu, Guatemala. Pye and Demarest (1991) report a mound 6.5 m in height located on the edges of the zone. They date the construction to late in the Ocos phase or early in the Cuadros phase. The identification of Mound 3 as ceremonial, and thus public, is based on its height and use of colored sands. Both aspects could, however, be products of the estuarine setting of the mound, and a more careful evaluation of the claim must await publication of details.

Significant alterations to the cultural landscape occur during the Cuadros and Jocotal periods (ca. 1200–900 B.C.). John Clark (personal communication, 1989) reports a 10 m tall mound more than 200 m long at the site of El Silencio on the Coatan River. This and other long mounds dating to the Cuadros and Jocotal periods may be associated with Olmec-style sculpture in the region (John Clark, personal communication, 1989).

By the beginning of the Middle Pre-Classic, there is a clear structure to the ways in which the environment is being modified. Widespread construction of monumental pyramidal mounds comes at 900 B.C., with the beginning of the Conchas phase. At this time, people in several sites in the Río Naranjo region

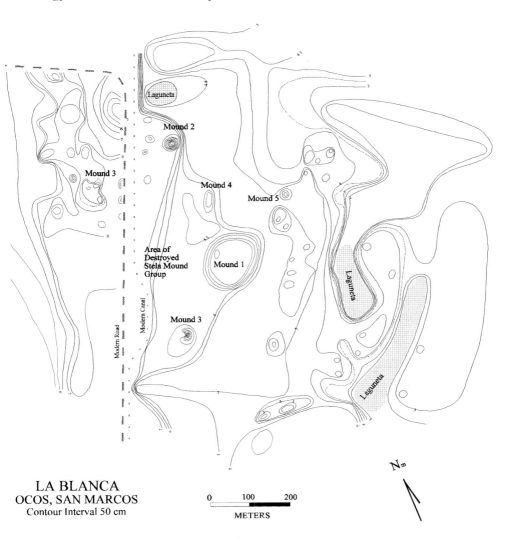

LA BLANCA
OCOS, SAN MARCOS
Contour Interval 50 cm

0   100   200

METERS

N

Fig. 4   Map of the northern sector of La Blanca.

constructed pyramidal mounds more than 15 m in height. The sites of La
Zarca, Infierno, and Valle Lirio all have single large mounds dating to this phase.
Mound 30a at Izapa should perhaps also be included in this group, as Izapa was
probably a secondary center within the La Blanca polity (Love n.d.a). La Blanca
has several mounds more than 5 m in height that appear to be ceremonial or at

Fig. 5 La Blanca Mound 1. Photograph courtesy of Edwin M. Shook.

least nonresidential (Fig. 4). The largest mound at the site was more than 25 m in height and 100 by 140 m at its base. Mound 1 was the largest construction ever built on the Pacific Coast of Guatemala and one of the largest of its time in Mesoamerica (Fig. 5).

There are some clear spatial correlates of these early monumental mounds. First, the distribution of secondary centers that have monumental architecture coincides fairly well with the limits of the Conchas ceramic complex, stretching from Izapa to the Río Ocosito. It may well be that these mounds mark the periphery of the polity dominated by La Blanca. Second, at La Blanca there may have been attempts to define spatial clusters by use of large mounds.

For La Blanca such spatial reconstructions are speculative. Many of the large mounds at La Blanca were severely damaged by road construction in 1972. Mound 1 was reduced to a stump, and many other large mounds were completely leveled. Given this damage it is difficult to say anything definitive about planning. The regular or formal arrangements of monumental architecture at La Blanca were apparently minimal, however. The relationship between Mound 1 and Mound 2 is the only one showing a significant directional orientation (magnetic north), and it is probable that a large plaza lay between them. The area west of Mound 1 was reported by Edwin Shook (personal communication, 1983) to have had several large mounds, one of which supported a stela.

The relationships between large mounds at La Blanca and the small mounds that surround them appear to me to be more significant, and I would suggest

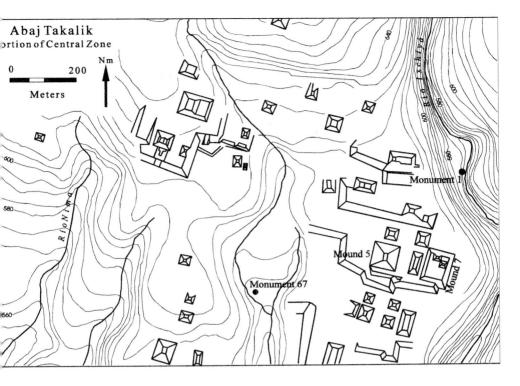

Fig. 6 Central zone of Abaj Takalik (after Graham, Heizer, and Shook 1978; 1984 reprint with new map).

that each of the large mounds is the shrine or temple of a residential group whose houses made up the small mounds around them. There is not enough direct evidence to establish such a pattern conclusively.

Although Mound 1 at La Blanca was the largest construction in Pacific Guatemala, other centers also had large ceremonial constructions. Abaj Takalik, whose Olmec sculpture shows that it was a major center contemporary with La Blanca, probably also had architecture on a grand scale (Fig. 6). No major excavated structure at Abaj Takalik has yet been securely dated to the early portion of the Middle Pre-Classic, but Mound 5 may have been built at that time. My opinion, which is frankly speculative, is based partially on the size of the mound; where excavations provide secure dates, the largest mound constructions in Pacific Guatemala are the earliest. In the Late Pre-Classic and later, monumental constructions combined smaller mounds arranged in formal groups.

139

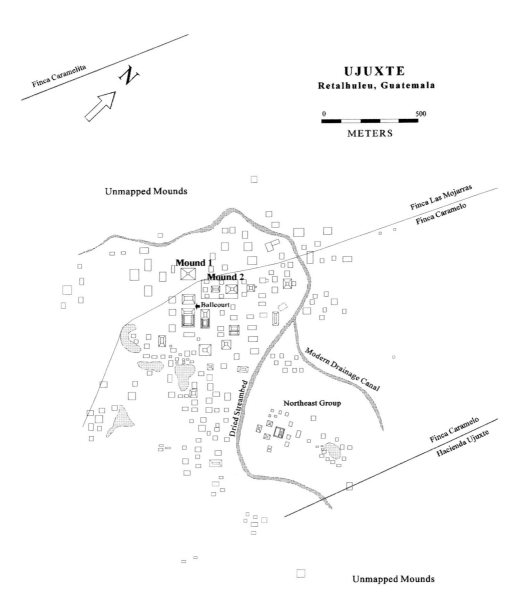

Fig. 7 Preliminary plan of Ujuxte, based on aerial photographs and ground survey.

Support for an early placement of Mound 5 comes from the fact that excavations within 100 m of the mound yielded the only lots of early Middle Pre-Classic material yet found at the site.

By the time of Ujuxte, spatial patterning had reached a zenith (Fig. 7). Ujuxte was in large part a planned city. Most of the city's mounds have an orientation about 35 degrees east of magnetic north. There are also Late Pre-Classic groups within the city whose mounds have an orientation of 55 degrees east of north. Both large mounds and small residential mounds are laid out with regular, nearly gridlike spacing, creating streets and boulevards.

The civic architecture of Ujuxte also follows a formal plan. The heart of Ujuxte's ceremonial center consists of Mound 1 and the Mound 2 Complex. The Mound 2 Complex proper consists of seven mounds on a large platform. Mound 1 is southwest of the group and probably had its stairway on the south side. The plan of the entire complex, including a smaller version of Mound 1, is duplicated at the nearby secondary center of Chiquirines. The largest mound at Chiquirines has its stairway on the west side, however. The plan of the Mound 2 platform is followed at the site of SM-142 as well, but lacks a large mound to the west. The SM-142 site might be classified as a tertiary center (Love n.d.c).

Ujuxte has many spaces with evident restricted access. Other spaces are enclosed in different structured ways. South of Mound 2 lies a massive ballcourt formed by Mounds 3 and 4. Both Mound 4 and the adjacent Mound 5 have enclosed patios on their east sides. An enclosed elite residential area may also be present near the core of ceremonial buildings. The tallest residential mounds within Ujuxte lie in a zone bounded by large ceremonial mounds and a now-dry streambed. These mounds have extremely high densities of ground stone tools and large quantities of decorated ceramics.

THE USE OF SCULPTURE IN STRUCTURED SPACE

Monuments and Space

The creation and use of monumental sculpture may also be usefully analyzed from the perspective of zonation of routine practices (compare Grove, this volume). Much sculpture was created during the Middle Pre-Classic, and most of it is recognizably "Olmec." I use the term *Olmec* solely as a stylistic label, without implying that the style has any geographical or ethnic connotations (see Love 1991). What is significant about Olmec sculpture in Pacific Guatemala is that it is found only at paramount sites such as Abaj Takalik and La Blanca. It thus marks them as distinctive places within their respective regions.

Only two small pieces are known presently from La Blanca (Figs. 8, 9). A

Fig. 8 La Blanca Monument 1.   Fig. 9 La Blanca Monument 2.
Photograph courtesy of Edwin M. Shook.

stela once present at the site was reportedly smashed by local residents in the 1970s. All three sculptural pieces come from a small area just west of Mound 1. The stela was reportedly set on top of a platform mound. The use of these unique features distinguishes this zone from the rest of the site. These facts suggest the use of sculpture to demarcate a restricted area of La Blanca as a ritual or sacred zone.

Abaj Takalik has a large corpus of Olmec sculpture, including two colossal heads (Figs. 10, 11). At Abaj Takalik, sculpture may well have been used as exclusionary markers: Monuments 1 and 68 (Figs. 12, 13) are both located on stream banks that would have been natural approaches to the site. Given the limited distribution of Middle Pre-Classic ceramics at the site, it is possible that the entire settlement lay within these boundaries. Other Middle Pre-Classic sculptures are found within this occupation zone (e.g., Fig. 14), although all were reset in later times, which leaves us without further avenue for investigation of Middle Pre-Classic patterning of sculpture within the site.

There is at present no sculptural corpus from Ujuxte other than two miniature (ca. 15 cm tall) potbellies found in surface collections in 1993. Given Ujuxte's immense size and its proximity to two great centers of sculptural production, Abaj Takalik and Izapa, this finding is strange. Smashed fragments from Chiquirines attest to the presence of sculpture near Ujuxte, and it is possible that Ujuxte once had sculpture that has been looted or destroyed.

Fig. 10 Abaj Takalik Monument 23.

Fig. 11 Abaj Takalik Monument 16/17.

Discussion

It is a long way from Structure 4 at Paso de la Amada to the ceremonial core of Ujuxte. The changes witnessed in architectural forms in the course of a thousand years bear striking witness to the social and cultural elaborations of the time. They also tell us much about the ways in which social interaction was shaped and modified by the world of material things.

In the Early Pre-Classic there were few attempts to shape the landscape. The modification of space was limited to the construction of dwellings on high ground. Some of these dwellings were apparently more elaborate than others and may have served as the scene of special actions or ritual acts. This is an important step, however, in that specific behaviors became fixed in space; they became associated with a locale. It was the first step toward segregating and regularizing activities in space.

143

Fig. 12 Abaj Takalik Monument 1.

Things changed fundamentally at the beginning of the Middle Pre-Classic. Monumental architecture of the type constructed at La Blanca, Abaj Takalik, and other centers has several effects on social interaction. First, these monuments warp social space much more than earlier constructions; they modify daily routines. Daily action includes space and is constituted in the routine use of certain spatial paths. In the trivial sense, these new monuments occupy space and therefore prevent the continuation of any daily routine that previously included the space upon which they are built. In a more significant sense, they become reference points for regionalization and the social categorization of space. That is, they become pivots for spatial segregation based on direction, distance, or other contingent factors. This referential quality differs from the locales of previous times in the size and durability of these monuments. Giddens maintains that the disciplinary power of locales is based upon their fixity; the ability to transform the novel into the habitual is based in part on durability. The size and durability of these monuments is significantly greater than anything that previously existed in Mesoamerica.

Abaj Takalik Monument
r Orrego Corzo 1990: 19).

Fig. 14 Abaj Takalik Monument 55.

Second, taken together, the monumental architectural constructions of the Middle Pre-Classic transformed and enlarged the concept of place. In the case of the Río Naranjo, the monuments at La Blanca and its secondary centers appear to define the center and peripheries of a polity. If this was true, the effects on daily activities would have been significant. The scale of social interaction would have been enlarged as the entire polity was materially redefined as a single locale. Thus an individual actor's daily routine might take place over a much larger physical and social space, though the space itself is more highly segregated. Such alteration of routine is evident in the spatial segregation of labor, for instance, in the development of special-function sites (Love n.d.b). At the same time, the possibilities for regionalization become much more pronounced as the number of groups and activities within the locale increase. Disciplinary aspects come into play as agents with differing social identities are forced into routinized co-presence and simultaneously restricted in their interaction with individuals and groups outside the locale's boundaries.

The built environment underwent another dramatic transformation during the time of Ujuxte. At this time, site planning was extended beyond the primary regional center into the hinterland. Secondary and tertiary centers became microcosms of the regional capital, extending referential spatial categorization to a more detailed level.

At Ujuxte itself, a very controlled social space was planned and constructed. Ceremonial zones of tightly clustered and precisely oriented mounds stand out clearly at the center of the city. Enclosed spaces, such as ballcourts and framed courtyards, were built within this precinct. Elite residences may be adjacent to the ceremonial core and segregated from the rest of the city.

The gridlike construction of Ujuxte's streets and avenues is especially salient. The grid could serve obviously as a means of spatial classification: every building and house stands in a well-defined relationship to others. But a grid also constructs a very precise spatial path through the city. The routine daily paths of every person at Ujuxte necessarily conformed to the regimen of the grid and thus were disciplined by the layout of the city.

A salient point in the above discussion is that, although much of the regionalization of space that took place in the Middle Pre-Classic was anchored on "ceremonial architecture," the social practices effected by this regionalization went far beyond ritual. Certainly these monuments were more than purely religious; they functioned as symbols of power, wealth, and prestige. More than that, however, their effect was to redefine all sorts of daily activities, including economic practices.

THE MICRO-SCALE: GROUP BOUNDARIES AND SOCIAL INTERACTION

The Middle Pre-Classic in Pacific Guatemala was thus marked by the pronounced regionalization and categorization of space. These processes were linked to dominance in that they affected how and where social interaction occurred. The size and durability of monuments, both architectural and sculptural, served to fix these new routines by indelibly altering the landscape in which interaction occurred.

Many types of space can be specifically linked to elite practices. Ritual precincts were salient as space was carved up, and a key aspect of domination was undoubtedly the ways in which the elite controlled access to and use of these settings. Elite residential zones were also present, both in an urban-rural dichotomy and the creation of elite residential zones within cities. The creation of these types of space had the net effect of constructing nonegalitarian forms of social interaction.

If the nature of when and where social interaction took place became more structured, so too did the quality of face-to-face encounters. In this context it is useful to analyze the material culture of individual households and the accoutrements used by their residents in the course of daily life. The data for this analysis is uneven but does provide some general outlines that complement the picture painted above.

Early Pre-Classic data suggest that there was little restriction on how various classes of material culture were distributed within society. Household assemblages show much less differentiation than in the Middle Pre-Classic. The presence of a ranked society is inferred from other lines of evidence, including settlement patterns, patterns of obsidian exchange, and the presence of craft specialization (Blake 1991; Blake et al. n.d.; Clark 1990, 1991; Clark and Blake 1989; Clark and Salcedo Romero 1989; Clark, Lesure, and Perez Suarez n.d.).

Data for the Middle Pre-Classic are similarly incomplete but nonetheless provide a consistent picture of significant social inequality. In addition to regional settlement data, excavations at La Blanca by Shook, Hatch, and myself, combined with Coe's (1961) excavations at La Victoria and surface collections from 60 Conchas phase sites, provide evidence for the emergence of inequality at the household level (Love 1991, n.d.a). Two households at La Blanca show signs of wealth and high status not present at any other locations in the site or region. These indicators include jade, jewelry of polished mica, and higher percentages of fine white-paste pottery.

These two households also have a unique array of decorative motifs on their pottery, including icons often labeled "Olmec." I have proposed previously that these ceramic motifs, along with items of personal adornment such as jewelry, were intended to mark social boundaries (Love 1991). They served as exclusionary tools that marked the emergent elite as a distinct group and erected symbolic social boundaries.

The presence of these artifacts in domestic refuse deposits along with domestic pottery, the remains of meals, and broken tools suggests that they were part of daily life. They were used and lost in the course of ordinary practices. Although the precise social context of their use cannot be certain, such artifacts strongly suggest that symbolism of social identity and standing had become an important aspect of social interaction between and within the social groups constituting Río Naranjo society. Such symbolism would have been instrumental in affecting the quality of social interaction, that is, in distinguishing dominator from dominated and in signaling the behaviors appropriate to such social encounters. Rather than shaping the time and place of co-presence, such symbolic expression serves to shape the nature of the encounter. In so doing, it is a vital part of structuration and a means by which dominance reproduces itself.

The data from Ujuxte are still being analyzed. Surface collections from 180 domestic mounds show some evidence for the differential distribution of ceramic motifs and type of ground stone tools. While many ceramic motifs seen at La Blanca continue to be present at Ujuxte, there are also important changes in the domestic assemblages that may reflect a general decline in ritual at the household level and an increased emphasis on public ceremony in explicitly defined ritual settings. Figurines, for instance, are nearly omnipresent at Conchas-phase sites, but by the time of Ujuxte they had nearly ceased to exist.

CONCLUSION

The interpretations and data presented here are intended to do little more than outline some productive lines of inquiry that await exploration. The lines that develop will surely be influenced by fresh bodies of data emerging from ongoing projects on the Pacific piedmont and coastal plain. But while recognizing the importance of new data, we must also explore new theoretical alternatives that offer compelling avenues of interpretation and inspiration for empirical study. For instance, while I have emphasized the spatial aspects of the work flowing from Hagerstrand's time-geography, the temporal aspects also need to be explored. At the same time social space was becoming more highly segregated during the Pre-Classic, the calendrical reckoning of time was also becoming more formalized and more elaborate. The disciplinary dimensions surrounding the control of time by the elite are enormous and had ramifications for every aspect of daily life.

The social world that existed in Pacific Guatemala after the Middle Pre-Classic was vastly different from that which had existed previously. Power relationships, reproduced and transformed over one thousand years, were more pronounced and more institutionalized than previously. Economic intensification had been achieved through an increased focus on maize agriculture, the rearing of the domestic dog, and specialization of labor (Love n.d.b).

Over that time the world of objects had also changed. Material culture had shaped the situations in which people came into contact with one another, the ways in which they became co-present in space-time. It affected the quality of those interactions as well. Far from being simply symbolic of social change, changing material culture remade the social world.

The elaboration of ritual, ceremony, and official cosmology were without doubt very significant aspects of the newly created social world of the Middle Pre-Classic. But equally important, if not more so, were the transformed daily routines of every member of society. The structures of habitus created and transformed over the course of a thousand years were what constituted the culture and society of Mesoamerican civilization.

Acknowledgments Fieldwork in Guatemala was made possible with the permission and assistance of the Instituto de Antropología e Historia de Guatemala. Erick Ponciano, head of the Departamento de Monumentos Prehispanicos deserves thanks for his help, especially with work at Ujuxte. The Río Naranjo project was made possible by a Fulbright-Hayes Doctoral Research Abroad Fellowship from the U.S. Department of Education, several grants from the University of California at Berkeley, and a National Science Foundation Dissertation Improvement Grant, BNS-8611064. The Ujuxte Project received funding from the H. Charles Heinz III Charitable Trust in 1993 and a Fulbright Senior Lecturing and Research Fellowship in 1994. Additional funds for the 1994 season were provided by the Kidder Chair of the Universidad del Valle de Guatemala. I also thank the Centro de Investigaciones Regionales de Mesoamerica for the use of their scanner to prepare some of the illustrations. Thanks also to Fernando Sanchez for the use of his computer and printer. An earlier version of this chapter was presented at the 1992 meetings of the American Anthropological Association in San Francisco in the session "Ideology, Power and Material Culture in Pre-Classic Mesoamerica." I wish to thank the discussants, Susan Kus and David Grove, for their comments on that version. Margaret Purser read all previous versions of this chapter and helped greatly with its development. All the above are absolved of responsibility for the chapter's final state.

BIBLIOGRAPHY

ASHMORE, WENDY
    1991   Site-Planning Principles of Directionality among the Ancient Maya. *Latin American Antiquity* 2: 199–226.

BERREMAN, GERALD
    1982   Social Categories and Social Interaction in India. *American Anthropologist* 74: 567–586.

BLAKE, MICHAEL
    1991   An Emerging Early Formative Chiefdom at Paso de la Amada, Chiapas, Mexico. In *The Formation of Complex Society in Southeastern Mesoamerica* (William R. Fowler, ed.): 27–46. CRC Press, Boca Raton.

BLAKE, MICHAEL, RICHARD G. LESURE, VICKI L. FEDDEMA, WARREN D. HILL, DENNIS C. GOSSER, JOHN E. CLARK, AND RONALD LOWE
    n.d.   Preliminary Report: 1993 Excavations at Paso de la Amada, Chiapas, Mexico. Report prepared for the Social Sciences and Humanities Research Council of Canada, 1993.

BOURDIEU, PIERCE
    1977   *Outline of a Theory of Practice.* Cambridge University Press, Cambridge.

CLARK, JOHN E.
    1990   Olmecas, Olmequismo, y Olmequizacion en Mesoamerica. *Arqueologia* (ser. 2) 3: 49–56.
    1991   The Beginnings of Mesoamerica: Apologia for the Soconusco Early Formative. In *The Formation of Complex Society in Southeastern Mesoamerica* (William R. Fowler, ed.): 13–26. CRC Press, Boca Raton.

CLARK, JOHN E., AND MICHAEL BLAKE
    1989   El origen de la civilización en Mesoamerica: Los Olmecas y Mokaya del Soconusco de Chiapas, Mexico. In *El Preclasico o Formativo: avances y perspectivas* (Martha Carmona Macas, coord.): 385–403. Instituto Nacional de Antropología e Historia, Mexico.

CLARK, JOHN E., MICHAEL BLAKE, PEDRO GUZZY, MARTHA CUEVAS, AND TAMARA SALCEDO ROMERO
    n.d.   Final Report to the Instituto Nacional de Antropología e Historia on the Early Preclassic Pacific Coastal Project, Mexico, 1987.

CLARK, JOHN E., RICHARD F. LESURE, AND TOMAS PEREZ SUAREZ
    n.d.   Investigaciones del Formativo Temprano del litoral Chiapaneco. Informe final entregado al Consejo de Arqueología, Instituto Nacional de Antropología e Historia, Mexico, 1994.

CLARK, JOHN E., AND TAMARA SALCEDO ROMERO
    1989   Ocos Obsidian Distribution in Chiapas, Mexico. In *New Frontiers in the Archaeology of the Pacific Coast of Southern Mesoamerica* (Frederick J. Bove and Lynette Heller, eds.): 15–24. Anthropological Research Papers 39. Arizona State University, Tempe.

COE, MICHAEL D.

1961   *La Victoria, an Early Site on the Pacific Coast of Guatemala.* Harvard University, Papers of the Peabody Museum of Archaeology and Ethnology 53. Cambridge, Mass.

1981   Religion and the Rise of Mesoamerican States. In *The Transition to Statehood in the New World* (Grant D. Jones and Robert R. Krautz, eds.): 157–171. Cambridge University Press, Cambridge.

DEMAREST, ARTHUR A.

1989   Ideology and Evolutionism in American Archaeology: Looking beyond the Economic Base. In *Archaeological Thought in America* (C. C. Lamberg-Karlovsky, ed.): 89–102. Cambridge University Press, Cambridge.

DRENNAN, ROBERT D.

1976   Religion and Social Evolution in Formative Mesoamerica. In *The Early Mesoamerican Village* (Kent V. Flannery, ed.): 345–368. Academic Press, New York.

FOUCAULT, MICHEL

1977   *Discipline and Punish.* Vintage, New York.

GIDDENS, ANTHONY

1979   *Central Problems in Social Theory.* University of California Press, Berkeley.

1982   *Profiles and Critiques in Social Theory.* University of California Press, Berkeley.

1984   *The Constitution of Society.* University of California Press, Berkeley.

1985   Time, Space, and Regionalization. In *Social Relations and Spatial Structures* (Derek Gregory and John Urry, eds.): 265–295. St. Martin's Press, New York.

GRAHAM, JOHN A.

1977   Discoveries at Abaj Takalik, Guatemala. *Archaeology* 30 (3): 196–197.

1979   Maya, Olmecs, and Izapans at Abaj Takalik, Guatemala. In *Actes du XLII Congrès des Américanistes* 8: 179–188. Paris.

1981   Abaj Takalik: The Olmec Style and Its Antecedents in Pacific Guatemala. In *Ancient Mesoamerica: Selected Readings* (John A. Graham, ed.): 163–176. Peek Publications, Palo Alto.

1989   Olmec Diffusion: A View from Pacific Guatemala. In *Regional Perspectives on the Olmec* (Robert J. Sharer and David Grove, eds.): 227–246. Cambridge University Press, Cambridge.

GRAHAM, JOHN A., AND LARRY BENSON

1990   Escultura Olmeca y Maya sobre canto en Abaj Takalik: su desarrollo y importancia. *Arqueologia* (ser. 2) 3: 77–84.

GRAHAM, JOHN A., ROBERT F. HEIZER, AND EDWIN M. SHOOK

1978   Abaj Takalik 1976: Exploratory Investigations. In *Studies in Ancient Mesoamerica,* pt. 3 (John A. Graham, ed.): 85–110. Contributions of the University of California Archaeological Research Facility 36. (Reprinted in 1984 with new site map.) Berkeley.

GROVE, DAVID C.

1981   The Formative Period and the Evolution of Complex Culture. In *Handbook of Middle American Indians,* suppl. (Victoria Reifler Bricker and Jeremy A. Sabloff, eds.) 1: 373–391. University of Texas Press, Austin.

HAGERSTRAND, TORSTEN

    1970   *What about People in Regional Science?* Papers of the Regional Science Association 24.

    1975   Space, Time, and Human Conditions. In *Dynamic Allocation of Urban Space* (A. Karlqvist, L. Lundqvust, and F. Snickars, eds.): 3–14. Saxon House, Westmead.

HODDER, IAN

    1982a   Theoretical Archaeology—A Reactionary View. In *Structural and Symbolic Archaeology* (Ian Hodder, ed.): 1–17. Cambridge University Press, Cambridge.

    1982b   *Symbols in Action.* Cambridge University Press, Cambridge.

    1991   *Reading the Past,* 2nd ed. Cambridge University Press, Cambridge.

JOHNSON, MATTHEW H.

    1989   Concepts of Agency in Archaeological Interpretation. *Journal of Anthropological Archaeology* 8: 189–211.

LOVE, MICHAEL W.

    1990   La Blanca y el Preclasico Medio en la Costa Pacífica. *Arqueología* (ser. 2) 3: 67–76.

    1991   Style and Social Complexity in Formative Mesoamerica. In *The Formation of Complex Society in Southeastern Mesoamerica* (William R. Fowler, ed.): 47–76. CRC Press, Boca Raton.

    n.d.a   Early Settlements and Chronology of the Río Naranjo, Guatemala. Ph.D dissertation, University of California, Berkeley, 1989.

    n.d.b   Economic Patterns in the Development of Complex Society in Pacific Guatemala. In *Pacific Latin America in Prehistory: The Evolution of Archaic and Formative Cultures* (Michael Blake, ed.): 89–100. Washington State University Press, Pullman.

    n.d.c   Informe preliminar sobre investigaciones arqueológicas en la Costa de Retalhuleu y San Marcos. Report submitted to the Instituto de Antropología e Historia de Guatemala, 1993.

LOVE, MICHAEL W., AND CAROL HERRERA

    n.d.   Exploración arqueológica en la region de El Ujuxte, Costa Sur. Paper presented at the VII Simposio de Arqueología Guatemalteca, Guatemala City, 1993.

MANN, MICHAEL

    1986   *The Sources of Social Power,* vol. 1: *From the Beginning to A.D. 1760.* Cambridge University Press, Cambridge.

MOORE, HENRIETTA

    1986   *Space, Text, and Gender: An Anthropological Study of the Marakwet of Kenya.* Cambridge University Press, Cambridge.

ORREGO CORZO, MIGUEL

    1990   *Investigaciones Arqueológicas en Abaj Takalik, El Astinal, Retalhuleu, Año 1988, reporte no. 1.* Ministerio de Cultura y Deportes, Instituto de Antropología e Historia, Guatemala.

PRED, ALLAN

    1985   The Social Becomes the Spatial, the Spatial Becomes the Social: Enclosures, Social Change, and the Becoming of Places in Skane. In *Social Relations and Spatial Structures* (Derek Gregory and John Urry, eds.): 337–365. St. Martin's Press, New York.

Pye, Mary E., and Arthur A. Demarest

    1991   The Evolution of Complex Societies in Southeastern Mesoamerica: New Evidence from El Mesak, Guatemala. In *The Formation of Complex Society in Southeastern Mesoamerica* (William R. Fowler, ed.): 77–100. CRC Press, Boca Raton.

Schele, Linda, and David Freidel

    1990   *A Forest of Kings.* William Morrow and Company, New York.

Scott, James C.

    1990   *Domination and the Arts of Resistance.* Yale University Press, New Haven.

Shanks, Michael, and Christopher Tilley

    1988   *Social Theory and Archaeology.* University of New Mexico Press, Albuquerque.

Soja, Edward W.

    1985   The Spatiality of Social Life: Towards a Transformative Retheorization. In *Spatial Organization and Social Structure* (Derek Gregory and John Urry, eds.): 90–127. St. Martin's Press, New York.

    1989   *Post Modern Geography: The Reassertion of Space in Critical Theory.* Verso, London.

From Stone to Symbols: Olmec Art in Social Context at San Lorenzo Tenochtitlán

ANN CYPHERS

UNIVERSIDAD NACIONAL AUTÓNOMA DE MÉXICO

IN THIS CHAPTER I ADDRESS CERTAIN questions concerning the reconstruction of Olmec ideology by focusing on an emerging body of data in which context, in a number of its various senses, is unusually well controlled. The specific archaeological contexts of monuments dating to the Early Pre-Classic (1200–900 B.C.), situated within larger spatial settings on the San Lorenzo plateau and at the hinterland site, Loma del Zapote, are the data to be examined. The ideology in question is clearly elite: the objects used in the inference are numerically quite rare, and their distribution within the sites is limited. The empirical basis of the definition of elites (Marcus 1992; Chase and Chase 1992) is the large-scale control of large quantities of imported rock, specialized production technologies, and the restricted manipulation of objects embodying ideological concepts.

The contexts and settings presented illustrate the mutual involvement of ideological legitimation and economics as a basis of elite interests. The display of rulership may be directly associated with the control of two resources, water and stone. The use and regular reuse of exotic materials reflects Olmec pragmatism in making important decisions affecting the display of ideology and its transformation through recycling.

An intense *in situ* focus on monument erection physically associated with a constructed water channel, as yet not fully excavated, suggests control of water sources as one potential power base in a clearly nonegalitarian social context. Moreover, I suggest that an elite monopolized the use of exotic stone in its own monuments. Such limitation of the distribution of exotic stone, combined with the consistent evidence of reuse and reworking of old pieces, may well indicate that such materials were themselves sacralized.

155

The settings under consideration will show how, on a piece-by-piece basis, Olmec sculptures provide the individual strands of a conceptual framework about the earth and the cosmos; yet when the sculptures are organized into visual displays, the symbols and concepts they evoke can be arranged and rearranged to achieve a variety of messages and effects. Stone monuments, arranged in groupings, thus constitute statements about ideology, statements that permitted considerable variation in symbols and concepts.

Artistic manifestations, analyzed mainly from the intrinsic meaning of the images, have from the beginning provided the characterization of the Olmec of southern Veracruz and Tabasco, the area from which the first large corpus of stone monuments was derived. Originally proposed rather casually by Stirling (1955), a "central Olmec myth" (Coe 1965) stood for many years as an unquestioned reconstruction of elite ideology. Much of this reconstruction was necessarily based on the comparative analysis of individual monuments, most recovered almost by chance as they eroded out of the banks of ravines, or located by other fortuitous means without archaeological context. The reconstructed elite ideology was enhanced by ethnohistoric and ethnographic analogy. Interpretations have been in effect imposed upon the Olmec, with no consistent methodology for testing any of them against each other or against a body of data beyond that of often individual objects widely separated in time and space. In a recent synthesis of major hypotheses regarding Olmec iconography, Coe shows how some interpretations have been modified and changed, and highlights the speculative quality of what he hesitatingly calls "Olmec ideology" (1989).

The focus on an "Olmec ideology" has remained central and has provoked debate on, first, what is Olmec, and second, what is ideology. If the "Olmec phenomenon" is geographically diverse, with its contexts varying from one area to another, it has also proven to be chronologically variable through its presumed span of at least one thousand years (among others, Berger, Graham, and Heizer 1967; Coe and Diehl 1980; Graham 1989; Grove 1984, 1989; Heizer, Drucker, and Graham 1968; Heizer, Graham, and Napton 1968; Lowe 1977, 1989; Piña Chan 1958; Sharer 1978). Isolated finds, and even controlled survey and excavation at single sites, because of their relative rarity, have not provided a sample size adequate for broad, comparative generalization. Furthermore, Olmec studies have been significantly influenced by both the theoretical perspectives and the substantive findings of research in other Mesoamerican areas and time periods. In consequence, earlier and later investigations and their respective conclusions may not be entirely comparable, and the "Olmec phenomenon" comes to look increasingly elusive. Like Stark (1991), I believe that a fine-grained analysis is necessary to eliminate temporal depth as a possible cause of distress about "Olmec."

Unfortunately, ideas are not directly recoverable from archaeological remains, but must be reconstructed or inferred from the by-products or remnants of human behavior that presumably are generated or influenced by ideology. As Demarest (1989: 96) has pointed out, many explanations automatically assign chronological or causal priority for economic, social, and political institutions over ideology. Certainly this is true for interpretations of Olmec art that derived from an explicit Marxist perspective. Regardless of theoretical orientation, the impact of ideology and its attendant rituals must be explored with scrupulously accurate chronological controls in order to establish sequentiality and to infer causality. Basic to this approach is rigorously defined archaeological context as a necessary point of departure.

A major problem has been one of context or, more specifically, its absence. Like *Olmec* and *ideology, context* is a surprisingly ambiguous term with many, not entirely comparable, referents. It is a hierarchic term with a range from broad and general to highly specific; as such it is difficult to operationalize. Clearly an isolated monument, a chance find, has no context. Objects demonstrably or ostensibly from the same geographic location share at least that context, but if chronology is not simultaneously controlled, the context is of limited analytic utility. Objects comprising elements in a controlled sample will share that as a context, depending on how the sample was constructed. Ideally a "context" implies not only the single object, but those objects found together with it, including constructed architecture and/or modified landscapes, immediate or more remote. It also implies association with some individuals or groups: is the object widely distributed, with a variety of other objects, in numbers of differentiated spaces, or is its distribution restricted? Especially in nonegalitarian societies, such questions address the nature of sociopolitical differentiation, including that of how we recognize and define an elite—the necessary first step in explaining how, perhaps, an elite comes into being (compare Love, this volume).

The problem arises, in the particular case of ideology because symbols cannot be interpreted in isolation; they necessarily derive their meaning as parts of a network or web of contrasts. For Olmec, the consistent identification of such complexes of symbols has been difficult, as noted above: it is often context, both archaeological and sociological, that provides the necessary network, which the investigator can then use to suggest some potential readings as more probable, as having more internal support, than other readings.

When specific contexts become available, the evidence from the specific location of objects is best situated in yet broader settings. Rapoport defines a setting as "a milieu which defines a situation, reminds occupants of the appropriate rules and hence of the ongoing behaviors appropriate to the situation defined by the settings, thereby making co-action possible" (1990: 12). Setting is indispensable for discussing the interplay of function and meaning and for defining social context. In reconstructing how activities are conducted and the way in which they are ordered on a larger scale, the study of very specific context leads to the definition of activities and activity systems that have key facets such as order or sequence, nature, and participation. Activities give shape to space (Rapoport 1990).

SAN LORENZO TENOCHTITLÁN AND ITS HINTERLAND

Located in the municipality of Texistepec in southern Veracruz, the site called San Lorenzo Tenochtitlán by Stirling (1955) encompassed the plateau of San Lorenzo, the high ground of Tenochtitlán, and the community of Potrero Nuevo. Stirling implicitly recognized the difficulty in establishing site boundaries in this area because of the type of soil accumulation and ground cover. Stirling did not define individually bounded sites but rather a broad area where archaeological remains were evident but not visually continuous on the surface. Today, on the basis of recent research, I would modify Stirling's definition slightly, as the visibility problems have improved somewhat in the last 50 years. The great plateau of San Lorenzo, the Early Pre-Classic regional center, has evidence for habitation spilling down onto the terraced sides and into the lower lands. Evidence for Olmec occupation under the later period occupations of Tenochtitlán certainly exists but is highly inaccessible at present, leaving the magnitude or importance of this focus unknown. Another important focus of population in the immediate hinterland is Loma del Zapote, located on the narrow band of elevated lands between two branches of an ancient river located 4.5 km south of the San Lorenzo plateau. Loma del Zapote includes the contemporary community and ejido of Potrero Nuevo, some private lands, and the Tenochtitlán ejidal annex. With monumental architecture and stone monuments, Loma del Zapote newly proclaims its importance as an Early Pre-Classic site.

The San Lorenzo Tenochtitlán Archaeological Project has benefited from work previously conducted in the area by Stirling (1955), Coe and Diehl (1980), and Beverido (n.d.). Basic to the explorations since 1990 are the detailed topographic map, the regional aerial photographs and restitutions (Coe and Diehl 1980), as well as detailed presentations of excavations and stratigraphy (Coe and Diehl 1980; Beverido n.d.).

The San Lorenzo Tenochtitlán Archaeological Project was developed on the basis of a theoretical focus differing significantly from those of previous explorations in the region. The emphasis from the beginning was explicitly on settlement pattern at both regional and community levels of analysis, that is, the documentation, and eventual explanation, of the differentiated use of space through time by a human population. Thus the goals have been the delineation and excavation of domestic, workshop, storage, and ceremonial areas of sites. Moreover, extensive regional surveys were designed to suggest, eventually, how center and hinterland were functionally interrelated. Investigation of the ancient environment will facilitate explanation of landscape utilization for subsistence and other purposes—again, a focus on space as context, as shaping and being shaped by, differentiated human behavior.

Several excavations therefore explored the contexts of monumental sculpture in order to date monuments and define the specific localities in which they were situated. These explorations have been highly productive and in one place were well guided by the detailed stratigraphic descriptions published by Coe and Diehl (1980). Fortunately, the contexts of several newly discovered monuments at Loma del Zapote were able to be explored with controlled archaeological excavations. Observations beyond what is possible solely from the style and iconography of the individual monuments can be submitted as evidence of how the Olmec may have perceived and expressed a conception of cosmic and earthly order.

MONUMENT CONTEXTS AND SETTINGS

Two areas on the San Lorenzo plateau will be examined here. The Group E setting of monumental features provides specific contexts from the central area of the plateau which may be related to rulership. Monument recycling activities in Group D show evidence for stoneworking and sculptural transformation. In the hinterland, the Loma del Zapote site provides two contexts of monuments excavated *in situ* as well as a newly discovered monument.

The Group E Setting

The area designated Group E is marked by the intersection of the B3, B4, C3, and C4 quadrants of the San Lorenzo plateau topographic map (Coe and Diehl 1980, 1: map 1), a clear hotspot of elite activity manifested in the vicinity of Laguna 8 (Fig. 1), and may be defined by the presence of the following features:

(a) *Monument 14,* the largest tabletop throne (Grove [1973] modified the concept of altars to thrones) known in the corpus of Olmec art; it bears a

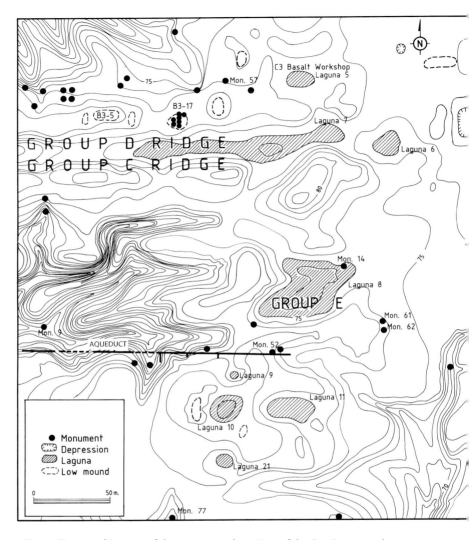

Fig. 1 Topographic map of the west central portion of the San Lorenzo plateau showing the location of Groups E and D and other features mentioned in the text. Drafted by Cesar Fernandez, based on Coe and Diehl 1980, 1: map 1.

central figure within a niche on the front, a right lateral figure with jaguar paw headdress insignia, and a left lateral partial human head removed by a broad erasure and rectangular coffers (Stirling 1955).

   (b) *Monument 61,* a colossal head (Brüggeman and Hers 1970) situated approximately 46 m southeast of Monument 14.

Fig. 2 Monument 77, a human–feline sculpture found in a ravine south of Group E.

(c) *Monument 62,* found next to Monument 61; this is a fragment of a possible circular monument (Brüggeman and Hers 1970).

(d) *The possible origin point of the 171 m long basalt aqueduct line* (Coe and Diehl 1980; Krotser 1973); several other monuments were associated with it at one time (such as Monuments 9, 52, and 77).

(e) *Monument 9,* the duck fount (Stirling 1955).

(f) *Monument 52,* an alleged rain deity with a hollowed troughlike interior (Coe and Diehl 1980: 361–363).

(g) *Monument 77,* a human–feline supernatural sculpture recently discovered near the aqueduct and probably related to it (Cyphers 1992b, n.d.c) (Fig. 2).

This particular area provides a special study case since archaeological excavations on the aqueduct (Coe and Diehl 1980; Krotser 1973; Cyphers n.d.d), on Monuments 61 and 62 (Brüggeman and Hers 1970), and at the Monument 14 location (Cyphers 1992b, n.d.d) provide archaeological information on specific context.

Any consideration of this area immediately raises the question of the antiquity of Laguna 8, a prominent central surface feature. Although Krotser proposed it as a source of water for the aqueduct (1973: 48), recent explorations in and around Laguna 8 show that this large pond postdates the Early Formative occupation and may, in fact, have altered some Early Pre-Classic features such as the context of Monument 52. Placed directly on the ancient ground surface, the main aqueduct line is located at 2.65 m below surface at Station 0+65, near Monument 52, which was reported at a depth of 1.4 m (Coe and Diehl 1980: 361 and fig. 83). Even though the hollowed-out form of Monument 52 may seem morphologically related to the trough stones of the aqueduct, this sculpture itself was not found in primary context when discovered in 1968, but had been disturbed either when Laguna 8 was dug out after the Pre-Classic period or at some time subsequent to this.

The reconstruction of the ancient topography shows that the aqueduct and Monument 61 were at the same level. This ancient surface rises north of Monument 14, dipping slightly to the level of Monuments 61 and 62 and the aqueduct, and then rising again immediately south of the main aqueduct line where the proposed feeder lines, or possibly overflow drains, were found. As we see it today, the ground surface does not resemble its Pre-Classic configuration mainly because of the large-scale alteration represented by Laguna 8.

In the Group E setting, several key contexts were clustered together within a maximum distance of 75 m of each other. The first of these is the aqueduct. East of the final trough located by Krotser, a ditch, designed to hold the troughs as they neared the water source, became apparent and was followed 18 m eastward. Even though the 1993 expedition did not locate the origin point of the aqueduct, the change in width and depth of the ditch indicate that explorations are undoubtedly close to it. A spring or well might be the ultimate source of sweet water for the aqueduct (Cyphers 1992b). Another season of exploration should confirm or disprove this as well as Krotser's proposal of an ancient buried laguna (1973).

Curiously, the newly discovered continuation of the aqueduct line, as an orange clay-filled ditch without trough stones, may never have been finished and dedicated. Or perhaps the missing section was removed for other reasons, including possible termination rites causing the cessation of the system. I hope that future excavations can clarify these questions.

Through the diligence of Coe and Diehl (1980), the original location of many monuments already removed from the site were marked on their map 1. One of these, Monument 14, was plotted in the northeastern corner of Laguna 8. Stirling (1955: 15) reports that during most of the year, the piece was submerged and became visible during the dry season when the water level in the laguna dropped. In 1993 explorations at the Monument 14 location revealed that, despite both Stirling and Medellin's work there in exposing and removing the estimated 28-ton throne, large portions of the ancient context remained intact. The throne may originally have rested on the floors described below.

Explorations found the edge of the floor and penetrated well into Laguna 8. Nevertheless, the presence of a red sand-plastered standing mud wall at the north of the excavations defines one side of a construction, possibly a walled patio, in which the throne was situated. Photographs in the National Geographic Archives suggest that the base of the throne faced south-southeast toward the water source of the aqueduct and Monument 61, the colossal head. Numerous vessel offerings were found on the yellow sand floor. Below it, resting on a red sand-plastered floor only a few centimeters below, were numerous vessels, broken figurines, and evidence of burning of human and animal bone. Of particular interest are burnt secondary bone offerings identified as human infant and bird, perhaps suggesting some kind of sacrifices.

In the Group E setting, several characteristics of the contexts suggest the existence of dedication and termination rituals (see Freidel and Schele [1989] on the Maya). The resurfacing of the red patio with yellow sand was preceded by the placement of objects such as vessels and ritual sacrifices; perhaps one day it will be possible to define these past actions as accession or enthronement rituals, offerings to the ancestors or calendrical ceremonies. At the time of abandonment, the yellow floor was littered with vessels and figurines. Monument 14 may have been turned on its back as part of the same event, but unfortunately we have no way of knowing this because the piece was removed from context.

In a similar fashion, Monument 61, the colossal head, was found resting on its left side and facing west toward the aqueduct. Monument 62, found next to it, may have been utilized in the levering and maneuvering operations when it was tipped over. Because of the mottled stratum it was found in, Brüggeman and Hers (1970) suggested that the head was deposited in a large pit, but stratigraphic maps provided by Hers, photographs from the 1970 excavations, and recent tests do not show the existence of such a feature. The head may have rested on the original Early Pre-Classic ground surface.

Proposed as ancestors, rulers, shamans, warriors, and ballplayers (Bernal 1969; Clewlow et al. 1967; Clewlow 1974; Coe 1965, 1972; de la Fuente 1975; Piña Chan and Covarrubias 1964; Stirling 1955; Westheim 1963; Wicke 1971), the colossal heads from San Lorenzo have never before been considered in context. Monument 61 is a unique colossal head for two reasons. First of all, its stratigraphic position is known, and second, unlike Monuments 53 and 2 from San Lorenzo which are clearly recarved from thrones (Porter 1989), it seems to have been originally sculpted from a boulder. Although not without cupping, it is the most perfectly conserved head known from San Lorenzo, a fact that, when considered in conjunction with the setting in which it was found, points to a possible first phase carving located *in situ*. Following Stirling's original evaluation of these heads as portraits (1955), Monument 61 located only some 45 m from the throne (Monument 14), suggests that this may indeed be a portrait perhaps of a ruler, his predecessor, or ancestor. The consistency of the colossal head category, despite the individuality represented in each one, and the repetitive form of rectangular tabletop thrones with frontal niches and personages, reinforce the belief that the office of ruler was institutionalized.

This description of the Group E setting shows the interpenetration of felines, water, and rulership. Monuments 52 and 77 have morphological felinelike traits, and their shape indicates a relationship to the aqueduct system. Child and bird sacrifices, as seen between red and yellow floors at Monument 14, are known ethnohistorically for Central Mexico and for the Maya (Broda 1971; González 1985; Márquez and Schmidt 1984; Román Berrelleza 1990; Ruz 1968; Thompson 1970). Several Olmec monuments relate children and dwarfs with water, rulership, and felines. In La Venta Altar 5, the niche figure with three raindrops in his headdress holds an inert infant; lateral narrative relief shows adults holding active infants. The highly mutilated Monument 20 from San Lorenzo has a central niche figure holding a child. Monument 18 from San Lorenzo and Monument 2 from Potrero Nuevo show dwarfs, fantastic beings related to water (Covarrubias 1957).

Further archaeological evidence for this association comes from burials. Even though a possible burial, now entirely disintegrated, may have been present in front of La Venta Altar 4 (Drucker 1952: 23–26), the closest comparison can be made with the table-top throne of Chalcatzingo excavated *in situ* with associated architectural patio and sacrificial burials (Fash 1987). This monument fulfilled a dual function, that of throne and mortuary monument. Of a total of 16 Cantera phase burials, five are children and one is an infant. Fash relates the child sacrifice there to later period rites of rain, water, fertility, and mountains. Consistent and recurrent evidence for child burials near thrones points to sacrifice, a repetitive ritual event associated with rulership and the patron supernatural. The Chalcatzingo throne is located approximately 100 m west of the El Paso stream and its 7 m high diversion dam (Grove and Cyphers 1987: 41). The proximity of the monument to a water control structure parallels the context described for Monument 14 at San Lorenzo with its proximity to the aqueduct.

Based on the context discussed, the rituals and symbolism of rulership were intimately linked to the figure of a patron water supernatural. It is not unreasonable to infer that these rulers regulated water control systems and, by extension, the water itself. The so-called were-jaguar symbolism and the syncretic feline-human metamorphosing bodies thus express a link between water, ruler, and patron supernatural.

It is misleading to assume, even implicitly, that given San Lorenzo's location in the humid tropics, its inhabitants would have faced a relatively uniform physical environment in which considerations of water would not have been especially challenging to survival. Preliminary analyses of the Olmec period topography have strongly suggested that comparatively slight differences of land elevation and water table may have significantly affected the settlement pattern, almost certainly because such differences account for variation in productivity and/or security. The rhythms of the Olmec environment have to do with water in all its manifestations. Rain, fluvial systems, and the water table were all aspects that the elite sought to control one way or another. The prediction of rain may have been the most difficult aspect of their job, but control of groundwater was well within their grasp. Pure water was important for ceremony (Krotser 1973) as well as for drinking purposes.

The existence of multiple drain systems at San Lorenzo suggests that the position and depth of the water table were highly variable, making any high point in the water table a circumscribed resource. This is true in the region today where the *norias* are the prized source of drinking water. The implications of the control of drinking water are obvious and multiple. Beyond the initial labor investment to procure the material, manufacture the troughs, and build the channels, subsequent social relations had to be organized for its continued maintenance. As a probable source of pure drinking water used not just for ritual purposes but also, more significantly, for generalized human consumption, the aqueduct was an integral material component of an economic, social, and political mechanism for the distribution of water. Water distribution systems often function with stipulations of maintenance responsibilities for participants and, for nonparticipants, the creation of debts in exchange for water. Water debts can form the basis for the control of social labor, as exists in the region today.

Group D Setting

Located west of the central area of the plateau, Group D is well known as the site of the explorations conducted by Coe and Diehl (1980), which discovered seven *in situ* monuments at the B3-17 location. Their investigations around B3-17 concentrated on the exposure and definition of the stratigraphic position of these monuments, an extraordinary discovery of datable Olmec monuments. In 1991 the San Lorenzo Tenochtitlán Archaeological Project examined this area as a possible locus for additional stratigraphic excavations. As testing

Fig. 3 View of the 1992 excavations of B3-17 on Group D showing two new large stones awaiting recycling. Previous excavations by Coe are located to the right.

proceeded, the structural features noted by Coe and Diehl were noted to have been associated with suggestive evidence of stoneworking. Accordingly, I decided to explore this structure more extensively in the following field season. These 1992 excavations revealed not only the extent of the edifice but also four additional large worked stones, numerous fragments, small debitage, and tools.

Excavations were conducted on all sides of the seven monuments (23, 34, 37, 38, 40, 41, 43) bringing to light several more worked stones. West of Monuments 34 and 23, an immense broken bottle-shaped column, a large rectangular stone, and a peculiar rectangular basalt, slablike stone with multiple depressions were found resting on or inserted into the red sand-plastered floor, along with abundant flakes, medium-sized fragments, and tools (Fig. 3). Along the east side of Cut 2 of Coe and Diehl's Monument 23 Excavations, the continuation of the red floor and more sculpture fragments were found. To the north, a large stone in process of reduction and reshaping was found outside the structure and associated with numerous by-products, tools, and abrasives. Numerous whole vessel offerings, including pots with Calzadas motifs, were interspersed among the rocks and may be interpreted as evidence of the continued sacredness of the rock, even as it was being recycled.

On Group D alone, a total of 39 broken "monuments" have been located (Stirling 1955; Coe and Diehl 1980; Beverido n.d.; Cyphers 1992b, n.d.a, n.d.b, n.d.d). There are six sculptures in-the-round, 12 flat rectangular stones (stelae, lápidas, flat broken pieces), 11 architectural elements (columns, troughs, benches, and slabs of sedimentary rock), and ten sizable fragments. Monuments were stored here while awaiting their recarving. The amount of workshop material, such as flakes, abrasives, and tools, suggests that reworking was conducted at this locality, less than 100 m west of the C3 "Basalt Workshop" (as labeled on Coe and Diehl 1980, 1: map 1), most likely a discard area where more than 6 tons of largely basalt with some metamorphic waste has been recovered.

The architectural context of the monuments discussed above is particularly important because three separate structures, located about 25 m apart, seem to form a group of related dwellings. West of B3-17, where the sculptures and fragments were found, is a red-floored, mud-walled structure carefully delimited by a lightly sloping cobbled pavement. East of B3-17 is the Red Palace, located at the site of Monument 57. Even the limited exposure of about 60 sq m of the red floor, including only one edge to the structure, shows that a sculpted basalt column must have functioned as a roof support. Step-coverings and limestone and bentonite slabs found collapsed in the structure seem to indicate their architectural use. This structure, based on its construction features, is clearly elite. Interestingly, there is a probable thick rammed-mud wall running from the western edge of the Red Palace toward B3-17, forming a possible enclosure for the sculpture workshop. The C3 Basalt Workshop is found just 50 m east of the Red Palace. These data seem to indicate that the recarving activity and specific kinds of stoneworking were "attached" both physically and socially to elite patrons (Brumfiel and Earle 1987).

There is at present no evidence of where primary carving of monuments took place—whether stone would have arrived at San Lorenzo in partially or even in completely finished form. The elite group that consumed, and presumably commissioned, these sculptures would have dictated their contents. The presence at Group D of large rocks and of sculptures, in process of or awaiting recarving, implies that the restricted contexts, physical and sociological, of stone sculpture in exotic materials were retained even when individual pieces had "outlived their usefulness" and were destined for recycling. As noted above, the association of monumental stone sculpture—necessarily in exotic materials that would have incurred high transport costs—with a sociopolitical elite evidently sacralized the stone itself.

The convergence of the pragmatic—a scarce resource, obtainable only at a distance (Coe and Fernández 1980) and enormously demanding of labor in its transport—with the symbolic is both striking and not expected. Quite obviously, given its relative expense, such materials would have been systematically reused and fragments hoarded. At different levels of inclusiveness—from grinding and pounding stone conserved in most households excavated on the plateau, through smaller sculptural pieces reworked in another workshop in the southwestern A4 sector, to the large pieces recarved at Group D—the recycling of this resource seems to have been consistent within the community.

Loma del Zapote Settings

Located about 3 km south of the San Lorenzo plateau, Loma del Zapote is the secondary settlement focus in the San Lorenzo hinterland (Fig. 4). The site includes the ejido of Xochiltepec y Anexos, the private ranch "El Azuzul" and others, and the ejidal annex of Tenochtitlán. It is characterized by extensive habitation, monumental public and transportation architecture, large-scale workshops, and monumental sculpture.

The archaeological site overlies the elevated lands north of the juncture of two ancient river courses. The present-day estuary, known as El Azuzul, is part of an ancient river course that once pertained to the Coatzacoalcos River system. Early Pre-Classic occupation follows closely along this ancient course in a linear fashion, as evidenced by the monumental earthworks at Loma del Zapote and Potrero Nuevo. The Loma del Zapote site is strategically located at the fork of two rivers to take advantage of transportation and communication.

The following discussion touches upon monumental sculpture from three areas on the Loma del Zapote site. Two contexts were archaeologically investigated, and a third is a fortuitously discovered key sculpture. These monuments form an important basis for interpretation, and the fact that this is hinterland site of the regional center at San Lorenzo makes the contrast even more interesting.

The first case is a new monument from Loma del Zapote (Cyphers 1992a, 1992b) (Fig. 5). Although it has no context, it is important for clues it gives about function. It is a decapitated and dismembered human sculpture, seated with one leg crossed and the other one hanging down, and therefore had to be positioned on an elevated surface. With one arm held up and the other forward, the sculpture is strikingly similar to the highly adorned figure of Painting No. 1 of Oxtotitlán cave, which is seated upon the stylized earth-monster immediately above the cave mouth (Grove 1970). Perhaps this monument was designed to be placed atop a stone throne. The position of the arms recalls the

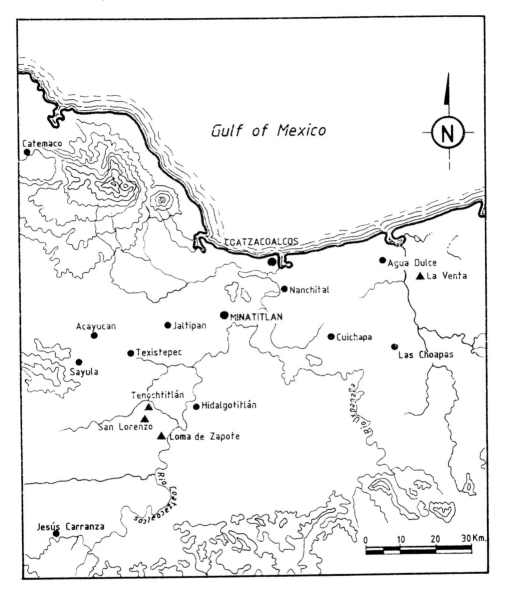

Fig. 4 Regional map showing the location of Loma del Zapote in relation to the San Lorenzo plateau. Drafted by Cesar Fernandez.

Fig. 5 Monument 11 as it was found, Loma del Zapote.

possibilities suggested for the ratcheted articulations of Monument 34 from San Lorenzo (Coe and Diehl 1980: 343).

Second, the discovery of the Rancho Azuzul sculptures on the Loma del Zapote site (León and Sánchez 1991–92) provides convincing evidence that Olmec sculptures were arranged in ensembles to display themes and events scenically. Four monumental sculptures occur on the southern side of the Azuzul acropolis at the juncture of the upper and lower stages of the man-modified hillside. Two distinct types of monuments occur here. To the west, positioned one behind the other and facing east, are two nearly identical human figures (Figs. 6, 7). To the east and northeast of these are two nearly identical felines. All these monuments were originally positioned on a pavement at the corner of monumental public architecture.

Each and every monument on the Azuzul Acropolis is spectacular because they are all largely intact and extraordinarily well preserved, making the an-

Fig. 6 The twin human sculptures and small feline of the Azuzul Acropolis, Loma del Zapote.

Fig. 7 Oblique view of the large feline located just a few meters from the twins and small feline, Azuzul Acropolis, Loma del Zapote.

171

cient setting in this place of incalculable historic value. As they must have been viewed in ancient times, they undoubtedly formed a spectacular sight when seen by people disembarking at the nearby river. Each human figure with classically Olmec features measures one meter tall. Both sculptures are identical in size and form, with only a slight difference evident in the facial characteristics, to the same degree that "identical twins" are really exact copies of each other. Representing young males, each figure is similarly mutilated to erase probable identifying insignia on the headdress. Holding a short bar, each twin stares ahead in a forwardly inclined seated position that gives the impression of imminent movement.

More differences between the two felines can be described than between the human twins. Nevertheless, the overall form and shape of both felines obey the same concept or canon. The differential sizes of the feline sculptures are the most notable contrast between them (1.20 m and 1.64 m high respectively), with details of the mouth and teeth as well as finely engraved lines marking minor differences. Several traits, such as the stilted posture, hammer marks, and vestiges of remnant surfaces, indicate that these felines are recarved monuments (Cyphers and Botas 1994; Cyphers 1992b). Unfortunately, there is no good hint to the nature of the earlier phase sculptures. Recalling Furst's treatise on human-to-jaguar transformations—"the jaguar beneath" (1968)—recarving monuments into felines may be viewed as a metaphor for shamanistic animal transformations, a perception in accord with animistic interpretations of Pre-Classic religion (Pohorilenko 1977; Marcus 1989).

The physical arrangement and characteristics of human figures and felines bear uncanny symbolic resemblances to later period myths from the Maya and Central Mexican cultures about twins and jaguars. Like the young heroic twin gods of the Popol Vuh (Edmonson 1971) who are associated with sun and light, these twins face east, the direction of sunrise and the first source of light. The jaguar associations with Quiché kingship seem to be echoed by the felines and are reminders that feline–ruler connections have been documented throughout Mesoamerican prehistory (among others, Coe 1972; Matos 1984; Thompson 1970; Schele and Freidel 1990).

Perhaps the parallels are mere coincidence, or perhaps this scene represents a very ancient myth that dates to the Early Pre-Classic. Associated with public architecture, the scene may be interpreted as a vestige of a ritual reenactment in which monuments were utilized to portray a possible historical or mythical event with astronomical significance or symbolism. The lack of dedicatory offerings with the four sculptures may indicate that this is an abandoned visual display, an explanation that does not negate the possibility that it is a ritually dedicated offering.

The third case is the excavation of a monument *in situ* on the western edge of the Loma del Zapote site (Los Treinta locality). Decapitated and dismembered, the human torso was at one time seated or kneeling. As found, it was facing directly west toward the setting sun (Fig. 8). Propped on a pedestal of sedimentary rocks, it was located on the eastern edge of a structure. The first bentonite pavement, a well-made surface with curious faced stones forming lines and canals, was covered by a later bentonite pavement. Between the two pavements, two secondary burials without offerings were recovered. One was partially disturbed by a later intrusion, but the other was completely sealed between the pavements. Perhaps that of a sacrificial victim, the burial includes skull and feet that are 2–3 m from the flexed limbs and articulated bones of the torso. Evidence for other associated rituals comes from a nearby shallow circular feature 3 m in diameter which is reminiscent of ritual baths. Interestingly, later period intrusions of pottery vessels around the monument show that it

Fig. 8 Front view of Monument 5, a decapitated and mutilated human torso wearing a cape and pectoral, excavated at the Los Treinta locality of the Loma del Zapote site.

173

was subject to periodic offerings through time.

This monument and its specific context add another note of diversity to settings and at the same time shows the multidimensional aspects of monument mutilation (see also Grove 1981; Porter 1989). In contrast to the display at Rancho El Azuzul, this monument was brutally mutilated, sacrificed to, and then set in its final display where it was subject to continuing ritualistic activities through time.

CONCLUDING OBSERVATIONS

To summarize, scenic display, recycling, and rulership revolve about a general concept of transformation. The specific processes of material and symbolic transformation discussed here point to a changing, fluctuating, or cyclical milieu in San Lorenzo society. The transformation of objects and concepts, a time-consuming and labor-intensive business, entailed work in planning, production, and redistribution. Recycling and scenic displays went hand in hand to create definite social obligations and organizations. Because transformed symbols used repetitively in rites were relocated for celebrations, ceremonies and their accompanying labor obligations were likely predictable events, even though their ideological content may have varied according to the needs perceived by the elite. Scenic display fomented the integration and participation of all sectors, creating a reproductive Olmec social identity. Ritual reenactment of mythical or historical dramas using sculpture and architecture permitted the Olmec successfully to combine ceremony, rulership, and cosmology.

This chapter has offered a broader and more precise concept of context for the analysis of Olmec monumental sculpture in relation to postulated ritual behavior and the associated social and belief systems. In contrast to the frequently faute-de-mieux attempts to reconstruct an underlying ideology through the iconography of single objects often only loosely anchored in time and space, I suggest, in however preliminary a form, a potential methodology for generating interpretative statements that can be tested against each other and against an enormously expanded body of data.

It is apparent that the spatial context of monumental sculptures regularly included other such sculptures. This observation raises the probability that the "meanings" of each piece may have been multivocal, modifiable in terms of what other pieces were placed where and in what association with it. An isolated piece would thus convey one set of possible symbolic significances; that same piece relocated to an architectural setting could acquire a different set of meanings. Associated offerings, moreover, may help to differentiate meanings—

are they, for instance, apparently one-time or repetitive?—and potentially shed light on conceptions of history. It is one thing to plug in the ethnohistorically documented (for other peoples and much later times) view of history as cyclical and repetitive, quite another to point to a series of offerings or repeated architectural modifications as direct material evidence of such a conception.

Attention to spatial context similarly permits interpretation of other aspects of Olmec culture. The restriction of monumental sculpture to only certain areas within a site not only documents and helps to confirm the nonegalitarian nature of society (a long-standing interpretation clearly based on other evidence as well), but suggests a specific elite power base that can be investigated. Control of water, in this case drinking water, is implicated in the association of sculptural groups with a carefully fashioned canal line with troughs of imported stone. This point may be important especially in view of the conventional assumption that, in the human Gulf Coast environment, water is seldom, if ever, a limiting factor.

Chronological context, from the perspective of this chapter, may also influence meaning and must be taken into account as we attempt to infer or reconstruct such meaning. If the symbolic significance of any monument is modifiable by its association with other monuments, it then follows that a piece may "mean" one thing at one time, something quite different at another. The San Lorenzo Tenochtitlán Archaeological Project has documented the regular, systematic reuse, recarving, and recycling of stone sculpture. Understandable intuitively— the necessary raw materials are exotic and their procurement was relatively expensive in direct labor costs and the more indirect costs of maintaining certain types of sociopolitical institutions—this observation has still wider implications. The storage spaces and workshops involved in such undertakings are also spatially restricted, associated physically and by extension socially with elite buildings. There would clearly have been a supporting, justifying ideology in association with this behavior. Less directly perhaps, I imply that the material itself was in some sense sacralized and thus conserved and curated for reuse. Because any such recarvings would have altered symbolic meaning, one wonders about the specific histories of particular monuments and speculates on the extent to which such meanings may have been cumulative.

Persistence of a single belief system over a time span of some one thousand years and across an enormous and diverse geographic expanse would be unlikely. Within even any single Olmec site there would have been a distinctive history of social, political, economic, and religious changes, and, accordingly, variation would be expected in the relative size and status of social groups and institutions at any site. Whatever sort of interrelationship between social groups and belief systems or ideologies that existed seems predictably variable at the intrasite as well as intersite levels. It becomes fruitless to attempt to reconstruct a single overarching "Olmec ideology"; the stylistic and formal variability that makes it so difficult to specify an "Olmec style" is in fact telling us something. In view of these considerations, the increased attention to context as advocated here could help to detail this variability and thus eventually help to explain it.

Acknowledgments The research reported here was made possible by the American Philosophical Society, the National Endowment for the Humanities, the National Geographic Society, the Consejo Nacional de Ciencia y Tecnología, the Instituto de Investigaciones Antropológicas, and the Dirección General de Asuntos del Personal Académico de la Universidad Nacional Autónoma de México. I am grateful for comments on this research from Barbara Price and Rebeca González. I also appreciate the profiles and verbal information on the excavation of Monument 61 so kindly provided by Marie-Areti Hers. Access to the National Geographic photographic archives of the Stirling expedition was graciously facilitated by George Stuart.

BIBLIOGRAPHY

BERGER, RAINER, JOHN A. GRAHAM, AND ROBERT F. HEIZER
   1967   A Reconsideration of the Age of the La Venta Site. In *Studies in Olmec Archaeology*: 1–24. Contributions of the University of California Archaeological Research Facility 3. Berkeley.

BERNAL, IGNACIO
   1969   *The Olmec World*. University of California, Berkeley.

BEVERIDO, FRANCISCO
   n.d.   San Lorenzo Tenochtitlán y la civilización olmeca. M.A. thesis, Universidad de Veracruz, Jalapa, 1970.

BRODA, JOHANNA
   1971   Las fiestas aztecas de los dioses de la lluvia (una reconstrucción según las fuentes del siglo XVI). *Revista Española de Antropología Americana* 6: 245–327.

BRÜGGEMAN, JÜRGEN, AND MARIE-ARETI HERS
   1970   Exploraciones arqueológicas en San Lorenzo Tenochtitlán. *Boletín del Instituto Nacional de Antropología e Historia* 39: 18–23. Mexico.

BRUMFIEL, ELIZABETH M., AND TIMOTHY K. EARLE
   1987   Specialization, Exchange, and Complex Societies: An Introduction. In *Specialization, Exchange, and Complex Societies* (Elizabeth Brumfiel and Timothy K. Earle, eds.): 1–9. Cambridge University Press, Cambridge.

CHASE, DIANE Z., AND ARLEN F. CHASE
   1992   An Archaeological Assessment of Mesoamerican Elites. In *Mesoamerican Elites: An Archaeological Assessment* (Diane Z. Chase and Arlen F. Chase, eds.): 303–317. University of Oklahoma Press, Norman.

CLEWLOW, C. WILLIAM, JR.
   1974   *A Stylistic and Chronological Study of Olmec Monumental Sculpture*. Contributions of the University of California Archaeological Research Facility 19. Berkeley.

CLEWLOW, C. WILLIAM, JR., RICHARD A. COWAN, JAMES F. O'CONNELL, AND CARLOS BENEMANN
   1967   *Colossal Heads of the Olmec Culture*. Contributions of the University of California Archaeological Research Facility 4. Berkeley.

COE, MICHAEL D.
   1965   The Olmec Style and Its Distribution. In *Handbook of Middle American Indians,* vol. 3: *Archaeology of Southern Mesoamerica,* pt. 2 (Gordon R. Willey, ed.): 739–775. University of Texas Press, Austin.

   1972   Olmec Jaguars and Olmec Kings. In *The Cult of the Feline: A Conference in Pre-Columbian Iconography* (Elizabeth P. Benson, ed.): 1–18. Dumbarton Oaks, Washington, D.C.

   1989   The Olmec Heartland: Evolution of Ideology. In *Regional Perspectives on the Olmec* (Robert J. Sharer and David C. Grove, eds.): 68–84. Cambridge University Press, Cambridge.

COE, MICHAEL D., AND RICHARD A. DIEHL
   1980   *In the Land of the Olmec*. University of Texas Press, Austin.

Ann Cyphers

COE, MICHAEL D., AND LOUIS A. FERNÁNDEZ
    1980   Appendix 2: Petrographic Analysis of Rock Samples from San Lorenzo. In *In the Land of the Olmec*, vol. 1 (Michael D. Coe and Richard A. Diehl, eds.): 397–404. University of Texas Press, Austin.

COVARRUBIAS, MIGUEL
    1957   *Indian Art of Mexico and Central America*. Alfred A. Knopf, New York.

CYPHERS GUILLÉN, ANN
    1992a   Escenas escultóricas olmecas. *Antropológicas* 6: 47–52.
    1992b   Investigaciones arqueológicas recientes en San Lorenzo Tenochtitlán, Veracruz: 1990–1992. *Anales de Antropología* 29: 37–93. Universidad Nacional Autónoma de México.
    n.d.a   Informe del proyecto "Espacios Domésticos Olmecas en San Lorenzo Tenochtitlán, Veracruz, Mexico: Temporada 1990." Field report for the Instituto Nacional de Antropología e Historia (INAH), Mexico, 1990.
    n.d.b   Informe del proyecto "Espacios Domésticos Olmecas en San Lorenzo Tenochtitlán, Veracruz, Mexico: Temporada 1991." Field report for INAH, Mexico, 1991.
    n.d.c   Informe del proyecto "Espacios Domésticos Olmecas en San Lorenzo Tenochtitlán, Veracruz, Mexico: Temporada 1992." Field report for INAH, Mexico, 1992.
    n.d.d   Informe del proyecto "Espacios Domésticos Olmecas en San Lorenzo Tenochtitlán, Veracruz, Mexico: Temporada 1993." Field report for INAH, Mexico, 1993.

CYPHERS GUILLÉN, ANN, AND FERNANDO BOTAS
    1994   An Olmec Feline Sculpture from El Azuzul, Southern Veracruz. *Proceedings of the American Philosophical Society* 138 (2): 273–283. Philadelphia.

DE LA FUENTE, BEATRIZ
    1975   *Las cabezas colosales olmecas*. Fondo de Cultura Económica, Mexico.

DEMAREST, ARTHUR
    1989   Ideology and Evolutionism in American Archaeology: Looking beyond the Economic Base. In *Archaeological Thought in America* (C. C. Lamberg-Karlovsky, ed.): 89–102. Cambridge University Press, Cambridge.

DRUCKER, PHILIP
    1952   *La Venta, Tabasco: A Study of Olmec Ceramics and Art*. Smithsonian Institution, Bureau of American Ethnology, Bulletin 153. Washington, D.C.

EDMONSON, MUNRO S. (ED.)
    1971   *The Book of Counsel: The Popol Vuh of the Quiché Maya of Guatemala*. Tulane University, Middle American Research Institute, Publication 35. New Orleans.

FASH, WILLIAM, JR.
    1987   The Altar and Associated Features. In *Ancient Chalcatzingo* (David C. Grove, ed.): 82–94. University of Texas Press, Austin.

FREIDEL, DAVID A., AND LINDA SCHELE
    1989   Dead Kings and Living Temples: Dedication and Termination Rituals among the Ancient Maya. In *Word and Image in Maya Culture* (William F. Hanks and Donald S. Rice, eds.): 233–243. University of Utah Press, Salt Lake City.

Furst, Peter
    1968   The Olmec Were-Jaguar Motif in the Light of Ethnographic Reality. In *Dumbarton Oaks Conference on the Olmec* (Elizabeth P. Benson, ed.): 143–174. Dumbarton Oaks, Washington, D.C.
    1981   Jaguar Baby or Toad Mother: A New Look at an Old Problem in Olmec Iconography. In *The Olmec and Their Neighbors* (Elizabeth P. Benson, ed.): 149–162. Dumbarton Oaks, Washington, D.C.

González, Yólotl
    1985   *El sacrificio humano entre los Mexicas.* Fondo de Cultura Económica and Instituto Nacional de Antropología e Historia. Mexico.

Graham, John
    1989   Olmec Diffusion: A Sculptural View from Pacific Guatemala. In *Regional Perspectives on the Olmec* (Robert J. Sharer and David C. Grove, eds.): 227–246 Cambridge University Press, Cambridge.

Grove, David C.
    1970   *The Olmec Paintings of Oxtotitlán Cave, Guerrero, Mexico.* Studies in Pre-Columbian Art and Archaeology 6. Dumbarton Oaks, Washington, D.C.
    1973   Olmec Altars and Myths. *Archaeology* 26: 128–135.
    1981   Olmec Monuments: Mutilation as a Clue to Meaning. In *The Olmec and Their Neighbors* (Elizabeth P. Benson, ed.): 49–68. Dumbarton Oaks, Washington, D.C.
    1984   *Chalcatzingo: Excavations on the Olmec Frontier.* Thames and Hudson, London.
    1989   Olmec: What's in a Name? In *Regional Perspectives on the Olmec* (Robert J. Sharer and David C. Grove, eds.): 8–16. Cambridge University Press, Cambridge.

Grove, David C. (ed.)
    1987   *Ancient Chalcatzingo.* University of Texas Press, Austin.

Grove, David C., and Ann Cyphers Guillén
    1987   The Excavations. In *Ancient Chalcatzingo* (David C. Grove, ed.): 21–55. University of Texas Press, Austin.

Heizer, Robert, Philip Drucker, and John Graham
    1968   Investigations at La Venta, 1967. In *Papers on Mesoamerican Archaeology*: 1–39. Contributions of the University of California Archaeological Research Facility 5. Berkeley.

Heizer, Robert, John A. Graham, and Lewis K. Napton
    1968   The 1968 Investigations at La Venta. In *Papers on Mesoamerican Archaeology*: 127–154. Contributions of the University of California Archaeological Research Facility 5. Berkeley.

Krotser, Ramon
    1973   El agua ceremonial de los olmecas. *Boletín* 2: 43–48. Instituto Nacional de Antropología e Historia, Mexico.

León, Ignacio, and Juan Carlos Sánchez
    1991–92   Las gemelas y el jaguar del sitio El Azuzul. *Horizonte* (Año 1) 5–6: 56–60.

Lowe, Gareth W.
    1977   The Mixe-Zoque as Competing Neighbors of the Early Lowland Maya. In

The Origins of Maya Civilization (R.E.W. Adams, ed.): 197–248. University of New Mexico Press, Albuquerque.

1989   The Heartland Olmec: Evolution of Material Culture. In *Regional Perspectives on the Olmec* (Robert J. Sharer and David C. Grove, eds.): 33–67. Cambridge University Press, Cambridge.

MARCUS, GEORGE

1992   The Concern with Elites in Archaeological Reconstructions: Mesoamerican Materials. In *Mesoamerican Elites: An Archaeological Assessment* (Diane Z. Chase and Arlen F. Chase, eds.): 292–302. University of Oklahoma Press, Norman.

MARCUS, JOYCE

1989   Zapotec Chiefdoms and the Nature of Formative Religions. In *Regional Perspectives on the Olmec* (Robert J. Sharer and David C. Grove, eds.): 148–197. Cambridge University Press, Cambridge.

MÁRQUEZ, LOURDES, AND PETER J. SCHMIDT

1984   Osario infantil en un chultun en Chichén Itzá. In *Investigaciones recientes en el área Maya. XVIII Mesa Redonda* 2: 89–103. Sociedad Mexicana de Antropología, Mexico.

MATOS MOCTEZUMA, EDUARDO

1984   The Templo Mayor of Tenochtitlán: Economics and Ideology. In *Ritual Human Sacrifice in Mesoamerica* (Elizabeth Boone, ed.): 133–164. Dumbarton Oaks, Washington, D.C.

PIÑA CHAN, ROMÁN

1958   Tlatilco. *Serie investigaciones* 1, pt. 1. Instituto Nacional de Antropología e Historia, Mexico.

PIÑA CHAN, ROMÁN, AND LUIS COVARRUBIAS

1964   *El pueblo del Jaguar (los Olmecas arqueológicos).* Consejo para la Planeación e Instalación del Museo Nacional de Antropología, Mexico.

POHORILENKO, ANATOLE

1977   On the Question of Olmec Deities. Journal of New World Archaeology 2 (1): 1–16.

PORTER, JAMES B.

1989   Olmec Colossal Heads as Recarved Thrones: "Mutilation," Revolution, and Recarving. *Res* 17–18 (Spring–Autumn): 23–30.

RAPOPORT, AMOS

1990   Systems of Activities and Systems of Settings. In *Domestic Architecture and the Use of Space* (Susan Kent, ed.): 9–20. Cambridge University Press, Cambridge.

ROMÁN BERRELLEZA, JUAN ALBERTO

1990   *Sacrificio de niños en el Templo Mayor.* Instituto Nacional de Antropología e Historia, Mexico.

RUZ LHUILLIER, ALBERTO

1968   *Costumbres funerarias de los antiguos Mayas.* Universidad Nacional Autónoma de México.

SCHELE, LINDA, AND DAVID FREIDEL

1990   *The Forest of Kings: The Untold Story of the Ancient Maya.* William Morrow and Company, New York.

SHARER, ROBERT J. (ED.)
  1978   *The Prehistory of Chalchuapa, El Salvador.* University of Pennsylvania Press, Philadelphia.

STARK, BARBARA
  1991   Book review of *Regional Perspectives on the Olmec. Journal of Field Archaeology* 18: 234–238.

STIRLING, MATTHEW
  1955   *Stone Monuments of the Río Chiquito, Veracruz, Mexico.* Smithsonian Institution, Bureau of American Ethnology, Bulletin 157: 1–23. Washington, D.C.

THOMPSON, J. ERIC S.
  1970   *Maya History and Religion.* University of Oklahoma Press, Norman.

WESTHEIM, PAUL
  1963   *Arte antiguo de México.* Fondo de Cultura Económica, Mexico.

WICKE, CHARLES
  1971   *Olmec, an Early Art Style of Precolumbian Mexico.* University of Arizona Press, Tucson.

Pre-Classic Cityscapes: Ritual Politics among the Early Lowland Maya

WILLIAM M. RINGLE
DAVIDSON COLLEGE

> Religious change from particularism to greater universalism has its
> own momentum rather than being a mere correlate or after-effect of
> other transformations. (Werbner 1977: xxiii)

THE THEMES OF THIS VOLUME FIND strong resonances in two of the most
dynamic facets of recent Maya archaeology, research into ancient Maya
ideology and investigations of the roots of Maya civilization. Fieldwork carried out from the mid-1970s onward has dramatically altered our
ideas about the size and complexity of Late Formative lowland Maya centers.
Initial discovery of Late Formative monumental architecture at Uaxactun[1]
(Ricketson and Ricketson 1937) was amply confirmed by substructures encountered in the North Acropolis trench at Tikal (W. R. Coe 1965). Further
discoveries of substantial Late Formative public architecture are now well known
from Cerros, Komchén, Cuello, Nakbe, El Mirador, Tikal, Uaxactun, Lamanai,
and elsewhere (Fig. 1). In most cases the associations of these structures are
hard-won, being often buried beneath later construction phases, but a few sites—
Cerros (Robertson and Freidel 1986; Scarborough 1991a), Cuello (Hammond
1991), Komchén (Andrews and Ringle 1992), and El Mirador (Dahlin 1984;
Matheny and Matheny 1990)—are largely free of later overburden and provide
some insight into community organization during the period. Settlement surveys at several sites have shown that Late Formative occupations frequently eclipse

---

[1] Although the earliness of E-VII-Sub was appreciated at the time, further excavations
were undertaken in 1940 to confirm this. The exploratory trench into E-VII-Sub yielded
a surprisingly small number of sherds, 29 of 30 being Chicanel (Smith 1955: 20).

Fig. 1 Map of the Maya Lowlands showing major archaeological sites (after Andrews 1990: map 1.1, used with permission of the Middle American Research Institute, Tulane University). Courtesy of E. W. Andrews V.

those of the Early Classic period and occasionally even Late Classic densities.

In addition, recent research has imparted a deeper appreciation for the so-phistication and considerable ancestry of early Maya ritual. One striking fea-ture of what we know of Formative ritual life is the degree of continuity it exhibits with that of later times. Iconographic studies have demonstrated the Pre-Classic roots of many facets of Classic period ritual practice: human sacri-fice (Laporte and Fialko 1990, 1995; Hammond, Clarke, and Estrada Belli 1992: 42; Hammond, this volume), deities such as the "Jester God" (Fields 1991; Freidel 1990), costume (Freidel and Andrews n.d.), and office (Freidel and Schele 1988). In the best of cases we can reconstruct at least some aspects of the Late Forma-tive belief system (Schele and Freidel 1990: chap. 3). Aspects of temple archi-tecture and decoration likewise continue into the Classic period, and excavations have demonstrated that in some cases Formative sacred places endured for cen-turies, good examples being the North Acropolis and Mundo Perdido of Tikal. This suggests that early in their history the Maya developed certain organiza-tional principles, and certain ways of symbolically expressing them, which were flexible enough to order the significantly more complex societies of the Clas-sic and Post-Classic periods.

My own perspective on the themes of this volume has been heavily influ-enced by the opportunity to do fieldwork at two Formative sites, Komchén in northwest Yucatan (E. W. Andrews V, director) and El Mirador in Guatemala (Bruce H. Dahlin, director). But it is the architecture and site layout of the Classic period site of Ek Balam, where George Bey and I have been working for a number of years, that stimulated my interest in site layout and caused me to reexamine earlier sites. I maintain that the clear continuities between the Formative and Classic sites are due in part to the persistence of segmentary organization among many Maya polities. As several commentators have noted, ritual tends to play a prominent political role in such societies because central-ized political leadership is often weak and bureaucracies underdeveloped (Southall 1988; Wolf 1982). Organization is typically pyramidal, with consider-able replication of functions. Thus one reason that early urban templates could persist was that later growth was largely additive and did not force a drastic hierarchical restructuring of society.

GENERAL COMMENTS ON RITUAL AND IDEOLOGY

In this chapter I consider the generative role of ritual and religion in the rise of Maya civilization. The majority of recent discussions on the topic empha-size the coercive nature of ideology, religion and ritual being seen mainly as vehicles for elite legitimation and propaganda. While there can be no doubt that they were, we must remember that religious rationales for inequalities of wealth and status are usually embedded in a larger vision of social cohesion. A simple legitimation model can only partially explain the elaboration and particular configurations of Maya ritual. More important, such models say little about why ritual should have been an effective vehicle for social control. In particular, it is difficult to see how legitimation alone can engender belief. Rather, legitimation would seem to depend upon a prior system of beliefs, which only later could have been appropriated and modified for political ends. Thus we must look elsewhere for the roots of ritual.

In my view, we need to examine more closely the expressive and organizational roles of religion in Maya culture. During the Formative period especially, when avenues of information exchange were fewer, simpler, and rapidly becoming overburdened by population growth, religion provided institutional means for expressing order and accommodating change. For a preliterate society lacking formal legal codes, religion and ritual provided visible statements of the obligations linking its members to each other and to the cosmos. As discussed below, ideology provided a set of metaphors whose application to society grew and changed over time, but nevertheless continued to reflect their Formative roots. At the same time, religion was a developing institution with its own internal conditions of growth, providing some of the earliest opportunities for specialization and status differentiation. Temple construction indicates the increasing involvement of religion in the management of labor and resources. Finally, as will be shown, religious expansion accompanied significant changes in residential organization. As such, it cannot simply be reduced to the "epiphenomenal" result of certain configurations of production and social organization, but was itself an active agent of social change.

Since the changes wrought during the Late Formative were so substantial, and since the period lasted several hundred years, the mature Formative ritual complex does not appear full-blown nor everywhere concurrently. At least two horizons seem identifiable. The first construction of monumental architecture begins near the Middle-to-Late Formative transition. This correlates with the appearance of domestic compounds, but in my view occurs within a still largely egalitarian society with limited differences of rank (see Hammond, this volume; Hendon, this volume; Ringle n.d. for evidence as of 1985). A second stage occurs during the last two centuries B.C. and is manifested by the spread of a particular iconographic complex in the southern lowlands, particularly temples faced with monster masks, ballcourts, *sacbeob,* and imagery associated with rulership. At this time, earlier metaphors begin to be applied to status differences, resulting in the complex stratified societies so apparent during the Classic period.

The question of monumentality is a related issue. Why did the Pre-Classic Maya, like several other formative civilizations, invest inordinate amounts of energy in constructing monumental architecture? Here the achievements of the inhabitants of El Mirador are particularly impressive, since the Late Formative Tigre and Danta complexes are two of the largest examples of monumental architecture from the entire span of Mesoamerican prehistory. In light of recent work at Nakbe, Tikal, Lamanai, and elsewhere, however, these no longer seem exceptional but part of a broader impetus toward monumentality.

Again, materialist approaches have stressed the role of elite legitimation. Mendelssohn (1971), discussing the early appearance of pyramids in Egypt, saw these vast construction projects as a means of divorcing peasants from their subsistence base, insuring their future dependence on elites. Pharaohs organizing such projects were literally inventing the state, using continual pyramid building as a means of uniting a workforce that could be bent to the will of the state, and in the process engulfing formerly independent "tribal units." Trigger (1990), forwarding a "thermodynamic" perspective, sees monumental architecture as examples of conspicuous consumption by elites, as Flannery (1968) argued some time ago with regard to the buried mosaic pavements of La Venta:

> Monumental architecture and personal luxury goods become symbols of power because they are seen as embodiments of large amounts of human energy and hence symbolize the ability of those for whom they were made to control such energy to an unusual degree. Furthermore, by participating in erecting monuments that glorify the power of the upper classes, peasant laborers are made to acknowledge their subordinate status and their sense of their own inferiority is reinforced. (Trigger 1990: 125)

To me it seems improbable that Formative elites could somehow hoodwink an entire populace into building massive reminders of their humble station in life. Monuments may have conveyed this message subliminally, but I do not think it could have been their inspiration. Nor does Formative monumental construction appear to be accompanied by cults of individual rulers, which appear only later. I think we must instead remind ourselves that for the ancients, no less than for ourselves, monumental construction expressed aspects of communal life that were of deepest importance. This is not to deny their employment as tools of power and social coercion, for surely they were, but in a much more sophisticated and oblique manner than most materialist explanations would suggest.

One limitation of our attempts to understand the ritual role of architecture is a tendency to regard monumental architecture as "ritual materialized and *petrified*" (Wilson 1988: 134–135, emphasis mine). We have been content to imagine monumental buildings functioning as restored, but essentially inert, versions of the ruins we investigate today. Broda (1987), however, reminds us that while monumental architecture does have an autonomous symbolic existence, its role as a backdrop to ritual performance is every bit as important, if not more so. Buildings, far from being petrified, are constantly being transformed by the particular ceremonies enacted within their precincts (compare Cyphers, this volume).

It is not just that buildings were stages with constantly changing sets, for motion had a much deeper significance in Mesoamerican ritual. Motion was an inherent quality of life, and energy and spirit continually moved through the twin fields of time and space. Ritually this was manifested by the many pilgrimages and processions that moved through a series of prescribed stations according to a ritual calendar. Deities and destinies too were shaped by their associations with particular dates and directions. This restless, ceaseless flow between the dialectical extremes of experience is everywhere evident in Mesoamerican imagery and has much to tell us about the organization of monumental architecture.

THE MIDDLE-LATE FORMATIVE DEMOGRAPHIC AND RESIDENTIAL TRANSITION

Pre-Classic monumental construction must first be seen within the context of some general trends in Formative settlement patterns. Evidence suggesting precocious Early Formative developments in Belize has recently been reexamined, resulting in a significantly shortened lowland Formative chronology (Andrews and Hammond 1990; Andrews 1990). Andrews V (1990) doubts any lowland ceramic complex is truly Early Formative, the earliest instead beginning sometime at the outset of the Middle Formative.[2] The initially distinct Swasey, Eb, and Xe complexes, representing the earliest settlers, were replaced sometime during the seventh century by the Mamom sphere, whose makers spread rapidly throughout the lowlands and were responsible for first colonizing the north. The similarity of Mamom complexes is such that Andrews believes actual population movements were responsible for its spread, at least into northern Yucatan. I have speculated that this expansion may have been spurred in part by the availability of Nal-Tel maize hybrids capable of thriving in the humid lowlands (Ringle n.d.), but Formative macrobotanical remains are still

---

[2] Hammond, Clarke, and Estrada Belli (1992) argue for an earlier start, perhaps ca. 1200 B.C.

males and females are present, although the latter seem to predominate. Although figurines are of unknown function, scholarly consensus favors a ritual use (compare Hendon, Joyce, Marcus, all in this volume). Rands and Rands (1965) speculate they may have been part of a fertility cult, while Hammond (1989), following Grove and Gillespie's (1984) analysis of Middle Formative figurines from Chalcatzingo, has suggested they may be elite portraits used for unknown ritual purposes. The important fact, however, is that there is little, if any, evidence for more centralized ritual activity (see Hendon, this volume, for similar conclusions).

The figurine tradition ends just when household architecture becomes more permanent and formally arranged, and as construction of monumental architecture begins. Although the timing of this transition varies somewhat from region to region, residential reorganization and monumental construction seem closely related developments—at least it cannot be said that monumental construction was a later development. The process seems to begin in the south toward the close of the Middle Formative period. Mound B-IV at Altar de Sacrificios is placed by Smith (1972: 111) in the late San Felix subphase (500–300 B.C.), at which time it was a 5 m tall mound faced with *almeja* coating. However, because this early construction phase was encountered at the base of a 1.5 m square test pit and not further exposed, we have little idea of its extent. During the Escoba phase (600–300 B.C.) at nearby Seibal, Willey (1990: 195) indicates the construction of small temple pyramids in several localities, as well as a possible locus of public architecture deep beneath Group A, although no architectural remains confirm this.

---

figurines from Nakbe very similar to those from Uaxactun. It is unclear from the report whether these come from domestic contexts and predate the substantial architecture reported from the site.

Some suggestion of a later continuance comes from Cuello, where Hammond (1991: 177, 232–233) states figurines continue in limited use during the Cocos Chicanel, although again with the possibility of redeposition. Willey (1978: 7–8) notes similarities of the Seibal and Altar types with those of San José I, Copan Archaic, Jenny Creek, and Barton Creek phases of the Belize River survey, and Dzibilnocac II, all of which postdate the Middle Formative. A few figurine fragments were found in Tigre excavations at El Mirador (Hansen 1990: 269), mostly in mixed Middle-Late Formative fill, but a few pieces are placed in the Late Formative. In contrast, Formative figurines were not reported from Monos (Copeland 1989) or Danta complexes (Howell 1989), the latter of which had almost no Middle Pre-Classic sherds. Figurines appear to be absent from Cerros, which had occupation only from the Late Formative onward.

Figurines are very rare at northern sites, perhaps because of the scarcity of Middle Formative deposits. None were found in the Komchén excavations, and none of the figurines from Dzibilchaltun could be securely dated as Formative (see Taschek [1994: 203–208] for a more extended comparative treatment of the evidence from northern Yucatan).

At El Mirador, Copeland's (1989) excavation in the lowest terrace of the Monos Complex yielded a nearly pure Middle Formative assemblage beginning a meter below the surface in a deposit 3.85 m deep. However, the radiocarbon date (3220 B.P. ± 60; CALIB 397 B.C.) obtained from very nearly the bottom of this excavation indicates it was built very late in the Middle Formative. The profile (Copeland 1989: fig. 4) indicates that this earlier structure may have been only 1 to 1.5 m above bedrock. No Middle Formative structural remains were found in either the Danta (Howell 1989) or Tigre (Hansen 1990: 208–209) excavations. More impressive remains of Middle Formative ceremonial architecture come from the initial stages of the Mundo Perdido complex at Tikal (Laporte and Fialko 1990, 1995). Laporte and Fialko state that the earliest architecture, a radial pyramid and a rectangular platform west of it, probably was built during the Late Eb period (600–500 B.C.). Both were later greatly enlarged during the Tzec phase (500–250 B.C.). The results from Nakbe, where remains of substantial Middle Formative architecture are claimed, may dramatically revise this scenario, but Don Forsyth (personal communication, 1994) informs me that excavations as of that date indicate early monumental construction dates to the later Middle Pre-Classic.

The earliest monumental architecture in the north is less impressive and somewhat later, but shows the same close correlation with residential reorganization. Radiocarbon dates from three of the major buildings of Komchén (Figs. 2, 4) suggest construction began early in the Late Nabanche phase (350–150 B.C.). A sample from a midden below the lowest construction of 23F1 yielded a date of 2330 ± 80 B.P. and was associated with ceramics of the Kin complex (450–350 B.C.), as was a date of 2310 ± 180 B.P. from below 24G1. A radio-carbon date of 2200 ± 90 B.P. came from Construction Period 3A of Str. 25O1, the major building at the other end of the *sacbe* (Andrews and Andrews 1980: 55). During this Late Nabanche construction phase the pyramid was considerably enlarged, but the plaza before it had not yet been filled in and raised.

The earliest building stage of 21J1 (Fig. 2), the main ceremonial platform, sealed a pure Early Nabanche deposit.[7] The dimensions of the earliest building stage are difficult to determine due to later destruction, but the platform measured at least 39 m east-west and supported a pyramid more than 22 m across. The pyramid was preserved to a height of 2.8 m above the platform, but its

---

[7] Information on 21J1 comes from an unpublished excavation report by E. W. Andrews V and Kathy Rowlands in the Middle American Research Institute archives. Andrews will be preparing the final report on this work. Another date of 3275 ± 80 B.P. came from the surface below the building, but is considered too early.

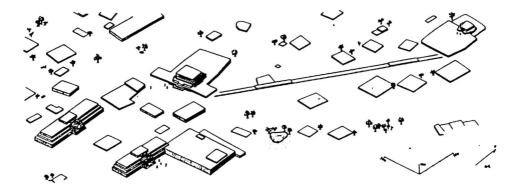

Fig. 4 Reconstruction drawing of the central plaza and *sacbe* of Komchén viewed from the southeast (after Andrews and Ringle 1992: fig. 2, with permission of the Middle American Research Institute, Tulane University). Courtesy E. W. Andrews V.

original height is unknown. Several additional construction stages and intervening periods of apparent abandonment occurred throughout the Formative. A radiocarbon date of 2215 ± 80 B.P. follows a major stage of construction activity during which 21J1 approached its maximum extent. Smaller modifications follow, but virtually all appear to have been Late Nabanche or earlier.

Komchén was not an isolated phenomenon, but few subsequent projects in the north have been concerned with Formative occupations. Important Formative public structures have been identified and excavated at Yaxuna by David Freidel, Charles Suhler, and Traci Ardren and are in the process of being reported (e.g., Suhler n.d.). Our own unpublished reconnaissance in the vicinity of Ek Balam has resulted in the tentative identification of at least one Late Formative center with monumental architecture, X-Huyub, based upon limited excavations and surface collections.

An intermediate level in the religious hierarchy also appears during the Late Formative, the local or minor temple. These smaller pyramids occur singly or in association with domestic groups. At Seibal, Tourtellot (1988: 277–284, 381) notes a regular distribution of minor temples (his Class M structures) in the peripheries during the Early Cantutse phase (300 B.C.–A.D. 1), each about 560 m apart. Our settlement work at El Mirador demonstrated small temples peppered the countryside there as well (Figs. 3, 5). At Komchén, substantial platforms supporting secondary platforms, such as 15R2 and 25O1, were found at some distance from the center while Str. 603 of the nearby Mirador Group of

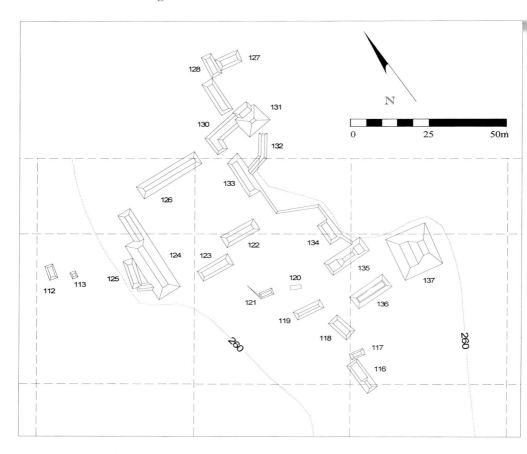

Fig. 5 Plaza Plan II group at El Mirador. Courtesy of Bruce Dahlin.

Dzibilchaltun (Fig. 6; Andrews and Andrews 1980: 20–40) might be classified as a local temple because of its size and placement within a formally arranged plaza.

The deployment of local temples within domestic compounds or among clusters of house mounds suggests the involvement of a now more centralized and hierarchically organized cult in this reorganization of residential life. One arrangement common in the Peten during the Classic period, Becker's (n.d.) Plaza Plan II, may have had its genesis at this time since so many of the plazuela groups at El Mirador had this pattern (Figs. 3, 5). Another common Formative pattern, perhaps related to Plaza Plan II units, was to place large platforms

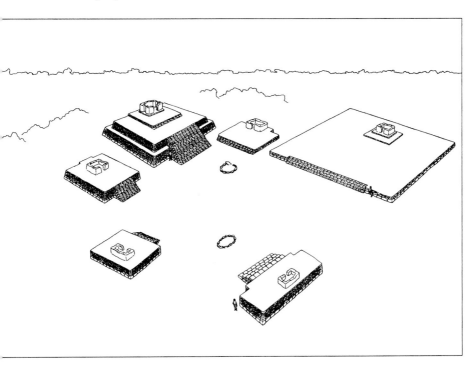

Fig. 6 Mirador Group, Dzibilchaltun viewed from the west (after Andrews and Andrews 1980: fig. 4, used with permission of the Middle American Research Institute, Tulane University). Courtesy of E. W. Andrews V.

adjacent to local temples. This arrangement characterizes the hearts of Komchén (Strs. 21J1 and 24G1; Fig. 2) and the Mirador Group of Dzibilchaltun. In the latter, the 3.5 m high pyramid Str. 603 was adjacent to Str. 605, at that time apparently a large low platform without superstructures. The pattern is true for Seibal as well, where minor temples tend to be associated with Class L platforms (Tourtellot 1988: 376), either adjacent to or across from the temple. (Class L structures are large basal platforms with "substantial height . . . in many cases but most notably a large ground area . . . and proportionately large upper surface" [Tourtellot 1988: 274]). Another pattern was to combine pyramidal and platform into a single structure, as with 25O1 and 21J1 at Komchén (Figs. 4, 9).

Local temples may have been prominent in domestic organization because organizational solutions developed elsewhere in Mesoamerica were inapplicable or undesirable. In many highland centers, occupational *barrios* provided a means of marking differences and organizing residence, perhaps as far back as the late Early Formative (e.g., in Oaxaca: Pires-Ferreira 1976; Flannery and Marcus 1976: 376). But if I am correct in my characterization of the Formative Maya economy, this was generally not possible in the lowlands. Nor were overt ceramic markers of ethnic or residential identity, such as have been suggested for Formative Oaxaca (Pyne 1976) and Copan (Fash 1991), well developed among the Mid-Late Formative lowland Maya, although the material record is rather limited. Mamom and Chicanel phase ceramics are relatively homogeneous over large areas, even as far as northern Yucatan, and begin to diverge substantially only toward the close of the Late Formative period. While there are differences from site to site, and from region to region, the impression is rather a conscious desire to minimize ethnic or political distinctions. This conformity in the material record may also be reflected in the relative lack of linguistic diversification across the peninsula, all of which may have acted as an incentive to exchange, political alliance, and population movements.

Local temples seem instead to have served as residential organizational nodes in the lowlands. I would agree with Tourtellot's statement that they pertain to "a series of long-established local corporate social groups each with its own idiosyncratic service center or 'chief's establishment'" (1988: 377). In many cases, temples are also associated (or combined) with open areas or platforms that were perhaps used for dances or public ceremonies. The association of temples with adjacent large platforms is a hallmark of the "temple assemblage," a group believed to be the site of lineage activities and ritual during the Late Classic and Post-Classic periods (Fox 1989; Proskouriakoff 1962; Bey and Ringle n.d.; Ringle and Bey n.d.). Hence this pattern may also have a Formative origin, indicating the importance of centralized performance and display at this early date.

ASPECTS OF THE SACRED

The central issue relating residential reorganization and ceremonial construction was, it seems to me, the emergence of hierarchy. The inability of egalitarian communities to deal with increasing population levels and perhaps the dwindling availability of land demanded some concentration of authority. To me, the plans of Maya urban centers into the Post-Classic period seem to be extended meditations on the problematic relation of the center to the whole. It was a question of more than idle speculation, given the importance of population recruitment and retention to these early polities, and one whose dimensions were constantly evolving as differentials of wealth and power increased. If the segmentary model is correct, the problem was acute because there were multiple centers of power, often with conflicting agendas and differing commitments to the paramount. Thus we cannot speak simply of center and periphery.

This ultimately became a religious question for two reasons: first, the segmentary divisions were clear points of potential conflict, and hence demanded the sanctions and boundaries that the sacred could confer. Second, religion provided a means of representation, of thinking about the problem. The peculiar power of religious explanation, aside from its claims of ultimate authority, is its metaphoric ability to connect the disparate fields of experience. The commonplaces that religion links individuals to the cosmos, or that religion mirrors society, become somewhat more interesting if we consider how metaphors achieve those links. In the following section I suggest some metaphoric transformations of this problem of hierarchy and their resultant expression in civic layouts.

A fundamental role of ideology in general and ritual in particular is to express a vision of social cohesion. General experience in societies of any complexity is of a series of differences—distinctions of occupation, status, class, and so on. What then provides a sense of belonging, a sense of identity and equality with one's fellow citizens? Victor Turner (1969, 1974) has brilliantly shown how these are in fact two polarities of the sacred. On the one hand is what Turner would define as "communitas," a direct, egalitarian, unstructured experience of social bonding. On the other is a rationale for hierarchy and difference:

> To simplify a complex situation, it might be said that ancestral and political cults and their local embodiments tend to emphasize ancestral cults representing crucial power divisions and classificatory distinctions within and among politically discrete groups, while earth and fertility cults represent ritual bonds between those groups and even . . . tendencies toward still wider bonding. The first type stresses exclusiveness, the second inclusiveness. The first emphasizes selfish and sectional interests and conflict over them; the second, disinterestedness and shared values. (Turner 1974: 185)

He further shows that these two poles are spatially segregated in many complex agricultural societies. Being associated with hierarchy and power, political/ancestral rituals usually occupy the central ground and fertility rituals the peripheries. This was not completely true for Mesoamerica, as can be seen in the twin temples of Huitzilopochtli and Tlaloc in the Aztec Templo Mayor, but their very pairing at the center of the empire indicates the power of this dialectic, and, as discussed below, there were many instances where this spatial pattern was indeed followed.

The degree to which social distinctions, roles, and categories are embedded in the sacred is frequently a measure of the degree to which they are perceived as sources of potential conflict. Strong taboos and sanctions may be created to discourage the crossing of these bounds. Nevertheless, individuals move through a series of social categories in the course of their lives, and such boundaries must often be mediated. Most often this is done by rites of passage, which commonly involve a series of inversions, of "antistructure" and "liminality," following which the initiate enters his or her new station (Turner 1969, 1974). Thus, paradoxically, antistructure reaffirms structure. This is also a fruitful way to look at community, since similar communal rituals are periodically needed to rekindle a sense of communitas on the one hand and to delineate the bounds of power on the other. Important to this discussion is Turner's (1974) demonstration that in more complex agricultural societies, collective pilgrimages play an equivalent structural role to rites of passage for the individual.

Several widespread Mesoamerican ideas concerning the sacred suggest the conceptual, or metaphoric, basis for mediating communitas and hierarchy. A concept of spirit in Mesoamerica whose wide distribution suggests great antiquity is known in lowland Maya languages as *ch'ulel* or *k'ulel,* a *mana*-like sense of numen or vital force infusing all important aspects of life (Vogt and Vogt 1970). *Ch'ulel* has obvious similarities to the Zapotec conception *pèe* (Marcus, Flannery, and Spores 1983: 37–39), Mixtec *ini,* and Nahuatl *teotl* (Townsend 1979). The strong communal bond of *ch'ulel* not only links different social ranks[8] but crosses other significant boundaries as well. As a quality of animals, plants, and places it spans the culture/nature boundary, while as a quality of deities it links the occupants of this world with the supernatural.

As explained by Vogt, *ch'ulel* is located in the heart and circulates through the bloodstream (see Stuart 1988 for related imagery). The circulatory aspect links it with another widespread concept, the belief in the efficacy of motion mentioned earlier. This animating power of spirit is expressed most powerfully on page 1 of the Codex Fejérváry-Mayer (Fig. 7a) and the related image on pages 75–76 of the Codex Madrid, where motion follows a path uniting time— here the *tonalamatl*—with the four world directions defining space. However, the direction is not circumambulatory, but at each station bends inward toward the center. This animating flow from periphery to center is reinforced by the

---

[8] During the Classic period, rulers and places were marked with this quality, as were deities and other denizens of the underworld (Ringle 1988). The degree to which this marked an appropriation of this quality by elites remains to be understood.

Fig. 7a Codex Fejérváry-Mayer, page 1 (after Anders, Jansen, and Peréz-Jimenez 1994: 183).

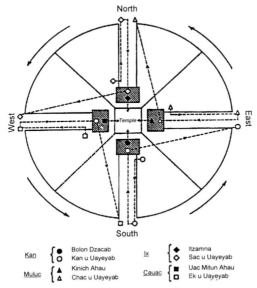

Fig. 7b Uayeb ritual circuit (after M. D. Coe 1965: fig. 1).

flow of blood from symbols of Tezcatlipoca at each of the four corners in toward the center (Leon-Portilla 1985; Anders, Jansen, and Peréz-Jimenez 1994). Thus the pattern of motion outlined in the two codices is an attempt not only to circumscribe time and space but to solve the relation of center to periphery.

The manifestations of *ch'ulel* are not always benign, and hence culture is viewed as a buffer between humans and the forces of nature. This is not only a contrast between civilization and the powers of the surrounding forests, mountains, and bodies of water, but also reflects man's dual nature. This duality is reflected in another widespread belief, that of the animal companion (Nahuatl *tonal,* Maya *way*) whose parallel life in the wild intersects that of his civilized counterpart only at moments when the structure of everyday life is imperiled (Vogt and Vogt 1970). The importance of this concept during the Classic period is clear from inscriptions and iconography (Houston and Stuart 1989), and its wide distribution again suggests a Formative origin, if not earlier.

Among Mesoamerican peoples, certain natural features such as mountaintops, cenotes, and caves have traditionally been regarded as extremely powerful, in part because they function as thresholds to the underworld. Central to the process of experiencing or propitiating the forces dwelling in these remote natural spots was the journey. Such pilgrimages mark a transition from the protective sphere of culture to the very edges of the world, and hence involve danger and structural inversion. The importance to the Maya of such spots, and of journeys to them, is clear from the archaeological, iconographic, and ethnographic record. Stuart's (1987) decipherment of the *witz* (mountain) glyph, for instance, has shown the importance of such spots in Classic ritual. Bassie-Sweet (1991) provides a useful overview of Maya cave ritual and argues for their central role in the scenes depicted on Classic period Maya sculpture. Although our knowledge of Pre-Classic nature shrines is scant, such rituals should logically be among the oldest practices. An example might be the northern Maya cave of Loltun (Velázquez 1980; Andrews 1986: 29), where excavations in cave chambers uncovered Middle and Late Formative ceramics. Although their ritual use has not been established, some of the earliest northern Maya relief images are carved above one of the entrances (Freidel and Andrews n.d.) and on bedrock outcrops before it.

But there is also a mimetic path to harnessing and experiencing the sacred, less fraught with danger because it occurs within the sphere of culture. This is reflected in yet another pan-Mesoamerican practice, that of ritual impersonation. By donning the garb of a particular deity, speaking the necessary words, and dancing the necessary steps, the celebrant—ruler or slave—succeeds in invoking the deity's presence. The practice of costuming celebrants, victims, and effigies as deities is perhaps best known for Aztec ritual (*teixiptla*; see Townsend 1979: 23–36), but masked figures are common in the art of Oaxaca, the Maya area, and elsewhere. In Townsend's view, particular vestments are used not so much to imitate this or that deity (or historical figure) as to signal the particular configuration of spirit being invoked:

> It is questionable that they represented gods in any conventional sense of the term. What they were connected with was designated in two ways: first, by the word *teotl,* and, second, by a metaphoric cult name. . . . *Teotl* expresses the notion of sacred quality, but with the idea that it could be physically manifested in some specific presence—a rainstorm, a mirage, a lake, or a majestic mountain. . . . And for ritual purposes, of course, a *teixiptla* especially acted as a talismanic token of the sacred. (1979: 28)

> *Teixiptlas* did not primarily advertise a personality, though the reliefs of emperors and kings were doubtlessly accompanied by dates and name-glyphs; rather, *teixiptlas* commemorated a lasting relationship between a community—personified by its leader—and the animating spirits of the universe. (1979: 34)

Like Vogt's (1964) conception of structural replication, ritual impersonation is at base simply another metaphoric process. Since teixiptlas may also be effigies, this suggests that the concept may be applied to other human creations as well. It may therefore be useful to look at the arrangement of ceremonial architecture, the "cityscape," as a similar imitation establishing a set of correspondences between the sacred geography of the natural world and the sacred, but built, topography of the community.

It is now abundantly clear from epigraphy and comparative ethnohistoric accounts that earlier suggestions (Vogt 1964; Holland 1964) that Maya pyramids were ceremonial mountains are true.[9] Much as the ideal landscape consists of a center fringed by a ring of enclosing mountains, so too the central temple of many Maya centers was surrounded by a lesser series of temple "mountains." The construction of artificial caves is another example of the imitation and appropriation of natural portals. Brady and Veni (1992) report the excavation

---

[9] Similar suggestions have been made for elsewhere in Formative Mesoamerica, for example, Heizer's (1968) suggestion that La Venta Complex C was a volcano effigy and Grove's (this volume) discussion of Chalcatzingo. The idea is unlikely to have been a Mayan innovation, given the priority of monumental construction outside the Maya Lowlands.

of tunnels at several highland Maya sites in which the form, the offerings, and the traces of fire clearly demonstrate their ritual use. What is particularly interesting is that several of these are excavated directly beneath main plazas. As the authors (1992: 160) note: "This would impart the impression that the very layout of the central ceremonial complex was ordained by the cave below it."

The cityscape therefore stands in the same mimetic relation to the otherworld as does the *teixiptla*: much as *teixiptla* acts to configure and channel spirit, so too the "cityscapes" of Maya centers may be viewed as templates for the direction of similar energies. But the imitation of the natural landscape by the center is in reality a double metaphor: on the one hand there is the opposition between culture and nature, symbolized by the central temple-wilderness shrine dyad. But within the realm of culture there is a further opposition, between the "mountain(s)" of the central precinct and those of the urban peripheries. Just as the pilgrim's trek to a mountain fastness is a prerequisite for spiritual renewal, so too a similar "journey" must periodically be made between the temple "mountains" of the community. Although this latter journey takes place entirely within the sphere of culture, moving as it does from the temple "mountains" of the center to those of the periphery, it involves crossing boundaries no less significant, although they are of human making (compare Grove, this volume).

PROCESSIONS AND SACBE SYSTEMS

In short, I am suggesting an additional correspondence between pilgrimages and ritual processions. Processions are of course reflected in the distinctive Maya practice of linking major architectural groups by means of *sacbeob*. Present evidence from two sites, Komchén and Cerros, indicate these causeways first appeared during the Late Formative period. Cerros Sacbe 1 (Fig. 8) has been assigned an early Tulix date (50 B.C.–A.D. 150), and although the dating of the second *sacbe* is not specifically discussed, it is apparently contemporary (Scarborough 1991a: 151, fig. 3.7). At Komchén (Figs. 2, 4), a trench through the *sacbe* suggests its construction during the Xculul phase (150 B.C.–A.D. 150). Xculul sherds were found throughout the loose rubble fill, but in low frequencies, perhaps indicating it was built early in the phase. Another site near Komchén, Tamanche, has two causeways thought also to be Late Formative in date (Kurjack and Garza 1981: 301). In the southern lowlands, Jones' (n.d.) excavations of some of the El Mirador *sacbeob* places much of the construction during the Late Formative. An intersite causeway apparently links El Mirador to Nakbe (Graham 1967), while an internal *sacbe* connects the two major groups of Nakbe (Forsyth 1993: fig. 2), which face each other along its axis. Dates for either have yet to be published.

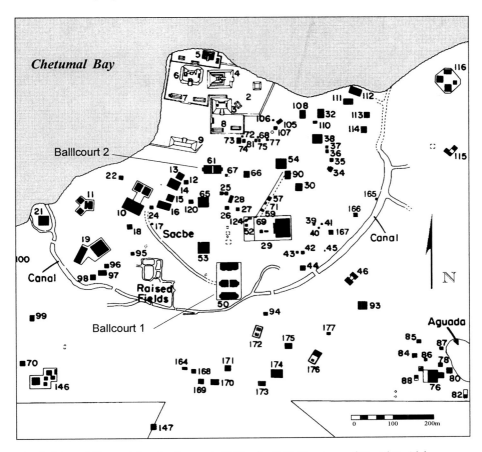

Fig. 8 Map of Cerros (after Scarborough 1991a: fig. 2.1). Courtesy of David Freidel.

The ritual function of most of these *sacbeob* is indicated by the type of structures they connect.[10] The Komchén *sacbe* connected two of the largest platforms, 25O1 and 21J1,[11] both of which undoubtedly had ritual functions.

---

[10] Scarborough (1991a: 150) argues that the Cerros *sacbeob* may also have served as dike walls for reservoirs within Cerros. Dennis Jones (n.d.: 73–79) suggests the *sacbeob* crossing the El Mirador *bajos* served several purposes, religious among them, although further exploration of the areas at the distal ends of these roads is necessary.

[11] The first structure designation is that of the Komchén Project (E. Wyllys Andrews V, director), the second that of the Dzibilchaltun Project. The earlier project explored only these two structures: Str. 25O1 was excavated in 1959–60 by Robert Funk, but planned excavations in 21J1 in 1961–62 had to be abandoned because of personnel problems (Andrews

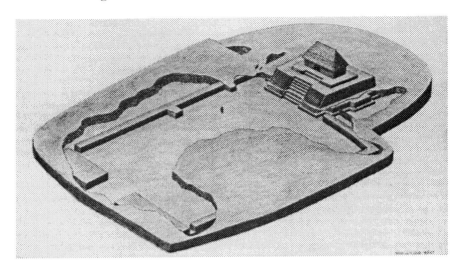

Fig. 9 Komchén Structure 25O1 (formerly Str. 450) (after Andrews and Andrews 1980: figs. 27 and 41, used with permission of the Middle American Research Institute, Tulane University). Courtesy of E. W. Andrews V.

The building of the *sacbe* also apparently correlates with major changes in 25O1, in particular the construction of a massive raised platform fronting the temple and burying an earlier enclosed court (Fig. 9; Andrews and Andrews 1980: 42–55). Cerros Sacbe 1, while it apparently skirted areas periodically inundated, connected three special-purpose architectural groups, Strs. 10,[12] 16, and 50. The last of these is a ballcourt, and in later times ballcourts and *sacbeob* were closely associated (Ringle and Bey n.d.). Sacbe 2 unites a large "civic facility," Str. 29, with two other large mounds, Strs. 54 and 90, also apparently civic/ritual in function.

and Andrews 1980: 42–58). Str. 25O1 was not reexamined by the Komchén project, but E. W. Andrews V and Kathy Rowlands intensively excavated 21J1 throughout the 1980 season.

The original Formative phase designations and their spans have been revised twice since the excavation of 25O1. The temporal units used by the Komchén project are (Andrews 1988):

Early Nabanche	700–450 B.C.
Ek Complex	450–350 B.C.
Late Nabanche	350–150 B.C.
Xculul	150 B.C.–A.D. 250

[12] Although the secondary platforms are Early Classic, Scarborough (1991a: 53) indicates the basal platform was built during the Tulix phase. However, the ceramic samples seem equivocal (Scarborough 1991a: 52–55).

The function of *sacbeob* has been a perennial topic of speculation, but it is noteworthy that the appearance of road systems accompany the changes in residential and monumental architecture previously mentioned. Kurjack (1979) has suggested that intersite *sacbeob* represent kinship links, specifically elite marriage ties. We (Bey and Ringle n.d.; Ringle and Bey n.d.) believe they primarily represent political axes, linking segments with the center. These views need not be mutually exclusive since segments were undoubtedly allied by means of marriage. But it is significant that the vast majority of *sacbeob* are radial, connecting center and peripheries, whereas a more complex system connecting outlying architectural complexes might be expected if kinship links alone were being commemorated.

These interpretations, however, neglect the performative aspect of *sacbeob,* the fact that they were in effect extended stages for ritual. While we may be forever ignorant of the specifics of such rituals, they surely involved processions, as we know they did in the Uayeb year-end rites of later centuries (Fig. 7b). This movement from center to periphery and back is, I believe, intended as an imitation of the dynamic of *ch'ulel* discussed above. There is a remarkable homology, for instance, between the cardinally oriented processions of Uayeb rituals and the first page of the Codex Fejérváry-Mayer (Fig. 7a–b). While the codex depicts the actual flow of spirit, the Uayeb procession marks the transport of deities from temples of the center to one of the peripheral shrines and back again. This flow is equally applicable to single *sacbe* systems since the fundamental component is the reciprocal movement linking the center with its peripheries.

The importance of performance also appears to be reflected in the type of buildings connected by *sacbeob*. At both Komchén and Cerros, the *sacbeob* reach large platforms supporting pyramids at one end (Str. 29 at Cerros, Strs. 21J1 and 25O1 at Komchén). In all cases, the large open terraces of the basal platforms face the *sacbe*. The evolution of Komchén Str. 25O1 is particularly interesting in this respect (Andrews and Andrews 1980: 42–55). Initially a small platform was fronted by a broad, low terrace delimited by a series of low, wide walls. During the Xculul phase, approximately at the same time the *sacbe* was built, the terrace was filled in and raised to create a substantial basal platform. It seems likely that such terraces were areas of public assembly and the locations of ritual dances involving substantial numbers of people. While it cannot be proven at this point, the association of possible large dance plazas with *sacbeob* suggests that such structures may have been prototypes of the *popolna,* the architectural setting for lineage dance rituals during the Post-Classic and Classic periods that were also often linked to *sacbeob*.

Like the pilgrimage, the procession serves to link and mediate structural opposites. Like pilgrimage routes, *sacbeob* occasionally link the community with natural portals. The most famous example is Chichén Itzá Sacbe 1, which leads from the Gran Nivelacíon to the Cenote of Sacrifice. (Recent work by Peter Schmidt and Rafael Cobos, of the Instituto Nacional de Antropología e Historia, has discovered other *sacbeob* linking structures with cenotes at this site.) At Ek Balam, the eastern *sacbe* also leads to a small architectural group around the rim of a large cenote. Similarly, Landa (Tozzer 1941) indicates that Uayeb rituals were associated with *sacbe* processions, and the Uayeb ritual on Dresden page 27 shows an "opossum impersonator" standing in what is probably a symbol for "cenote" (Fig. 10).

However, *sacbeob* far more often lead to outlying groups of elite architecture, and in the examples from Ek Balam and Chichén Itzá there seems to be an attempt to "mix metaphors" by equating the symbolic associations of processions and pilgrimages. Although the cultural opposition being mediated by the latter may simply be the conflict between authority and egalitarianism, as Turner suggests, the northern *sacbe* systems of the Classic period suggest that segmental oppositions were the more specific concern. Later northern *sacbe* systems (and indeed those of Komchén and Tamanche) seem frequently to lead from specific buildings of the center to outlying complexes, for example, there is no common point of convergence. The implication is that *sacbeob* do not necessarily link the center with an undifferentiated periphery, nor the periphery with an undifferentiated center.

We believe that in such cases *sacbeob* instead link different aspects of the same segment. If the segmentary model is correct, a key point of structural conflict would be between the roles of elites as segmentary lords and their

Fig. 10 Dresden Codex New Year Ceremonies, page 27, showing "Opossum Imitator" standing in cenote symbol (after Villacorta and Villacorta 1977).

roles as polity leaders. Such tension would have been particularly great for the paramount segment. Thus I would hazard the guess that even these early *sacbeob* did not link two ranked segments, but instead mediated the public and seg-mental personae of its ruling lineage. Implicit is yet another mediation be-tween communitas and hierarchy, but complicated by the fact that while hierarchy and privilege are exemplified by the center, in a segmentary society the center is also the sole point of political solidarity. Likewise, while the peripheries are usually associated with communitas, in fact segmental conflict is a chief threat to social coherence. Perhaps for these reasons, the movement between center and periphery is a reciprocal one.

BALLCOURTS

In linking the public and segmental roles of elites, *sacbe* systems are clear statements of the reciprocal relations of power in such societies. This is sup-ported by another component of the emerging cityscape, ballcourts. Ballcourts appeared most probably midway through the Late Formative, although only three have yet been excavated: Cerros (Scarborough 1991a, 1991b; Schele and Freidel 1990), Pacbitun (Healy 1992), and Colha (Eaton and Kunstler 1980). The role of the leader as hero (impersonator) in the ball game through reenact-ment of the defeat of death by the Hero Twins has been ably explained by a number of commentators. What I wish to comment upon briefly are some liminal aspects that the ball game seems to share with pilgrimages and proces-sions.

As a game ostensibly involving some element of chance and risk, the ball game invites the abandonment of structure. Although at one level the game is a ritual drama (or re-creation), on another the advantages of rank are aban-doned in a contest of athletic ability. The game is also about motion, given the metaphorical associations of the ball with heavenly bodies. And like remote mountain or cave shrines, the ballcourt was conceived of as a portal to the underworld. The association of human sacrifice makes the transformative as-pect of the game explicit.

Examination of where ballcourts are placed with respect to monumental architecture confirms their involvement in this "meditation on the center." Gillespie (1991) and Scarborough (1991b) have demonstrated the role of ball games as boundary markers. Bey and I (Ringle and Bey n.d.) have further shown that ballcourts are typically placed along *sacbeob*, further associating them with transition and liminality. Although the Formative evidence is slight, there is a convincing body of evidence from Classic and Post-Classic sites and images to show their involvement with segments and interpolity relations (Gillespie

1991; Ringle and Bey n.d.). Closer examination shows ballcourts usually occur at the extremes of *sacbeob,* either marking the entrance to outlying architectural complexes or the articulation of *sacbes* with the center. This pattern is true for the major Cerros ballcourt, Str. 50, which is found at the southern end of the primary north-south axis of the ceremonial center and also at the southern terminus of Sacbe 1. Although the Pacbitun ballcourt is not associated with a *sacbe,* it is at the northern fringe of the main ceremonial compound. The second Cerros ballcourt, Str. 61, would seem to be an exception in that it is located near the center of the site and is unassociated with roadways. Nevertheless, the fact that it somehow served a mediatory function is indicated by its location along the north-south axis (as was Str. 50) and its position midway between the northern acropolis and the major temple complex, Str. 29. The placement of the ballcourt along the borders of the ceremonial center, often at the juncture of causeways, suggests again the metaphoric mediation of structural fault lines.

MONUMENTAL ARCHITECTURE

While the above aspects of ritual practice were expressive of the segmental divisions of society, others, perhaps even more evident, expressed the primacy of the center. Some comments are therefore necessary concerning the monumentality of Formative constructions, the largest examples of which were the equals of any later period in the lowlands. While some low platforms of the Middle Formative may have had ritual functions (see Hendon, this volume), the Middle to Late Formative transition witnessed a geometric rise in the ratio of temple to domestic architectural volumes. Nor were temples the sole recipients: large earthworks at sites such as Becan and El Mirador, and ditches, again at Becan and perhaps Cerros, served to define and protect ceremonial precincts.

Theories mentioned earlier, stressing elite legitimation, attribute monumental temple building to elite strategies for impressing, intimidating, and exploiting their subjects. In other words, temple construction is viewed as a *local* strategy of subordination. Such Cecil B. DeMille-like visions of sweating helots bending to the lash of the overseer seem, however, as unsatisfying for the Maya as they do for Egypt. It is doubtful for one thing that Formative elites had the means necessary to exact such labor coercively without risking rebellion, and a purely local focus does not explain why temple construction spread so widely so rapidly.

To return to a point made earlier, recruitment would have been of special concern to emerging centers. Since in most cases tribute and command over labor would seem to have been the bases of Formative wealth, revenues would have varied directly with population size. Hence mechanisms for attracting new followers (and retaining them) would have been of special interest. Yet the political administration of tribute networks must have presented great obstacles for the as yet small-scale Formative polities. As Hicks (1991) demonstrates for the Aztecs, the alternatives of hegemonic or politically administered "empires" each had their drawbacks: direct political or military administration was costly in resources and personnel, although greater amounts of surplus could be forcibly extracted. Hegemonic relations had the advantage that the bureaucratic investment was less, but they were inherently less profitable. Reciprocal relations meant that lower levels of surplus production could be demanded, "gifts" were necessary to maintain tribute relations, and frequently there were several layers in the process, each extracting its own cut. Finally, it was easier for subject territories to assert their independence, demanding costly wars of reconquest.

The sponsorship of religious cults was a third possible pathway to social complexity, involving neither the military costs of political administration nor the reciprocal obligations of a tribute system. As cults expanded their membership, and as cult objects became of more than local significance, they could have provided powerful incentives to recruitment. Cultic practice would have been especially valuable in providing a prior language of hierarchy and inequality that could easily have been transferred to the economic and political spheres. Such metaphors were also significant in that they operated at both the individual and regional level, providing models for the development of secular status differences and settlement hierarchies.

At the outset of monumental construction, near the Middle-to-Late Formative transition, we are not yet speaking of "world religions"—the later appearance of stucco masked temples across the Peten may mark this horizon—but rather of regional cults. As defined by Werbner (1977: ix), regional cults "are cults of the middle range—more far-reaching that any parochial cult of the little community, yet less inclusive in belief and membership than a world religion in its most universal form." Two aspects of this inclusiveness are of interest: the demographic inclusiveness of the cult itself and the inclusiveness of the cult objects, in other words, the scope of their spiritual and cosmic spheres of influence. Although we have little evidence of the nature of cult objects at this time, the disappearance of figurines from domestic contexts does suggest their replacement by figures with power over wider aspects of the community and nature. By the time religious imagery becomes widespread in the mid-Late Formative, deities are clearly of universal import, such as the sun god or the jaguar god of the underworld.

Regional cults are attractive to a wider clientele, but as Werbner (1977, 1989)

211

emphasizes, this clientele is not necessarily coextensive with existing political or ethnic boundaries. Regional cults frequently cross-cut these limits, promoting the exchange of information, personnel, and goods, and thus may have been an initial vehicle in expanding religiopolitical boundaries beyond the limits of the community (for an early Andean example, see Burger's [1992: 192–203] discussion of the role of regional cults in the genesis and spread of Chavín ideology). And regional cults are frequently organized as a series of client shrines recognizing a central parent temple, oftentimes the locus of a particularly important event or the dwelling of the major spokesman or prophet. These central places frequently become significant sources of wealth. This is especially true of pilgrimage centers (compare Freidel 1983): markets and fairs frequently accompanied medieval European pilgrimages, and certainly the Sacred Cenote of Chichén Itzá drew objects from an enormous area in later times.

What might have initiated this process? Several recent discussions (compare examples in Earle 1991) of the rise of inequality downplay the functional or adaptive value of "big men" and chiefs, finding little evidence for their role in risk distribution or enhancement of political networks. Instead, conflict, exploitation, and individual intentionality and self-interest are emphasized. For instance, Hayden and Gargett (1990), in a recent discussion of the problem in Mesoamerica, pose the question of how early "accumulators" could have broken free from an egalitarian ethos and justified inequalities of power and wealth. They favor a model in which such differences arose in the contexts of cargo systems and the resultant competition for cargo positions. In cases where communities were able to generate surpluses, competitive feasting provided a privileged means for amassing wealth and personal prestige without incurring social opprobrium. Feasts would have been viewed favorably by all, they would have provided a means whereby the organizer could accrue debts from large numbers of people, and sponsorship would have provided potential "big men" with access to ritual or sacred positions (Hayden and Gargett 1990: 14–15).

I believe that this view, appropriately modified, has much to recommend it. The scope of such activities might first be criticized. Hayden and Gargett's model is essentially local in focus: competition occurs between rivals within a given cargo system. "It is precisely because there is no possibility of drawing in profit from outside the community that frenetic attempts by the highest community leaders to out-give each other . . . are curtailed" (Hayden and Gargett 1990: 14). Such a view does not consider the role of competitive intercommunity feasting and gift giving. Although that may have been a subsequent development, a mechanism that could organize resources from a wider area for purposes of display, such as a regional cult, would seem an equally powerful route to social ranking.

Also in their view the sacred was not a necessary component of this process, but more of a derived benefit. Perhaps one way that differentiation began to occur was through spiritual, rather than material, accumulation, however. My reading of the archaeological evidence suggests that the explosion in temple construction began before status differences became significant. Thus cults may be a preferable framework for the emergence of "big men." Cults share nearly all the same traits as cargo competitions: certainly ostentatious displays of wealth and power, as well as feasting, are well-known aspects of Mesoamerican ritual life, and human sacrifice and the destruction of other forms of material wealth are common to both.[13] The great advantage for sponsors is of course that such activities would be ritually sanctioned and ostensibly for the direct benefit of the community, and offerings would be for beings of recognized superior authority.

A necessary first step must have been the acceptance of imitation. Werbner (1989: 242) makes the interesting point that although Turner (1974) claims that earth or nature cults promote communitas, such cults are also "place-bound" and paradoxically more restrictive "because highly particularistic, not generic, bonds were required." Acceptance of metaphoric, rather than metonymic, relations with the spirit world would have permitted the recentering and replication of cults, moving religions toward "person-bound" systems (Werbner 1989: 239). Such recenterings of metaphoric mountains, caves, and other portals to the otherworld within the community of course placed them in contexts where communities and "big men" could directly benefit from cult activities. Much as mountains or caves could be accepted as imitations of sacred places, so too individuals must have been accepted gradually as imitations of sacred figures, eventually acquiring divine status.

As the material rewards of cult leadership began to be appreciated, centers may have been stimulated to greater investment in sacred displays. In my view, these served primarily to inspire a sense of spiritual identity and provide charismatic attractions for potential recruits, and only secondarily to humble subjects. But most important, this model emphasizes that monumental construction did not come from the expansion of the egos of local elites, but occurred within a framework of *regional* competition between neighboring regional cults.

---

[13] See Hammond, this volume, for a possible Late Formative example; Middle Formative (Tzec) dedicatory burials have been found in the second stage of Str. 5C-54, the main pyramid of the Mundo Perdido complex, Tikal (Laporte and Fialko 1995: 48).

A positive feedback cycle is easily imagined: to the extent that cult centers were successful in increasing tribute and labor, they could afford additional investments in ritual displays and sacred architecture. At some point, probably in the first two centuries B.C., regional rivalry seems to have resulted in the winnowing of less competitive cults and the emergence of yet more comprehensive "world" religions. Energies could then be redirected into purely economic or political arenas. Such cycles were probably not limited to the Formative, but reoccurred throughout the span of Maya history because of the instabilities inherent in segmentary organizations.

CONCLUSION

In this chapter I have tried to show how certain concepts of spirit may have influenced the layout of early Maya ceremonial centers. My approach has essentially been structural in attempting to show how this involved a series of metaphoric oppositions: a nature-culture opposition was equated with a center-periphery dichotomy, which was in turn applied to political oppositions. The utility of the approach derives from the fact that the Maya were themselves trying to solve structural problems involved with the appearance of hierarchy. At base, this "meditation on the center" concerned the fundamental opposition between communitas and privilege. But by the Late Formative, the basic armature of political organization was already in place, and the problem became the more specific one of the allocation of power between individual social segments and the authority of the paramount.

I have further attempted to show that these structural fault lines were mediated by architectural features such as *sacbeob* and ballcourts. But mediation could only be effected by the animation of these structures, hence the critical associations of movement and processions, and by extension with the experience of the pilgrimage. The flow of *ch'ulel* across the boundaries separating nature and culture thus became a direct metaphor for the passage of power between the central power of the polity and the peripheral power of the segmental leaders.

These ideas had less to do with legitimation than with providing a comprehensive vision of society. I suggest that these metaphors were primarily employed during the Pre-Classic to define the relations between segments and paramounts. Hence they played a key role in recruitment and organization of the growing population, although mortuary evidence suggests that status or class differences were as yet limited (see, for example, Hammond, this volume). But again the role of monumental architecture was not simply reactive. Monumental architecture fostered growth, prosperity, and political expansion. As such, it provided an example of what a wealth-driven, expansionistic social order might be like, in contrast to what for the most part were probably closed egalitarian communities.

During the Classic period, these same metaphors were borrowed and appropriately modified for the task of expressing economic differences. The *sacbe* complex is a good example. Axial organization, coupled with rotational rituals, provided a natural vehicle for polity expansion. New segments could simply be added as additional spokes and sacred "mountains" in the ritual cycle. And like good metaphors, it could be expanded into new realms. In northern Yucatan, sometime during the Classic period, the system was expanded to include intersite causeways. Kurjack and Andrews V (1976) present a strong case that such causeways marked polity limits. Again *sacbeob* were used to mark the passage to the liminal margins of a political unit, but in this case it is a different order of social integration and a new concept of the relation of the center to the periphery. Similar arguments may be made for the ball game (Ringle and Bey n.d.). But despite the significant organization changes, the metaphoric associations between successive applications provided the strong thread of continuity permitting us to trace their earlier Formative heritage.

BIBLIOGRAPHY

ANDERS, FERDINAND, MAARTEN JANSEN, AND GABINA AURORA PERÉZ-JIMENEZ
1994   El Libro de Tezcatlipoca, señor del tiempo: libro explicativo del llamado Códice Fejérváry-Mayer. Códices Mexicanos 7. Fondo de Cultura Economica, Mexico.

ANDREWS, E. WYLLYS, IV, AND E. WYLLYS ANDREWS V
1980   Excavations at Dzibilchaltun, Yucatan, Mexico. Tulane University, Middle American Research Institute, Publication 48. New Orleans.

ANDREWS, E. WYLLYS, V
1986   Olmec Jades from Chacsinkin, Yucatan, and Maya Ceramics from La Venta, Tabasco. In Research and Reflections in Archaeology and History: Essays in Honor of Doris Stone (E. Wyllys Andrews V, ed.): 11–49. Tulane University, Middle American Research Institute, Publication 57. New Orleans.
1988   Ceramic Units from Komchen, Yucatan, Mexico. Cerámica de Cultura Maya 15: 51–64.
1990   The Early Ceramic History of the Lowland Maya. In Vision and Revision in Maya Studies (Flora S. Clancy and Peter D. Harrison, eds.): 1–20. University of New Mexico Press, Albuquerque.

ANDREWS, E. WYLLYS, V, NORBERTO GONZALEZ CRESPO, AND WILLIAM M. RINGLE
1980   Map of the Ruins of Komchen, Yucatan, Mexico. Middle American Research Institute, Tulane University. New Orleans.

ANDREWS, E. WYLLYS, V, AND NORMAN HAMMOND
1990   Redefinition of the Swasey Phase at Cuello, Belize. American Antiquity 55: 570–584.

ANDREWS, E. WYLLYS, V, AND WILLIAM M. RINGLE
1992   Los mayas tempranos en Yucatán: investigaciones arqueológicas en Komchén. Mayab 8: 5–17.

BASSIE-SWEET, KAREN
1991   From the Mouth of the Dark Cave: Commemorative Sculpture of the Late Classic Maya. University of Oklahoma Press, Norman.

BECKER, MARSHALL J.
n.d.   The Identification of a Second Plaza Plan at Tikal, Guatemala, and Its Implications for Ancient Maya Social Complexity. Ph.D. dissertation, University of Pennsylvania, 1971.

BEY, GEORGE J., AND WILLIAM M. RINGLE
n.d.   The Myth of the Center. Paper presented in the symposium "Changing Views of Classic Maya Political Organization," 54th Annual Meeting of the Society for American Archaeology, Atlanta, 1989.

BRADY, JAMES E., AND GEORGE VENI
1992   Man-Made and Pseudo-Karst Caves: The Implications of Subsurface Features within Maya Centers. Geoarchaeology 7: 149–167.

BRODA, JOHANNA
1987   Templo Mayor as Ritual Space. In The Great Temple of Tenochtitlan: Center and Periphery in the Aztec World (Johanna Broda, Davíd Carrasco, and Eduardo

Matos Moctezuma, eds.): 61–123. University of California Press, Berkeley.

BURGER, RICHARD L.
1992   *Chavin and the Origins of Andean Civilization.* Thames and Hudson, London.

COE, MICHAEL D.
1965   A Model of Ancient Maya Community Structure in the Maya Lowlands. *Southwestern Journal of Anthropology* 21: 87–119.

COE, WILLIAM R.
1965   Tikal, Guatemala, and Emergent Maya Civilization. *Science* 147: 1401–1419.

COPELAND, DENISE E. R.
1989   *Excavations in the Monos Complex at El Mirador, Peten, Guatemala.* El Mirador Series, pt. 2 (Donlu Thayer, ed.). Papers of the New World Archaeological Foundation 61. Brigham Young University, Provo.

COWGILL, GEORGE L.
1975   On Causes and Consequences of Ancient and Modern Population Changes. *American Anthropologist* 77: 507–525.

DAHLIN, BRUCE H.
1984   A Colossus in Guatemala: The Preclassic Maya City of El Mirador. *Archaeology* 37 (3): 18–25.

DEMAREST, A., R. SHARER, W. FOWLER, E. KING, AND J. FOWLER
1984   Las excavaciones (Proyecto El Mirador de la Harvard University, 1982–1983). *Mesoamérica* 7: 1–160.

DRENNAN, ROBERT D.
1976   Religion and Social Evolution in Formative Mesoamerica. In *The Early Mesoamerican Village* (Kent V. Flannery, ed.): 345–368. Academic Press, New York.

EARLE, TIMOTHY (ED.)
1991   *Chiefdoms: Power, Economy, and Ideology.* Cambridge University Press, Cambridge.

EATON, J. D., AND B. KUNSTLER
1980   Excavations in Operation 2009: A Maya Ballcourt. In *The Colha Project: Second Season, 1980 Interim Report* (T. R. Hester, J. D. Eaton, and H. J. Shafer, eds.): 121–132. University of Texas, San Antonio.

FASH, WILLIAM L.
1991   *Scribes, Warriors and Kings: The City of Copán and the Ancient Maya.* Thames and Hudson, London.

FIELDS, VIRGINIA M.
1991   The Iconographic Heritage of the Maya Jester God. In *Sixth Palenque Round Table, 1986* (Merle Greene Robertson and Virginia M. Fields, eds.): 167–174. University of Oklahoma Press, Norman.

FLANNERY, KENT V.
1968   The Olmec and the Valley of Oaxaca: A Model for Inter-Regional Interaction in Formative Times. In *Dumbarton Oaks Conference on the Olmec* (Elizabeth P. Benson, ed.): 79–110. Dumbarton Oaks, Washington, D.C.

FLANNERY, KENT V., AND JOYCE MARCUS

    1976   Formative Oaxaca and the Zapotec Cosmos. *American Scientist* 64: 374–383.

FORSYTH, DONALD W.

    1993   The Ceramic Sequence at Nakbe, Guatemala. *Ancient Mesoamerica* 4: 31–53.

FOX, JOHN W.

    1989   On the Rise and Fall of *Tuláns* and Maya Segmentary States. *American Anthropologist* 91: 656–681.

FREIDEL, DAVID A.

    1983   Political Systems in Lowland Yucatan: Dynamics and Structure in Maya Settlement. In *Prehistoric Settlement Patterns: Essays in Honor of Gordon R. Willey* (Evon Z. Vogt and Richard M. Leventhal, eds.): 375–386. University of New Mexico Press, Albuquerque, and Peabody Museum of Archaeology and Ethnology, Harvard University, Cambridge, Mass.

    1990   The Jester God: The Beginning and End of a Maya Royal Symbol. In *Vision and Revision in Maya Studies* (Flora S. Clancy and Peter D. Harrision, eds.): 67–76. University of New Mexico Press, Albuquerque.

FREIDEL, DAVID A., AND ANTHONY P. ANDREWS

    n.d.   The Loltun Bas-Relief and the Origins of Maya Kingship. Manuscript in possession of the authors.

FREIDEL, DAVID A., AND LINDA SCHELE

    1988   Symbol and Power: A History of the Lowland Maya Cosmogram. In *Maya Iconography* (Elizabeth P. Benson and Gillett G. Griffin, eds.): 44–93. Princeton University Press, Princeton.

GILLESPIE, SUSAN D.

    1991   Ballgames and Boundaries. In *The Mesoamerican Ballgame* (Vernon L. Scarborough and David R. Wilcox, eds.): 317–345. University of Arizona Press, Tucson.

GRAHAM, IAN

    1967   *Archaeological Explorations in El Peten, Guatemala.* Tulane University, Middle American Research Institute, Publication 33. New Orleans.

GROVE, DAVID C., AND SUSAN D. GILLESPIE

    1984   Chalcatzingo's Portrait Figurines and the Cult of the Ruler. *Archaeology* 37 (4): 27–33.

HAMMOND, NORMAN

    1989   The Function of Maya Middle Preclassic Pottery Figurines. *Mexicon* 11: 111–114.

HAMMOND, NORMAN (ED.)

    1991   *Cuello: An Early Maya Community in Belize.* Cambridge University Press, Cambridge.

HAMMOND, NORMAN, AMANDA CLARKE, AND FRANCISCO ESTRADA BELLI

    1992   Middle Preclassic Maya Buildings and Burials at Cuello, Belize. *Antiquity* 66: 955–964.

HANSEN, RICHARD D.

    1990   *Excavations in the Tigre Complex, El Mirador, Peten, Guatemala.* El Mirador Series, pt. 3 (Donlu Thayer, ed.). Papers of the New World Archaeological Foundation 62. Brigham Young University, Provo.

HASSAN, FEKRI A.
1981   *Demographic Archaeology.* Academic Press, New York.

HAYDEN, BRIAN, AND ROB GARGETT
1990   Big Man, Big Heart? A Mesoamerican View of the Emergence of Complex Society. *Ancient Mesoamerica* 1: 3–20.

HEALY, PAUL F.
1992   The Ancient Maya Ballcourt at Pacbitun, Belize. *Ancient Mesoamerica* 3: 229–239.

HEIZER, ROBERT F.
1968   New Observations at La Venta. In *Dumbarton Oaks Conference on the Olmec* (Elizabeth P. Benson, ed.): 9–40. Dumbarton Oaks, Washington, D.C.

HICKS, FREDERIC
1991   Gift and Tribute: Relations of Dependency in Aztec Mexico. In *Early State Economics* (Henri J. M. Claessen and Pieter van de Velde, eds.): 199–213. Transaction Publishers, New Brunswick.

HOLLAND, WILLIAM R.
1964   Contemporary Tzotzil Cosmological Concepts as a Basis for Interpreting Prehistoric Maya Civilization. *American Antiquity* 29: 301–306.

HOUSTON, STEPHEN, AND DAVID STUART
1989   *The Way Glyph: Evidence for "Co-essences" among the Classic Maya.* Research Reports on Ancient Maya Writing 30. Center for Maya Research, Washington, D.C.

HOWELL, WAYNE K.
1989   *Excavations in the Danta Complex at El Mirador, Peten, Guatemala.* El Mirador Series, pt. 2 (Donlu Thayer, ed.). Papers of the New World Archaeological Foundation 60. Brigham Young University, Provo.

JONES, DENNIS C.
n.d.   The Crossroads Area of El Mirador: Causeways and Cityscape of a Maya Site in Guatemala. M.A. thesis, Department of Geography and Anthropology, Louisiana State University, Baton Rouge, 1985.

KURJACK, EDWARD B.
1979   *Sacbeob:* parentesco y desarrollo de estado maya. In *Los procesos de cambio en Mesoamerica y áreas circunvecinas,* vol. 1: 217–230. Sociedad Mexicana de Antropología, XV Mesa Redonda, Guanajuato.

KURJACK, EDWARD B., AND E. WYLLYS ANDREWS V
1976   Early Boundary Maintenance in Northwest Yucatan, Mexico. *American Antiquity* 41: 318–325.

KURJACK, EDWARD B., AND SILVIA GARZA T.
1981   Pre-Columbian Community Form and Distribution in the Maya Area. In *Lowland Maya Settlement Patterns* (Wendy Ashmore, ed.): 287–309. University of New Mexico Press, Albuquerque.

LAPORTE, JUAN PEDRO, AND VILMA FIALKO C.
    1990   New Perspectives on Old Problems: Dynastic References for the Early Classic at Tikal. In *Vision and Revision in Maya Studies* (Flora S. Clancy and Peter D. Harrision, eds.): 33–66. University of New Mexico Press, Albuquerque.
    1995   Un reencuentro con Mundo Perdido, Tikal, Guatemala. *Ancient Mesoamerica* 6: 41–94.

LEON-PORTILLA, MIGUEL
    1985   *Tonalamatl de los Pochtecas, Códice Fejérváry-Mayer.* Celanese Mexicana, México, D.F.

MARCUS, JOYCE, KENT V. FLANNERY, AND RONALD SPORES
    1983   The Cultural Legacy of the Oaxacan Preceramic. In *The Cloud People* (Kent V. Flannery and Joyce Marcus, eds.): 36–39. Academic Press, New York.

MATHENY, RAY T., AND DEANNE G. MATHENY
    1990   *Introduction to Investigations at El Mirador, Peten, Guatemala.* El Mirador Series, pt. 1 (Donlu Thayer, ed.). Papers of the New World Archaeological Foundation 59. Brigham Young University, Provo.

MENDELSSOHN, KURT
    1971   A Scientist Looks at the Pyramids. *American Scientist* 59: 210–220.

PIRES-FERREIRA, JANE W.
    1976   Shell and Iron-Ore Mirror Exchange in Formative Mesoamerica, with Comments on Other Commodities. In *The Early Mesoamerican Village* (Kent V. Flannery, ed.): 311–328. Academic Press, New York.

PROSKOURIAKOFF, TATIANA
    1962   Civic and Religious Structures of Mayapan. In *Mayapan, Yucatan, Mexico.* Carnegie Institution of Washington, Publication 619. Washington, D.C.

PYNE, NANETTE M.
    1976   The Fire-Serpent and Were-Jaguar in Formative Oaxaca: A Contingency Table Analysis. In *The Early Mesoamerican Village* (Kent V. Flannery, ed.): 272–282. Academic Press, New York.

RANDS, ROBERT L., AND BARBARA C. RANDS
    1965   Pottery Figurines of the Maya Lowlands. In *Handbook of Middle American Indians* (Robert Wauchope and Gordon Willey, eds.) 2: 535–560. University of Texas Press, Austin.

RICKETSON, OLIVER G., JR., AND EDITH B. RICKETSON
    1937   *Uaxactun, Guatemala.* Carnegie Institution of Washington, Publication 477. Washington, D.C.

RINGLE, WILLIAM M.
    1988   *Of Mice and Monkeys: The Value and Meaning of T1016, the God C Hieroglyph.* Research Reports on Ancient Maya Writing 18–19. Center for Maya Research, Washington, D.C.
    n.d.   The Settlement Patterns of Komchen, Yucatan, Mexico. Ph.D. dissertation, Tulane University, New Orleans, 1985.

RINGLE, WILLIAM M., AND E. WYLLYS ANDREWS V
    1988   Formative Residences at Komchen, Yucatan, Mexico. In *Household and*

Community in the Mesoamerican Past (Richard R. Wilk and Wendy Ashmore, eds.): 171–197. University of New Mexico Press, Albuquerque.

RINGLE, WILLIAM M., AND GEORGE J. BEY

n.d.   The Center and Segmentary State Dynamics. Paper presented at the Wenner-Gren Conference on the Segmentary State and the Classic Maya Lowlands, Cleveland State University, 1992.

ROBERTSON, ROBIN A., AND DAVID A. FREIDEL (EDS.)

1986   *Archaeology at Cerros, Belize, Central America,* vol. 1: *An Interim Report.* Southern Methodist University Press, Dallas.

SCARBOROUGH, VERNON L.

1991a   *Archaeology at Cerros, Belize, Central America, vol. 3: The Settlement System in a Late Preclassic Maya Community* (David A. Freidel, ed.). Southern Methodist University Press, Dallas.

1991b   Courting in the Southern Maya Lowlands: A Study in Pre-Hispanic Ball game Architecture. In *The Mesoamerican Ball game* (Vernon L. Scarborough and David R. Wilcox, eds.): 129–144. University of Arizona Press, Tucson.

SCHELE, LINDA, AND DAVID FREIDEL

1990   *A Forest of Kings: The Untold Story of the Ancient Maya.* William Morrow, New York.

SMITH, A. LEDYARD

1972   *Excavations at Altar de Sacrificios: Architecture, Settlement, Burials, and Caches.* Harvard University, Papers of the Peabody Museum of Archaeology and Ethnology 64 (2). Cambridge, Mass.

SMITH, ROBERT E.

1955   *Ceramic Sequence at Uaxactun, Guatemala,* 2 vols. Tulane University, Middle American Research Institute, Publication 28. New Orleans.

SOUTHALL, AIDAN W.

1988   The Segmentary State in Africa and Asia. *Comparative Studies in Society and History* 30: 52–82.

STOREY, REBECCA

1985   An Estimate of Mortality in a Pre-Columbian Urban Population. *American Anthropologist* 87: 519–535.

STUART, DAVID

1987   *Ten Phonetic Syllables.* Research Reports on Ancient Maya Writing 14. Center for Maya Research, Washington, D.C.

1988   Blood Symbolism in Maya Iconography. In *Maya Iconography* (Elizabeth P. Benson and Gillett G. Griffin, eds.): 175–221. Princeton University Press, Princeton.

SUHLER, CHARLES K.

n.d.   Excavations at Structure 6E-120, a Late Preclassic Ceremonial Building. Paper presented at the 47th International Congress of Americanists, New Orleans, 1991.

TASCHEK, JENNIFER T.

1994   *The Artifacts of Dzibilchaltun, Yucatan, Mexico: Shell, Polished Stone, Bone, Wood, and Ceramics.* Tulane University, Middle American Research Institute, Publication 50. New Orleans.

TOURTELLOT, GAIR, III

 1988   *Excavations at Seibal, Department of Peten, Guatemala. Peripheral Survey and Excavation: Settlement and Community Patterns* (Gordon R. Willey, ed.). Harvard University, Memoirs of the Peabody Museum of Archaeology and Ethnology 16. Cambridge, Mass.

TOWNSEND, RICHARD F.

 1979   *State and Cosmos in the Art of Tenochtitlan.* Studies in Pre-Columbian Art and Archaeology 20. Dumbarton Oaks, Washington, D.C.

TOZZER, ALFRED M. (ED. AND TRANS.)

 1941   *Landa's Relación de las cosas de Yucatán.* Harvard University, Papers of the Peabody Museum of American Archaeology and Ethnology 18. Cambridge, Mass.

TRIGGER, BRUCE G.

 1990   Monumental Architecture: A Thermodynamic Explanation of Symbolic Behavior. *World Archaeology* 22: 119–131.

TURNER, VICTOR W.

 1969   Humility and Hierarchy: The Liminality of Status Elevation and Reversal. In *The Ritual Process: Structure and Anti-Structure* (Victor W. Turner): 166–203. Aldine, Chicago.

 1974   Pilgrimages as Social Process. In *Dramas, Fields, and Metaphors: Symbolic Action in Human Society* (Victor W. Turner): 166–230. Cornell University Press, Ithaca.

VELÁZQUEZ V., RICARDO

 1980   Recent Discoveries in the Caves of Loltun, Yucatan, Mexico. *Mexicon* 2: 53–55.

VILLACORTA, C. J. ANTONIO, AND CARLOS A. VILLACORTA

 1977   *Códices mayas.* Tipografía Nacional, Guatemala.

VOGT, EVON Z.

 1964   The Genetic Model and Maya Cultural Development. In *Desarrollo cultural de los mayas* (Alberto Ruz L., ed.): 9–48. Universidad Nacional Autonónoma de México, Mexico.

VOGT, EVON Z., AND CATHERINE C. VOGT

 1970   Levi-Strauss among the Maya. *Man* 5: 379–392.

WERBNER, RICHARD P.

 1977   Introduction. In *Regional Cults* (Richard P. Werbner, ed.): ix–xxxvii. Association of Social Anthropologists, Monograph 16. Academic Press, New York.

 1989   *Ritual Passage, Sacred Journey: The Process and Organization of Religious Movement.* Smithsonian Institution Press, Washington, D.C.

WILK, RICHARD R., AND HAROLD L. WILHITE

 1991   The Community of Cuello: Patterns of Household and Settlement Change. In *Cuello: An Early Maya Community in Belize* (Norman Hammond, ed.): 118–133. Cambridge University Press, Cambridge.

WILLEY, GORDON R.

 1972   *The Artifacts of Altar de Sacrificios.* Harvard University, Papers of the Peabody Museum of Archaeology and Ethnology 64 (1). Cambridge, Mass.

1978   Artifacts. In *Excavations at Seibal, Department of Peten, Guatemala* (Gordon R. Willey, ed.). Harvard University, Memoirs of the Peabody Museum of Archaeology and Ethnology 14 (1): vii–189. Cambridge, Mass.

1990   General Summary and Conclusions. In *Excavations at Seibal, Department of Peten, Guatemala* (Gordon R. Willey, ed.). Harvard University, Memoirs of the Peabody Museum of Archaeology and Ethnology 17 (4): 175–276. Cambridge, Mass.

WILSON, PETER J.

1988   *The Domestication of the Human Species.* Yale University Press, New Haven.

WOLF, ERIC R.

1982   *Europe and the People without History.* University of California Press, Berkeley.

Olmec Ritual Behavior at El Manatí: A Sacred Space

PONCIANO ORTÍZ C. AND
MARÍA DEL CARMEN RODRÍGUEZ
INSTITUTO NACIONAL DE ANTROPOLOGÍA E HISTORIA, MEXICO

T HE CERRO MANATÍ JUTS FROM the otherwise flat floodplains of the lower Coatzacoalcos River basin in southern Veracruz and is distinctly visible from the Olmec center of San Lorenzo, 10 km to the west (Fig. 1). The Cerro Manatí was created by a deeply buried salt dome, a geologic feature common to the region (Coe and Diehl 1980: 11–13). Springs emerge from the base of the *cerro*. Those on its east side produce salty water, while clean fresh water flows from the western springs.

In 1987, villagers at the small modern hamlet of El Macayal selected one of the western springs as the location for two fish ponds they planned to construct (Fig. 2). As they excavated those ponds out of the mud of the spring area, they unexpectedly began to uncover an amazing quantity of wooden objects, human bones, greenstone axes, ceramics, and other artifacts interred within the mud. They reported their discoveries to the Veracruz Regional Center of Mexico's Instituto Nacional de Antropología e Historia (INAH), and in 1988 we traveled to this isolated area of rural Veracruz to verify the reported finds. Upon arriving at the village of El Macayal, much to our surprise, we were shown three extraordinarily preserved carved wooden busts. To our further astonishment, it was clear that these magnificent wooden sculptures were attributable to the ancient Olmec culture (1200–500 B.C.). Not only were the busts remarkable for their beauty and preservation, but they were also some of the oldest Pre-Hispanic wooden objects ever found in Mexico. The ceramics found associated with the heads helped verify their antiquity, for they were typical of the San Lorenzo (1000–900 B.C.) and Nacaste (900–700 B.C.) phases at San Lorenzo (Coe and Diehl 1980).

Late that same day, as dusk approached, we were taken to the site of the

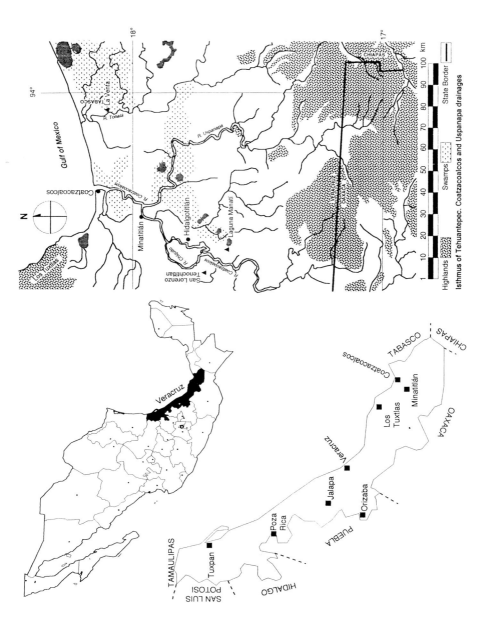

Fig. 1 State of Veracruz and Coatzacoalcos River basin, showing location of El Manatí. Drawing by Paul Schmidt.

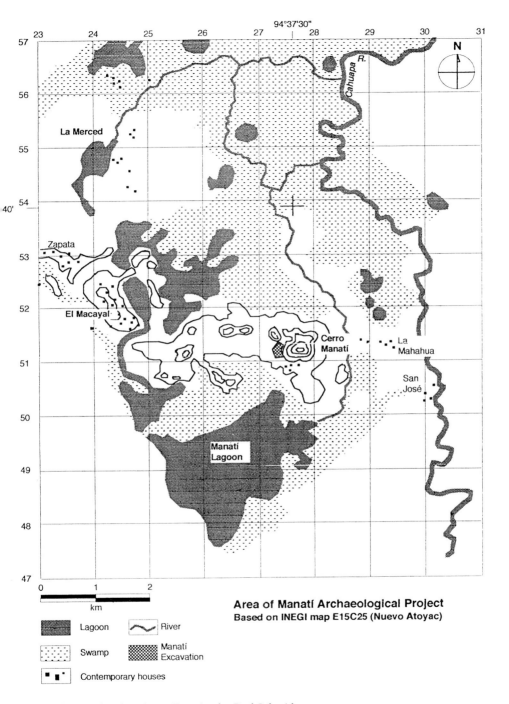

Fig. 2 El Manatí and environs. Drawing by Paul Schmidt.

discovery, a trip involving a canoe journey across lagoons and a long walk through savannah grasslands. The fish ponds, built to utilize water from the spring at the foot of the Cerro Manatí, measured 24 by 21 m, and 10 by 9 m. Both were filled with water at the time we first saw them, thus concealing from our view the areas that had yielded the unusual artifacts. We began excavations at El Manatí in 1988, and that research continued for several years thereafter. Although the spring deposits preserved the wooden busts and other organic remains, they also created extremely difficult excavation conditions, for rather than working on solid ground we were essentially excavating in gelatinous mud.

The springs, the mountain, and several other characteristics made El Manatí a sacred place and the scene of the ritual behaviors demonstrated by the archaeological record there. Our data suggest that the ritual use of the springs began as early as 1600–1700 B.C. and culminated about 1200 B.C. We believe that three phases of use occurred (Fig. 3). The first, Manatí A, is evidenced by stone axes, ceramic material, rubber balls, jade beads, and ground stone objects found dispersed across what we interpret as the bed of the spring. During the second, Manatí B, phase, axes occur in particular groupings of 2 to 11 pieces that were laid out along north-south and east-west axes. The final Macayal phase, about 1200 B.C., corresponds to the period of interment of the wooden busts. In this chapter we discuss some of the objects and patterns uncovered by our excavations. Details of the actual excavations, stratigraphy, and a plan view of the excavation units showing the location of Sculptures 1–9 has been published in Ortíz and Rodríguez (1989). In this chapter we report our results from the field seasons of 1988–89 and 1992, and reflects our data and analyses through the latter season.

THE HISTORY OF RITUAL USE OF A SACRED SPACE

Manatí A Phase

The earliest archaeological evidence for offerings at El Manatí is found in the area that we interpret to be the bed of the pond created by the spring. That bed is marked by sandstone rocks, the largest of which are positioned on a general north-south axis and have been modified with V-shaped ("ax-sharpening") grooves and ground circular depressions. The artifacts of this phase occur within Level X, a deposit of sandy sediment above and around the rocky bed (see Fig. 3). A sterile stratum of gummy yellowish clay underlies Level X. Two radiocarbon dates are associated with the earliest deposits: one 3740 ± 90 rya (Beta-637332), or 1790 ± 90 B.C. uncorrected; the other 3710 ± 110 rya (Beta-63735), or 1760 ± uncorrected.

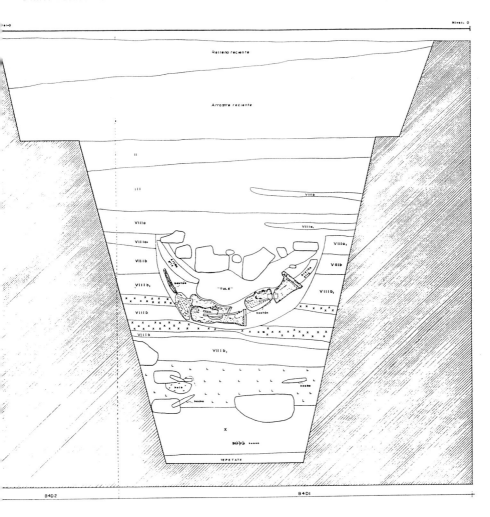

Fig. 3 Stratigraphic section showing evidence for three phases of use of springs. Sculptures 18, 19, and 20, belonging to the Macayal phase, are shown in their intrusive pit under a layer of organic remains (*tule*). Feature 31-92, a rubber ball and two axes belonging to the Manatí A phase, is shown at lower left.

The ceramic assemblage found within Level X is quite standardized, consisting basically of light cream-colored slipped tecomates with polished exteriors and extremely reduced mouths, and light cream-yellowish slipped flat-bottomed bowls with straight outslanting walls (some have a slight incised line on the interior). There are also fluted tecomates, red and dark reddish-brown slipped tecomates and flat-bottomed bowls, brushed and plain tecomates, smoked black tecomates and flat-bottomed bowls, and bichrome bottles. Some of these vessels still have traces of soot or carbon on their exteriors. We believe all of this assemblage is contemporaneous with the Bajío, Ojochi, and Chicharras phases at San Lorenzo (Coe and Diehl 1980) and that it exhibits many similarities to the ceramics of the Barra and Locona phases of Chiapas (Ceja 1984; Clark 1991, 1994; Lowe 1975).

"Domestic" artifacts in this level include fragments of shallow stone mortars and flat footless metates with rounded corners. The presence of fire-cracked rounded river rocks suggests particular food preparation practices. In addition, fragments of human and animal bone were found dispersed in this level. Only a few obsidian blades and one figurine fragment were found in this level, and obsidian artifacts and figurines are otherwise notable by their absence.

Isolated polished stone axes were found dispersed around the bed of the spring. Some seem to form groupings (although without forming patterns as in subsequent phases), and these we labeled "Features." Some of these are described below to provide an idea of the type of artifact clusters found in this, the deepest cultural level at El Manatí.

Feature 3-92 consists of a grouping of five highly polished green petaloid stone axes that were laid out side by side in a northeast direction with their bit edges all pointing west. These axes may be associated with two other axes that had been placed slightly further south. Feature 5-92 is composed of six axes laid horizontally, five of them with their bits oriented to the east, and the sixth set on its side with its bit facing south. Two isolated axes north of this group may also be part of the same feature. A third such ax group is Feature 25-92, four axes positioned horizontally, three with bits facing west and the fourth facing in the opposite direction. The smallest of the axes, 10 cm long and 4 cm wide, is a light cream color with dark veins, and the largest is of highly polished greenstone, 18.5 cm long and 5.5 cm wide. A third, measuring 15.5 cm long and 6.4 cm wide, is light green in color with dark green veins and well polished except for the butt. The fourth is also of light green color with dark green and white veins, and measures 13 cm long and 4.5 cm wide.

Two other ax groupings are highly significant, for they are each associated with another important artifact, a rubber ball. Feature 8-92 is composed of six axes above a rubber ball. The arrangement of the axes is irregular: the largest ax points to the south, another to the southwest, and yet another to the northeast; the next is located beneath the largest, placed on its side with its bit pointing west; the fifth is also on edge and facing west; and the sixth, with bit toward the north, lies beneath a large sandstone rock. The globular rubber ball (Fig. 4) is 10 cm in diameter and has small surface irregularities due to encrusted gravel. A rubber ball and two axes comprise Feature 31-92 (see Fig. 3). One of the axes lay above the rubber ball, with its bit pointing east. The other ax was nearby, oriented with its bit to the west. The rubber ball measures 22 x 18 x 10 cm. Its present flattish ovaloid shape was probably caused by the weight of overlying objects and deposits.

Fig. 4   Rubber ball from Feature 8-92, Manatí A phase.

Greenstone bead "clusters" also occur in Level X. During the 1989 field season, 56 jade beads were found in the same area as Feature 31-92. They were dispersed among the mud and sand in an area of approximately 2 sq m in association with the sandstone rocks of the spring bed. Each bead is distinct in terms of its size, quality of workmanship, and shape (rounded to semicylindrical), but all are perforated with a conical drill hole. More beads were recovered in the same area in the 1990 field season. These were jade and serpentine with different sizes and finishes. Their quantity indicates that they must have belonged to at least two different strands of beads or necklaces that had been thrown into the spring as an offering, and they may be part of the same 56-

Fig. 5 Six axes arranged in a flowerlike circle, Feature 11-92, Manatí B phase.

bead group excavated the previous season. The majority were found concentrated between the roots of an ancient tree that marks an old surface and around and beneath a large sandstone boulder within the sandy stratum of Level X.

A solid clay "baby-face" figurine fragment was found in association with the beads. The figurine head depicts cranial deformation, and some postfiring angular cut marks at the level of the ears suggest that this piece was reused, possibly as a pendant or pectoral. Its association with the beads suggests that it may have been part of a bead strand. A human molar and some human bone fragments were also found near the beads. Furthermore, this same area of the spring bed yielded fragments of what we originally believed to be highly overfired clay nodules, because of their similarity in texture to the scoria formed in kilns that reach high vitrifying temperatures. However, under inspection in the laboratory, we ascertained that these droplike fragments are apparently sandy concretions formed by water filtration in an open space or cave. They may indicate the existence of a cave or a rock shelter nearby in antiquity.

Manatí B Phase

The offerings and artifacts of this phase occur within Level VIIIb, a stratum separated from Level X by a muddy deposit, Level IX, which extends like a

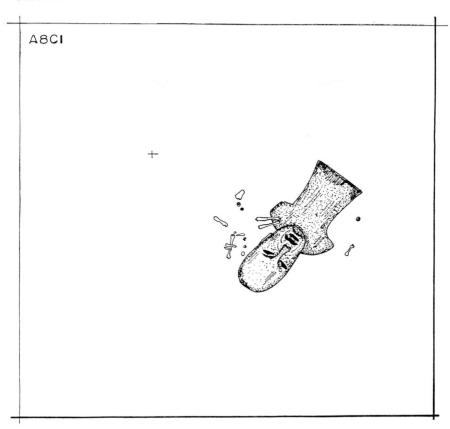

A8CI

PROYECTO MANATI 92
SITIO MANATI

N

Planta. (huesos.Infante y escultura 17).

Cuadro : A8CI

Elemento: 12   Nivel :200 - 220
Levanto : Zenaido Salazar B.
Dibujo : Irma Becerril Mtz
Responsables: Carmen Rodriguez Mtz.
                      Ponciano Ortiz   C.

0   10   30   50   70cm

Fig. 6 Sculpture 17, with associated bones of infant, as found.

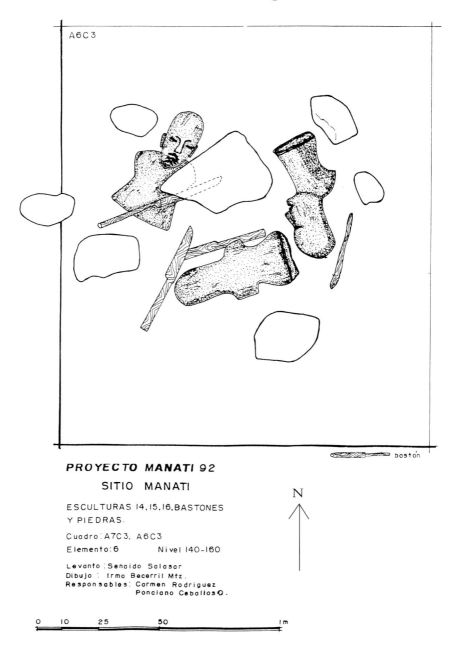

PROYECTO MANATI 92
SITIO MANATI

ESCULTURAS 14,15,16,BASTONES
Y PIEDRAS.

Cuadro:A7C3, A6C3
Elemento:6   Nivel 140-160

Levanto :Senaido Salasar
Dibujo : Irma Becerril Mtz.
Responsables: Carmen Rodriguez
              Ponciano Ceballos O.

N

Fig. 7 Sculptures 14, 15, and 16, with associated scepters and sandstone blocks, as found.

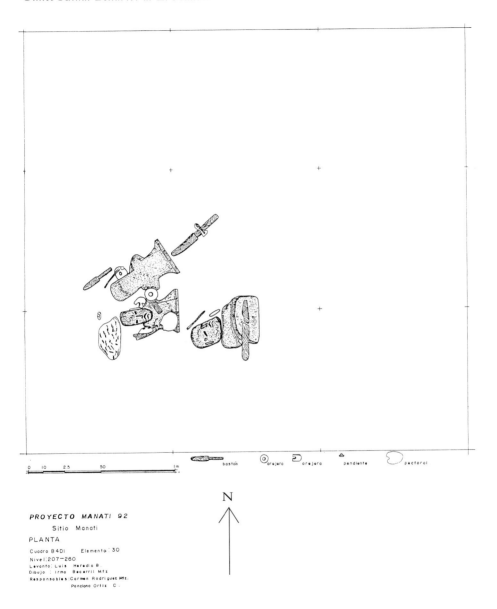

Fig. 8 Sculptures 18, 19, and 20, with associated ornaments and scepters, as found.

Fig. 9 Detail of Sculptures 19 and 20, showing the face of Sculpture 20, the round organic pectoral ornament of this sculpture at lower left, and traces of the earspool of Sculpture 19.

carpet over Level X and the rocky bed of the spring. Level IX was apparently created when the spring began to clog and fill with sediment. The ritual deposits of the Manatí B phase are principally characterized by more complex patterns in the arrangement of ax groupings. Several are described below.

A flowerlike arrangement of five axes, Feature 25-90, occurred 50 cm above the rocky spring bed in Level VIIIb. The axes had each been stuck into the mud at an angle, butts downward, to form a circle, as if each ax was the equivalent of one petal of the flower. All five axes are 13–15 cm long. Four of them were made from the same type of gray stone, and the fifth is dark green. A second flowerlike grouping of six polished axes, Feature 11-92, was also found (Fig. 5).

Feature 27-90 is a "square" created by five axes laid horizontally, one in each "corner" and the fifth in the center of the square. Two of the corner axes are oriented with bits to the southwest, the two other corner axes are oriented to the northwest, and the central ax has its bit to the south. Another cluster of five axes, Feature 29-90, occurs nearby. In this grouping, four were laid out horizontally together, and the fifth was 50 cm west and slightly higher. Of the four, three were side by side, touching one another, two with their bits to the east, the third to the west; the fourth was positioned facing southeast. The isolated ax was also laid flat, but with its bit to the northeast. It is possible that this feature, and the previously described Features 25-90 and 27-90, are somehow related, and they perhaps pertain in some manner to concentrations of greenish clay found slightly southeast of all of them.

The largest ax grouping is Feature 7-92, which consists of 12 axes occurring together as if they had been deposited as a bundle, although no organic remains that would suggest a wrapping were noted. The axes were positioned irregularly; taking into consideration the orientation of the edge, seven were placed with their bits to the west, and the others to the north, south, and east. While the features described above contain multiple axes, others such as Features 10-92, 16-92, and 29-92, consist only of ax pairs. Interestingly, within these pairs one ax is usually light green in color and the other dark green. Directionality of the bits in the ax pairs shows no consistent pattern.

Macayal Phase

The most spectacular artifacts found within the spring deposits at El Manatí are related to the Macayal phase and Level VIIIa. We refer specifically to the preserved wooden objects—busts, knives, staffs, and scepters—that make El Manatí unique among Mesoamerican sites (Figs. 6–9). Because all these wooden pieces are fragile and were in need of immediate conservation, they and other organic materials were frequently removed within a block of the surrounding clay matrix, and thus the field measurements and observations used in this chapter are at times incomplete. We have one radiocarbon date (GX-14765) for this period, 2990 ± 150 rya, or 1040 ± 150 B.C. uncorrected, obtained on wood from Sculpture 2, discussed below.

Sculpture 1 and Feature 1-88. The first wooden sculpture that our excavations uncovered, Sculpture 1, seems to represent a female and we nicknamed it Vicky (throughout this chapter we will refer to the sculptures by their field nicknames rather than feature numbers). When found, at a depth of 2.2 m, the sculpture was within a large block of clay that was part of a slowly collapsing sidewall, but we believe that this slumping did not alter the carving's original position by much more than 5 cm. The bust was lying horizontally, face upward, head oriented to the southwest. As we carefully cleared the facial area we observed that the mouth area was painted red. For fear of damaging this piece we did not remove the clay matrix from the remainder of the mouth nor the right side of the head, but left that delicate task to the INAH restoration laboratory.

An extremely unusual artifact, a carved wooden staff, was found to the right of Vicky's head, set in a vertical position. This was the first of many staffs to be recovered during our research (compare Figs. 7–9). The top of the staff reached above the height of the head, but we do not know how far below the base it continued since the bust and staff were removed together in the block of clay matrix. In addition a dark green ax, oriented east–west, lay just beyond the wooden staff.

A significant aspect of the Vicky bust is the evidence that it had received special treatment. Close inspection revealed that the bust had been wrapped in a woven fiber mat (or *petate*) of palm leaf or similar material and then tied with a string also of plant fibers (*ixtle*). The knots of that string could still be distinguished in the best-preserved sections of the bust. Unfortunately, most of this covering has disintegrated, and in general only dark green discolorations remain.

Sculpture 2 and Feature 15-88. Sculpture 2, which we nicknamed Fello, was found only 1.5 m east of Vicky, at a depth of 2.43 m. The Fello bust lay face down with the head oriented east. Unlike the Vicky carving, Fello was not associated with a wooden staff or stone ax, but instead had a large obsidian flake placed near its left ear. Slightly north of the obsidian piece was a concentration of red ochre or hematite that had significantly stained the clay around the bust in that area. Within the stained area there were small pieces of red ochre or hematite and smaller quantities of small balls of fine greenish-gray clay of obvious human manufacture. We could also ascertain purposely placed piles of leaves and plant bundles, and found some fragments of double-strand cord that had tied those bundles. Dispersed within this area were some fragments of human infant bones (see Fig. 6 for a similar association of infant bones with Sculpture 17). The bones were stained with the same red hematite pigment that also colored the surrounding clay matrix. Slightly beneath all of this was a hematite ball about 30 cm in diameter with the remains of a cord of two strands around its exterior, indicating that it too had been tied.

Fello was associated with a manmade feature common to a number of other sculptures, a pile of sandstone rocks that reached almost to the surface of the deposit (see Feature 16-89 below). To the east of this feature was the primary burial of an infant (possibly newborn), whose bone structure was similar to the bones described above.

Sculpture 4 and Feature 16-89. Toño (Sculpture 4) was discovered 2.3 m east of Fello associated with a stone pile (2.1 m high) similar to that adjacent to Fello. In similar stone piles throughout this phase, large stones (50–70 cm in diameter, weighing up to 100 kg) occur in the upper portions of the pile, and stone size decreases at the pile's base (to 10–20 cm in diameter). Toño was buried near the western base of the associated rock pile. Interestingly, this bust had been interred with its face to the east, but upside down. Between Toño and the stone pile, slightly higher than the sculpture, we uncovered a section of an unburnished flat-bottomed bowl, an ax, a seed fragment, and two small concentrations of fine greenish clay.

The Toño, Vicky, and Fello sculptures, and their respective rock piles—as well as the primary infant burial in the area between those rock piles—occur in an east-west alignment. It is therefore possible that they are essentially contemporaneous.

Sculptures 5, 6, 7 and Feature 17-89. The El Manatí sculptures not only occur individually but were interred in groups as well. This is exemplified by the grouping of three busts, Lulú (Sculpture 5), Chispa (Sculpture 6), and Poc (Sculpture 7). These sculptures were laid out on their sides, forming a crude semicircle, all facing toward the interior of the circle. These carvings were associated with organic material composed of branches and leaves, scattered human infant bones, and an incomplete wooden staff (see Figs. 7 and 8 for similar arrangements of Sculptures 14 to 16 and 18 to 20).

A cranium fragment was found near the center of this semicircular grouping together with pieces of plant stalks similar to a cane known as *junquillo*. Next to these we detected traces of dark organic remains from leaves or other plant materials. Associated with these were remnants of double-strand cord. This suggests that the junquillo canes and other plant remains had been tied in bundles that had been placed above the cranium and next to the sculptures as part of this ritual offering.

Furthermore, the remains of a covering or mat (*petate*) of reeds, along with cord fragments, could be detected around the face and part of the torso of Lulú, suggesting that this sculpture had also been wrapped as a bundle. Similar decomposed organic material occurred under the head and along the sides of Chispa. The third sculpture of this group, Poc, lay slightly deeper than Lulú and Chispa, and was found only these two had been removed. At Poc's neck we found an unusual pendant: a bead that had been made from tar. Indications of plant remains were also found around Poc's head and chest area, as were fragments of double-strand cord.

Sculptures 8, 9 and Feature 19-89. The busts that we nicknamed Nacho (Sculpture 8) and Polo (Sculpture 9) were found associated with another pile of sandstone rocks. Although this pile was smaller than those previously described, it nevertheless exhibits the same pattern, with smaller rocks near the base and larger stones at the top. A white slip, flat-bottomed flaring wall bowl (Coe and

Diehl's [1980: 177] Mina White) was associated with the stone pile. While there was no evidence with either Nacho or Polo of associated artifacts, plant bundles and cords, or skeletal remains, the sculptures do appear to have been covered by a layer of reeds and plant stalks (compare Fig. 3 for a similar feature found with Sculptures 18 to 20). The Nacho sculpture had been placed on its right side, head to the west and facing south, while Polo had been interred face down, head to the west.

Sculptures 12, 13 and Feature 28-89. We uncovered two additional wooden busts, Cruz (Sculpture 12) and Güicho (Sculpture 13), which were associated with yet another stone pile. The stone pile extended from a depth of 1.48 m to 2.4 m. The Cruz sculpture was buried south of the pile at a depth of 2.48 m. It had been interred in an upright position, facing east, and exhibited no evidence of having been wrapped or covered. To its east was a vertically positioned wooden staff with a lanceolate-shaped head and undulating tapered serpentlike body.

The Güicho bust was found beneath the stone pile, and the left side of its face was seriously indented by one of the stones. This sculpture was also positioned upright and facing east. Unlike Cruz, Güicho had been protected with reeds. This was particularly evident along the back of the head, where some woven reedlike fibers could be seen. These gave the appearance of having perhaps been a "hat" with curved rim, something not observed with the other sculptures. As with the Cruz bust, a serpent-shaped wooden staff, with lanceolate head with three angular cuts and rounded undulating body, was found just east of Güicho.

An infant burial was found beneath some stones slightly northwest of Güicho. The infant had been buried in a flexed position, on its right side, face to the east. All the bones were in anatomically correct position, indicating that it was a primary burial. Bone morphology indicates that the infant was newborn. Plant remains occurred above the burial, perhaps having served as a covering or an offering. The infant burial, Güicho sculpture, and the associated stone pile had been interred together, for they all occur within the same clearly identifiable intrusive pit. Although Sculpture 12, Cruz, occurs at essentially the same level as the former feature, it had been buried within a separate pit, and thus we cannot ascertain whether or not it is contemporaneous.

Sculptures 14, 15, 16 and Feature 6-92. This is a grouping of three wooden sculptures (Fig. 7) laid in a semicircle, an arrangement similar to that of the Lulú, Chispa, and Poc carvings of Feature 17-89 (see above). Sculpture 14 (Simon) was placed face down, head to the west. To the left of the head there was a wooden "dagger" with a north-south orientation, while another wooden dagger on the right side of the head and slightly lower pointed west. Sculpture 15

(Marti) lay on its left side, facing west, the head almost touching the base of the Simon sculpture. Another serpent-shaped staff, in poor condition, was found beside the head. Sculpture 16 (Mundo) was buried slightly deeper than the other two busts. It lay horizontally, with its face upward, and a large lanceolate staff lay across its chest and right shoulder, pointed to the east. A sandstone rock had been placed over the sculpture, and several other rocks lay around the carving. Both Marti and Mundo exhibit red and black paint around their mouth areas. This entire grouping had been covered by a thick layer of well-preserved organic material, *tule*, a treatment found with many carvings already described (see Fig. 3).

It is important to note that this grouping is in line with Sculptures 12 and 13 found in the 1990 season, and further indicates the existence of a pattern to the interment of the sculptures.

Sculpture 17 and Feature 12-92. Sculpture 17, Chico (Fig. 6), was found beneath a stone pile similar to those described above. Chico had been laid flat, face up, head toward the southwest. Black and red paint occur around Chico's mouth area, and tule-like organic material overlay the sculpture. Beginning about 20 cm above the sculpture, we found infant long bones, skull fragments, ribs, and vertebrae, all in association with organic remains. Among these were three infant crania, including one that exhibits an intentional U-shaped cut from which a double-strand cord hangs. Ribs and long bones continued as deep as the sculpture and also to its west, giving us the sense that body parts of several infants had been part of this offering. Lacking from the Sculpture 17 interment is a wooden staff, while included with the associated plant material were two small branches similar to those found with Sculpture 2 (Fello) and the Sculptures 4, 5, and 6 group.

Sculptures 18, 19, 20 and Feature 30-92. This group is composed of three sculptures, three wooden staffs, a ball of hematite, and 11 greenstone axes, all of which occur below a cluster of stones and within a pit intrusive from Level VIIIa into Level VIIIb (Fig. 8). A large number of thin layers of tule covered the sculptures, separating them from the stone cluster placed above them (Fig. 3). Sculpture 18, Fabian, was lying in a semi-inclined, head-down position facing west. On the left side of the chest was a rectangular object about 6 cm long, apparently a seed, which may have served as a pectoral. At each side of Fabian's face was a small "inverted t-shaped" pendant made from tar. Above the base of this sculpture was a wooden staff, butt pointing south.

A group of 11 axes were found below Fabian. Nine lay horizontally and two were positioned vertically. Of the former, one pointed east, six west, and two laid out north-south touched bit to bit.

Sculpture 19, Dani, was placed face down, with the head toward the west. On the chest area of the bust we found a circular pectoral of organic material, perhaps the base of a gourd. Dani was adorned with two circular earspools (material as yet unidentified). A bead of organic material was found by the left earspool. Both earspools hung from some sort of tar objects that had been stuck onto the earlobes. In addition, two wooden staffs were associated with the Dani carving. One lay above and to the west of the head, and the other had been placed at the base of the bust. Both staffs point toward the southwest. Sculpture 20, Macario, lay face up at the base of the intrusive pit, head to the west. Red paint occurs around the mouth area. As with the Dani sculpture, a circular (gourd base?) pectoral occurs on the chest, and earspools were noted at both sides of the head (Fig. 9). A plant stem, perhaps part of a larger bunch of vegetation, lay across the pectoral and right earspool. Finally, a 30 x 20 cm chunk of hematite lay just beyond Macario's head.

OTHER RITUAL OBJECTS AND OFFERINGS

Some objects found during our excavations do not appear to have had a direct association with the wooden sculptures, yet are worth noting.

Rubber Balls

The rubber balls recovered at El Manatí are extraordinary in and of themselves but are also important because many predate the offerings of wooden sculptures. We uncovered five such rubber balls within the Manatí A phase deposits along the rocky bed of the spring, and two of those, discussed earlier (Features 8-92 and 31-92; see Figs. 3, 4), were associated with polished greenstone axes. In addition, an isolated group of three rubber balls (Feature 21-89) was also unearthed. These balls vary in size from 8 to 13 cm in diameter, and were placed side by side in a southwest-northeast alignment. They lie atop Level IX, but within Level VIIIb, and are located essentially at the middle of the "rectangle" formed by Sculpture 2 (Fello), Sculpture 4 (Toño), Sculptures 5, 6, and 7 (Lulú, Chispa, Poc), and Sculptures 8 and 9 (Nacho, Polo) (see Ortíz and Rodríguez 1989: map 1). We know that during the construction of the fish ponds prior to our research, villagers found at least five other small rubber balls, presumably from Manatí A levels.

So far we have recovered only two rubber balls from Macayal phase deposits, and those were found in association with two wooden staffs (together Feature 24-89). The balls had been placed in an intrusive pit above one of the large worked stones that occur on the bed of the spring. This stone has extensive "ax-sharpening grooves" on its upper surface, as well as a ground "cup mark" 20 cm in diameter and 15 cm deep. However, we believe that the balls were only circumstantially associated with this worked stone.

The balls, both slightly oblong in shape (22 x 18 cm and 20 x 15 cm), lay side by side, touching, in an east–west orientation. A wooden staff pointing in a northerly direction lay above the west ball, and a second staff, also pointing north, lay beneath the same ball. The balls were covered by thin layers of a fibrous organic material, not as if they had been wrapped in the fibers, but rather as if the fibrous material was part of the offering. The fiber was highly decomposed, and only a small sample could be taken for identification in the laboratory.

Significantly, the excellent preservation of the balls has enabled us to ascertain their production technique. They were created by the layered wrapping of multiple strips of rubber, a technique similar to that used today to manufacture balls of string cheese. These rubber balls have a firm, compact texture. If we include the five balls found by local villagers, a total of 12 rubber balls have been found at El Manatí. One notable difference detectable in that sample is that the oldest rubber balls, those of the Manatí A phase, are generally smaller, from 10 to 14 cm in diameter, while balls of the Macayal phase measure 20–22 cm in diameter. Nevertheless, the presence of a dozen rubber balls among the offerings at El Manatí indicates their importance in the ritual activities that were carried out there.

Scepters

The largest wooden object recovered is Special Object 2, a long rodlike large wooden scepter or ceremonial staff, 110 cm in length and tapering from 3.5 to 2.5 cm in diameter. Protruding from the scepter's ovoid knoblike tip is a shark tooth. The knob is reminiscent of a bird's head with the beak represented by the shark tooth. In addition to its unusual knob, the scepter is of further interest because it had been painted a red-orange color, and at the moment of discovery the color still maintained an enamel-like shine. The color, most clearly seen on the knob, continues at least halfway down the scepter. Because this rare wooden object was encrusted with a hard sandy coating, we did not attempt to clean it. It is possible that the scepter has engraved designs, but we will not know until it is completely cleaned by the INAH conservation laboratory

The scepter occurred between Levels IX and X, with the top (knob) resting on the layer of organic material that represents Level IX, while the other end was within the sandy deposit of Level X. The scepter was oriented to the north and had been placed midway between Sculptures 5, 6, and 7 and Sculptures 8 and 9 (Ortíz and Rodríguez 1989: map 1), as if separating the two groupings. It

is therefore possible that it had been placed at the same time that both groupings were interred and that it is part of the same ceremonial complex.

Special Object 6 is a fragment of a wooden staff that is decorated with
white and red paint. The remnant is 25 cm long with a maximum diameter of
ca. 4 cm The staff is unusual, for it is octagonal in cross section, and the lengths
of each of its eight sides are decorated with excised rectangular depressions.
These sides were painted in red, and the rectangular excised depressions were
filled with a white pigment, creating an interesting contrasting decorative finish. One end of the staff fragment is thicker and ends in a flattish shape. This
latter is the best-preserved section of the staff and was probably the handle.
This object was found at a depth of 2.3 m, handle downward, penetrating into
the *tepetate* below the spring bed and extending upward through Level X. It
was an isolated object with no associated artifacts.

Ritual Knives

Excavations also uncovered a group of three unique stone knives (Feature
9-89) each consisting of a bifacial blade point embedded in a tar handle. Two
of the blades are of a milky gray obsidian and the other of flint or chert. The
latter knife occurred on the west side of the group. None of the knives shows
evidence of use. All three lay pointing south atop a block of fine-textured
yellow clay that was different from the yellow clay of the matrix.

Near to the knives, and in possible association (although 10 cm deeper) were
two concentrations of obsidian flakes. In both concentrations the flakes were
laid out in a triangular shape that pointed north. One concentration was composed of 27 fragments of gray obsidian, all possibly from the same core and all
probably reduction flakes from blade core preparation. All of the flakes exhibit
simple retouching that gave them projectile point shapes. The flakes were deposited directly on a layer of greenish clay, but the excavation profile of this
concentration suggests that the flakes had been held in a gourd bowl or some
other concave object of perishable material. The second concentration of flakes
was located 1 m to the southeast, and consisted of seven fragments of milky
gray obsidian, possibly all from the same core (since two pieces could be re-
joined). One of the fragments shows simple bifacial retouching, to give it the
shape of a projectile point. Directly north of the seven fragments was a small
concentration of yellow clay identical to the yellow clay of the block underlying the three knives.

Clay Blocks

Twenty-six clay blocks were found in the El Manatí deposits, indicating that these were another important type of artifact used there. The blocks are rectangular in shape, 20–30 cm long, and all have a very plastic consistency and vary from cream to greenish-gray in color. One two-section block gave the impression of having perhaps been a modeled bust, but there were no signs of a face. Eleven of the blocks each had a small serpentine ax embedded in their center, bit upward. We also have noted that some blocks were laid out in north–south lines. These blocks date to the same time as the sculptures, the Macayal phase, but occur as well in Level III, the stratum that covers the sediment in which the busts were interred.

BEHAVIORAL PATTERNS AND PERSISTENCE OF THE FEATURES

It is important to note several behavioral activities that seem to be constant in the rituals associated with the busts. First, it is clear that there is a pattern to the placement of the sculptures. Groupings were interred in north–south and east–west alignments, indicating that the ceremonies were carefully planned and executed. Furthermore, both the single sculptures and those buried in groups had been covered by plant materials similar to tule, and most of them were further protected by sandstone rocks.

Among the notable objects associated with the sculptures were wooden staffs. These occur in two general forms, serpentine and lanceolate, and their position vis-à-vis the busts varies. In addition, the skeletal remains of infants are associated with most, but not all, busts. Analysis suggests that these were probably newborns. Only one, below Sculpture 13, was a primary burial. A second, unassociated, primary burial was found in the area between Sculptures 2 and 4. The majority seem to represent infants whose bodies had apparently been dismembered and/or cut into sections (some with the extremities still articulated). These fragmentary infant remains occur dispersed around certain sculptures. In some instances the bones had been covered with powdered hematite. The most exceptional of these discoveries is the infant cranium found near Sculpture 17, with its manmade U-shaped cut and attached cord (Fig. 6).

Greenstone axes are rare in Macayal phase offerings, but 11 were found with the Sculptures 18, 19, and 20 group, and one was found with Sculpture 1. The Sculptures 18, 19, and 20 group was also associated with a ball of hematite, as was Sculpture 2. Finally, branches and bundles of plants were associated with Sculpture 2, with the Sculptures 5, 6, and 7 group, and with Sculpture 17 and thus form another group of objects sometimes associated with this ceremonial behavior.

While most of the sculptures seem not to have been decorated, 10 exhibit facial paint around the mouth area—red paint delimited by a black stripe. Sculptures 1 and 7 had wooden earspools that hung from an asphalt pendant, while Sculptures 18, 19, and 20 had circular earspools possibly made from a gourd and circular pectorals made of the same material (Fig. 9).

OBSERVATIONS AND DISCUSSION

The El Manatí site was located at a special place. The absence of ceremonial or domestic architecture, and the association of the cultural phenomena we uncovered there with natural features (the hill, the spring), allows us to consider this place a sacred space at which a series of religious practices were carried out. These practices varied in form and complexity over time (Ortíz and Rodríguez 1994).

We have not yet been able to determine the complete spatial extent of the area in which the ritual practices were carried out. Manatí A phase artifacts are found throughout practically the entire area excavated to date, and from test excavation data we believe that Manatí A phase ritual activities extended at least 30 m further north, 20 m west, and 18 m south (as measured from our central datum). It is highly probable that those activities encompassed an even larger area.

The axes characteristic of Manatí A phase offerings have a dispersed distribution across the spring bed. Although axes are sometimes near the edges of the ancient pool, most of the single isolated axes seem to be concentrated near its center, suggesting that they had been intentionally tossed into the deepest part of the pool. This suggests that they were offerings of an individual nature.

Another source of evidence for the ceremonial use of this area by the Olmec, beginning with the Manatí A phase, is the sandstone rocks found at the bottom of the bed. The rocks are generally the same size and have cuts or grinding marks on them. It is significant that the largest ones are aligned along a north-south orientation, indicating intentional placement. We initially postulated that the grinding marks on these stones were merely for sharpening axes. However, the data now lead us to believe it more likely that the grinding marks were related to a religious practice with the objective of obtaining the *mana* or magical power of the place. Similar grinding marks are found on two colossal heads and several other monuments at San Lorenzo (Coe and Diehl 1980: 298, 300–365) and on all four La Venta colossal heads (Clewlow et al. 1967: 71–76).

In addition to the axes recovered within the Manatí A phase level, we recovered domestic artifacts. Similar domestic artifacts were also recovered in excavations of shoreline areas beyond the spring. Because we have also carried out excavations of Olmec period houses at the nearby site of El Macayal, we have a good idea of the range of typical household artifacts used in daily lifeways, and thus note that certain types of domestic artifacts are absent in these early deposits at El Manatí. For example, domestic cutting instruments for preparing animal meat are absent. We note that many of the ceramics found are tecomates, the majority having extremely small mouth openings and lids. These could have been used as containers and may also have been used to boil tubers and seeds or to ferment fruit.

There are a number of explanations that could account for the types of domestic refuse found in the deposits at El Manatí. For instance, if these materials pertain to priests or special persons who were caretakers of this sacred place, the refuse suggests that they had dietary customs somewhat different from those of the rest of the population. In their search for closer ties with nature, their diet may have been more vegetarian—vegetables, tubers, and plants—thus eliminating the need for meat-cutting utensils. Alternatively, the domestic materials may have been brought by pilgrims who threw some of these objects into the pool, while materials occurring around the spring could have resulted from the occasional ritual preparation of foods. Whatever the case, it is clear that the El Manatí site had been a sacred place from at least the time of the Manatí A phase (1600–1700 B.C.).

In the following Manatí B phase, after the formation of Level IX at a time when sediment began to be deposited in the pool, ritual activities included the placement of groupings of axes following well-established patterns. These purposeful groupings varied in size from 2 to 12 pieces. In our final field season, in addition to east-west alignments of grouped axes, we found some interesting variations, including a "flower" created from 6 axes (Feature 11-92; Fig. 5) and a group of 12 stacked axes (Feature 7-92). These groupings immediately bring to mind the ax clusters and alignments found in Complex A at La Venta (Drucker, Heizer, and Squier 1959: 133–187) and at San Isidro, Chiapas (Lowe 1981). The Manatí B phase groupings obviously represent a purposeful patterned placement of axes, as opposed to the dispersed phase A axes that were apparently tossed, rather than carefully placed, in the pond. These purposeful ax deposits suggest a more developed form of ritual activity in phase B, one that would culminate in the offerings of a large number of sculptures carved in wood.

We have named the period of the ritual burial of wooden sculptures the Macayal phase, and associated ceramics and other artifacts indicate that it is contemporaneous with the Early Formative occupation of the nearby El Macayal site and with San Lorenzo A and B phases at San Lorenzo. The Macayal phase ritual area does not seem as extensive as earlier. We know, however, that it did probably extend somewhat farther north and south of the area we have excavated. In fact, our 1992 excavations found the Sculptures 18, 19, and 20 group some 12 m south of our central datum.

The majority of the wooden sculptures, in spite of their apparent individuality, follow the same formal model. This indicates that they were an ideological image, that is, a religious symbol, that was conceptualized following essentially the same pattern, a phenomenon also common in other religions of the world. At the same time, the individuality of the busts could indicate that they were representations of chiefs, rulers, or personas who achieved a high level of prestige, leading to an attempt to immortalize them with images. It is also possible that the wooden staffs associated with some of the busts were the insignia of the power the individuals enjoyed during their lives. Finally, the surface wear of the sculptures suggests that they must have served a specific function in ritual prior to their burial.

The bundles of leaves, plants, and reeds also clearly played an important role in the magico-religious ceremony of sculpture interment. Everything appears to indicate that the sculptures received a special burial treatment similar to that given to people: they were wrapped to form a funeral bundle, and they were buried in a careful and sophisticated ritual. One constant pattern to their placement, both singly and in groups, is that they seem to form three west-east alignments, toward the direction of the Cerro Manatí to the east.

The association of dispersed infant bones and two primary infant burials with the sculptures is also worthy of emphasis. We originally believed the bones to be those of monkeys and other animals that perhaps represented the spiritual animal companion of each sculpture. However, the bones have recently been identified as those of newborn (and possibly unborn) human babies (Valentin Maldonado n.d.). That identification elevates this cultural phenomenon to a higher level of complexity, as it is evidence of the human sacrifice of children and possibly of ritual cannibalism as well. We know from various examples of Olmec monumental art that infants played a fundamental role in Olmec religious ideology. We await the additional information that physical anthropologists can glean from these skeletal remains, for example, whether there are dismemberment cut marks or evidence of anthropophagy, and whether these had been healthy children or show signs of some pathology.

From the Spanish chroniclers (Durán 1967; Sahagún 1981), we know that at the time of Spanish contact, child sacrifice was a common practice and was especially associated with the worship of water and fertility. The recent discoveries at the Templo Mayor of Tenochtitlán (Román Berrelleza 1990) are particularly relevant in this regard. However, we have no way of ascertaining if the infants at El Manatí were dead (sacrificed?) prior to being interred with the wooden busts, or if they drowned in the pit dug to deposit the offering of sculptures. Whatever the case, it is interesting that these infant interments always take a secondary position in these offerings of sculpture and were not important on their own.

It is also interesting to note that rubber balls occur in offerings in both the earliest (Manatí A) and latest (Macayal) phases, showing continuity in the custom of offering these particular objects. The major change in the rubber balls over time seems to be in their size: as already noted, the earliest are also the smallest. The two rubber balls from the Macayal phase were associated with wooden staffs, indicating that they are contemporaneous with the busts and clearly formed part of the paraphernalia associated with this ritual complex. The fact that a total of nine balls were found indicates the importance of rubber balls in these offerings. It is the first time in the history of Olmec archaeology that overwhelming evidence is found for the use of this material and its importance in Olmec rituals.

While we had originally thought the rubber balls were simply another category of object associated with the rituals, a stone "yoke" was recently given to us by the villagers, and they assured us that it had come from El Manatí and had been associated with burials that they had uncovered. If that is indeed true, the yoke adds another interpretative possibility—a possible relationship of the El Manatí offerings with the ball game (Ortíz, Rodríguez, and Delgado 1992).

Many questions remain unresolved, which we hope to answer with further research at El Manatí. For example, we do not know if the offerings were the product of one single community or if there were various communities that worshiped at this place. The relative closeness of San Lorenzo, Tenochtitlán, and other important centers offers the possibility that various peoples or pilgrims used this sacred spot. Furthermore, although the data appear to us to indicate that the sculpture interment was carried out at essentially one period in time, we cannot discard the possibility that the site may have been used subsequently for other offerings and that what we have excavated corresponds to only one ritual moment.

It appears obvious that the offerings at El Manatí were related mainly to the worship of the water and the hill. El Manatí was clearly a sacred place, for several elements important to Mesoamerican concepts of sacred geography are found united here. Johansson (1992: 15) says of such sacred places:

> Son ... los espacios naturales, donde la epifanía formal del relieve o de
> la vegetación revela los lugares predilectos del culto, y *los recintos sagrados*
> que, por una parte, traen la naturaleza a la urbe, y, por otra, marcan los
> límites que separan el espacio sacro de su homólogo profano. . . . los
> primeros ritos serán esencialmente *miméticos,* ya que buscarán imitar las

manifestaciones naturales según el cuadro cultural del grupo.

> These are natural spaces where the formal epiphany of the relief or the vegetation reveals the favored places of worship and the sacred precincts that, on the one hand, bring nature to the city and, on the other, mark the limits that separate sacred space from its profane counterpart . . . the first rites must have been essentially mimetic, since they sought to imitate natural phenomena according to the cultural frame of the group.

The springs emerging from the base of the Cerro Manatí fed a pool of water into which axes, jade beads, and pottery were thrown. A similar phenomenon, an Olmec offering of jade objects in water, was also found at Arroyo Pesquero (Beverido n.d.). The Cerro Manatí itself would have been an important geographic feature, and the site's location at the foot of such a prominent hill is analogous to Chalcatzingo (Grove 1987), Las Bocas (Coe 1965), and Teopantecuanitlán (Martínez Donjuan 1986), where the communities settled on the west side of an important elevation in their respective areas. Furthermore, the Cerro Manatí is apparently a source of red pigment (possibly hematite), an important natural resource for both local and regional exchange. A reason for the economic demand for that pigment is that red color almost certainly symbolizes blood. That symbolic importance may have been yet another factor making El Manatí a sacred place.

CONCLUSION

The data obtained at El Manatí allow us to highlight some actions that later became an important part of the religious ideology of the Classic and Post-Classic peoples, up to the Spanish Conquest according to the chroniclers. We see these similarities as analogous, and it is not our intent to make direct comparisons between the Formative period ritual behavior at El Manatí and rituals carried out in later periods in Mesoamerica, for we realize the pitfalls (e.g., Kubler 1962; compare Diehl 1989).

The objects recovered at El Manatí are obviously the material reflection of important ceremonial activities, of which only some objects or paraphernalia remain preserved. We will probably never know what prayers, songs or music, or food and drink were included in the rituals. These objects undoubtedly had a semiotic meaning as signs or icons obviously charged with symbolism. But how can we interpret them if, for the most part, we lack the knowledge of Olmec social, political, and economic organization, which is precisely what gives substance to these manifestations? Perhaps it would be best to avoid subjective speculations and to merely describe these offerings while awaiting more information, for in archaeology there are few other alternatives.

It is clear that we have at El Manatí the remains of activities associated with the worship of natural elements, especially of water in the form of springs, of the hills as attractors of the clouds and the rain, and the possible linking of these with communication with the ancestors, here represented by images carved in wood (compare Chalcatzingo Relief 1; Angulo 1987: 133–141). One can also consider the possibility that the sculptures were like the assistants of Tlaloc, that is, the *tlaloques, chaneques* or dwarfs, inhabitants of the hills and springs, who provided and controlled the rains and who hit the clouds with their staffs so that the clouds would unload this vital element, perhaps represented by the small figures with staffs surrounding the personages on La Venta stelae 2 and 3 (Drucker 1952: fig. 49; Drucker, Heizer, and Squier 1959: figs. 67, 68). Personages carrying staffs are common on later stelae and their staffs have been interpreted as symbols of authority. That suggests, as we noted earlier, that the wooden busts might be images of chiefs.

A further analogy is found in the cult and tradition of child sacrifice in ceremonies associated with water and the worship of fertility that continued until the Spanish Conquest. The cries and tears of these sacrificed infants propitiated the rains. We know that children occupied a central role in Olmec iconographic representations. For this reason, some researchers have suggested that "child gods" born of the mountains, the hills, and the caves reflect an Olmec origin myth. As Joralemon speculates (1971: 19), some Olmec ceremonies possibly sought to bring the infantlike "rain god" back to the human world and "may have marked the beginning of the Mexican rainy season and [were] almost certainly accompanied by the sacrifice of infants and small children." The greenstone axes may have symbolized the drops of rain, the crystalline waters that reflect the verdant vegetation or even the sea.

The piles of stone above some offerings may also have had major significance, possibly symbolizing the sacred hill where the gods of water and the *tlaloques* live and/or can be found. Piles of stone were important and venerated at the time of Spanish contact, and as Landa (1978) reports for the Maya area, were related to the cardinal points and to roads.

In the Olmec area of southern Veracruz and Tabasco, including in the Coatzacoalcos Basin around El Manatí, the problem was not a scarcity of water but rather of fresh water such as that found in springs, as opposed to the unhealthy waters of the marshes. The inhabitants of these areas battled the marshes and the long rainy season that threatened to flood the villages and devastate cropland, causing serious crises due to the lack of basic resources. For this reason, springs and their supply of fresh water were both important and sacred spaces. What objective would ritual activities and ceremonies at El Manatí, charged with elements of worship of fertility, water, the hills, and so on, have had? Were they to incur favor or to ask for clemency against the constant floods? At this time, while we are evaluating our data, we continue to be struck by the abundance of water in this region and all its great threats to the peoples of the area, and believe that the ritual activities must have been a great plea that the gods of water be more benevolent to the people.

The El Manatí offerings imply elaborate ritual behavior involving the participation of many people and a great quantity of magical objects. The rituals were carefully planned and executed, and various communities may have participated in the activities. It is difficult to know the motive that drove these people to carry out this grand rite, the burial of dozens of wood sculptures, human infants, jadeite or serpentine axes, animals, and other sacred objects. The offering certainly surpassed the mere eagerness of propitiatory rites. It must have corresponded to an exceptional event. The discovery is extremely interesting, not only for the variety and artistic quality of the recovered objects, but also because a careful analysis of the context of the offerings and of the site will allow us to delve into the magico-religious thought of the Olmec communities, their beliefs, gods, mythology, and other almost unknown aspects of this enigmatic culture.

Acknowledgments This project was cosponsored by the Instituto Nacional de Antropología e Historia and the Instituto de Antropología de la Universidad Veracruzana. Funding was provided by the Instituto Nacional de Antropología e Historia and the National Geographic Society. The Facultad de Antropología de la Universidad Veracruzana, the Instituto de Investigaciones Antropológicas and the Instituto de Biología of the Universidad Nacional Autónoma de México, and the Unidad Regional de Culturas Populares de Acayucan also collaborated. Support for the radiocarbon dates reported here was provided by Betty Meggers (for the two dates obtained from Beta Analytic) and Robert Santley (for the date provided by Geochron).

Editors' note The basic translation of this chapter from Spanish to English was done by Yasha Rodríguez. The chapter was edited by David Grove, following both the Spanish and English versions to insure accuracy, and reedited by Rosemary Joyce. The editors accept responsibility for any errors or omissions.

in almost all aspects of its material culture (Grove 1987a: 435). Its inhabitants were presumably linguistically[2] and ethnically quite different from the Gulf Coast Olmec. Therefore, in appraising the spatial distribution of Chalcatzingo's monuments and architecture, some obvious questions emerge. Does that distribution follow a Gulf Coast Olmec template that was adopted along with the monument technology and artistic canons? Or is Chalcatzingo's template different, such that any Olmec elements it might contain were merely added to a preexisting (Central Mexican) sacred landscape at the site? Those questions are particularly pertinent to understanding the nature of Chalcatzingo's interaction with Gulf Coast Olmec sites.

To make such a comparison of organizational templates, it is obviously also necessary to reconstruct the Gulf Coast Olmec templates. As at Chalcatzingo, this can be done through an analysis of monument placements and architectural associations at the two best-documented Gulf Coast Olmec centers—La Venta, Tabasco, and San Lorenzo Tenochtitlán, Veracruz. In carrying out those analyses it is recognized that there are some inherent problems, but no more so than with almost any other archaeological data. An initial concern in analyzing monument placement is that of monument chronology. The monuments at the sites under consideration were apparently created and erected at differing times during a period of up to seven hundred years. Furthermore, during that time many of those carvings were perhaps repositioned, mutilated, recycled (see Cyphers, this volume), or buried, and the sites themselves enlarged and modified. Moreover, there is the basic problem of sampling, for in no case has any center been completely excavated to reveal all possible monuments.

This analysis is carried out to ascertain if viable patterns *do* exist, problems notwithstanding. It is aided by the fact that because sacred landscapes follow fundamental cosmological templates, they tend to be conservative and maintained for centuries. Thus, even though a site may have been physically rebuilt and modified over time, its cosmological template could have remained substantially unaltered. In fact, several interesting co-occurring patterns are observable at the three sites under discussion. Those patterns suggest that a basic template—the result of adherence to certain structuring principles—was operable at those sites, that the template was long-lived (conservative), and that any site modifications and monument repositionings over time probably reproduced the long-established template.

---

[2] Although Nahuatl was the common language of Morelos in the sixteenth century, several linguists, including Hopkins (1984: 30–52) and Manrique Castañeda (1975: maps 5, 7), have suggested that during the Formative period the peoples of Morelos and adjacent areas of Guerrero spoke a language of the Otomanguean family, a family common across Central Mexico and the Oaxaca area.

David C. Grove

The following analyses focus primarily upon large and relatively immobile stone monuments. At both La Venta and Chalcatzingo those have restricted distributions that form a zone of monumental art that I shall refer to in this chapter as the Major Monument Zone (MMZ). I do so to avoid using any term for that zone that might be misunderstood or give the appearance of being emic. Furthermore, this chapter deals only with monument placement and the reconstruction of the sacred landscape within that zone. What mundane uses the MMZ may also have had at the sites under analysis is not discussed, particularly because in most instances that use remains to be archaeologically ascertained.

For clarity and space considerations, bibliographic citations for the individual monuments mentioned in this chapter are presented in an Appendix.

CHALCATZINGO'S MONUMENTS AND THEIR DISTRIBUTIONS

Chalcatzingo is one of only two pre-500 B.C. sites in Central Mexico with both stone monuments and public mound architecture (e.g., Grove 1984, 1987c); the other site is Teopantecuanitlán, Guerrero (Martínez Donjuan 1982, 1985, 1986; Grove 1989: 142–145).[3] The Formative period village at Chalcatzingo was situated on a terraced hillside extending northward from the base of the Cerro Chalcatzingo and the Cerro Delgado, two imposing mountains that rise abruptly from the floor of the Amatzinac Valley in eastern Morelos. Most of the site's 31 known monuments occur in three spatially distinct settings: two major groupings on the Cerro Chalcatzingo and a third major cluster on several lower terraces within the settlement area (Fig. 1). Those three groupings define the Major Monument Zone, and the few solitary monuments at the site will not be considered in this general analysis. All of Chalcatzingo's monuments for which stratigraphic context can be ascertained were erected during the late Middle Formative Cantera phase, ca. 700–500 B.C. Those carvings that cannot be dated archaeologically can also be assigned to the Cantera phase on stylistic grounds (Grove 1987b: 426–430; 1989: 132–142).

The Cerro Chalcatzingo Carvings

The Formative period occupants of Chalcatzingo, and indeed the Pre-Hispanic peoples of eastern Morelos in general, most probably considered the Cerro Chalcatzingo to be a sacred mountain (see, e.g., Cook de Leonard 1967; Angulo

---

[3] The Teopantecuanitlán data are still being prepared for publication by Guadalupe Martínez Donjuan, and Kent Reilly has been independently investigating that site's sacred landscape. I have therefore not attempted an analysis of Teopantecuanitlán for this chapter.

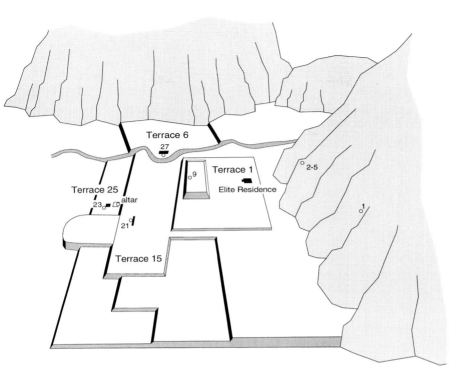

Fig. 1 Schematic view of Chalcatzingo, showing the platform mound (*center*) and monument distribution. North is to the left. Drawing by Marie J. Zeidler and David Grove.

1987: 157; Grove 1972: 36; 1987b: 430–432). It is important to note in this regard that the two groups of carvings specifically associated with that mountain are thematically "mythico-supernatural" (Grove 1984: 109–122).

Chalcatzingo's most famous bas-relief, "El Rey" (Monument 1; Fig. 2), is situated high on the mountainside, where it is the principal carving in a group of six bas-reliefs executed directly onto exposed rock faces there (Fig. 1). These reliefs occur adjacent to a natural watercourse for rainwater runoff, and rain is the major interrelating iconographic theme of these monuments. The "El Rey" carving depicts a personage seated within a large niche that is represented by a sectioned quatrefoil. That half-quatrefoil is marked with iconographic motifs that show it as the mouth of a supernatural creature and identify it as a "mountain cave." Rain clouds with falling !-shaped raindrops hang over the cave, and similar raindrop motifs also decorate the

259

Fig. 2 Chalcatzingo Monument 1, "El Rey."

costume of the personage. "Mist" scrolls are shown emanating from the mouth of the cave.

The other five small reliefs (Monuments 6/7, 8, 11, 14, and 15) occur as a linear series running eastward from Monument 1. While each of these carvings is slightly different in one or two minor details (Grove 1987b: table 27.1), they all depict the same basic scene: a small saurian creature crouched atop a scroll motif and peering upward at a rain cloud with falling !-shaped raindrops. In three of the five carvings a squash plant is depicted below the saurian and scroll. As Jorge Angulo (1987: 133) has noted, the linear arrangement of the bas-reliefs suggests that they may have composed a purposeful pictorial sequence. Because they are spaced several meters apart, it also means that they cannot be viewed simultaneously as a group. To see them, a viewer must walk from carving to carving, a positioning of monuments that I shall refer to throughout this chapter as a "processional arrangement."

The cerro's second cluster of carvings also consists of six bas-reliefs, but they are executed on boulders and stone slabs on the talus slope at the foot of the mountain (Fig. 1). Five of these carvings occur in a linear, spaced, processional arrangement. They are relatively large carvings and primarily depict supernatural zoomorphic creatures dominating generalized human figures: a large reptilianlike creature grasping a human figure in its mouth (Monument 5); two felines with supernatural features, pouncing with claws extended onto two prostrate humans (Monument 4); a recumbent feline beside a cactuslike plant (Monument 3; Angulo [1987: 144] has discovered a probable subordinate human figure in a damaged area of the carving); and a recently discovered carving showing a snarling feline atop a prone human figure (Monument 31; Fig. 3). These reliefs probably illustrate a sequence of mythical events important in the cosmogony of the peoples of Chalcatzingo.

The fifth relief (Monument 2), at the west end of the series, is best described as depicting a ritual involving four human actors. Three of them are standing and masked; the fourth is seated, and his mask has been turned to the back of his head. The headdress worn by one of the standing participants in the ritual replicates the motifs adorning the head of one of Monument 4's felines. This correspondence suggests that the ritual scene was related in some manner to the mythological events displayed by the other monuments in the sequence.

Fig. 3 Chalcatzingo Monument 31.

A sixth talus carving, Monument 13, was found downhill from the larger boulder reliefs. It portrays a supernatural anthropomorphic being with a cleft head, seated within the quatrefoil mouth of a supernatural creature. The carving is therefore iconographically similar to Monument 1, higher on the same hillside.

Monuments within the Habitation Zone (Fig. 1)

The hillside terracing begins at the base of the cerro's talus slopes. The Formative period settlement is situated on these terraces, and the uppermost major terrace (Terrace 1) was apparently a principal precinct of the Formative period village. It was the location of Chalcatzingo's major elite residence (PC-Structure 1), at its southern edge. Its northern edge is dominated by the settlement's largest public architectural construction, a massive 70 m long, 7 m tall Formative period earthen platform mound (PC-Structure 4). The platform mound and the elite residence on Terrace 1 are separated by a 1 ha "plaza" area. It is notable that no monumental art has been discovered within that plaza area.

At least one carving, Monument 9 (Fig. 4), had apparently been erected atop the large platform mound (Grove and Angulo 1987: 124; Prindiville and Grove 1987: 63). This large stone slab is decorated with a supernatural's frontal face created by a quatrefoil mouth surmounted by eyes and eyebrow elements. The cruciform center of the quatrefoil is hollow, and wear along the lower edge of the gaping mouth might have been caused during the monument's ritual use as a passageway (Angulo 1987: 141; Grove 1984: 50).

The three terraces immediately downhill (north) from the imposing earthen platform mound constitute the third major monument locality (Fig. 1). Each of these terraces (Terraces 6, 15, 25) is the location of a low stone-faced Cantera phase platform structure. The platform dimensions range from 15 to 20 m in length and 0.5 to 1.3 m in height. A carved stela had been erected adjacent to each platform: Monument 21 (Terrace 15), Monument 23 (Terrace 25), and Monument 27 (Terrace 6). Two additional stelae (Monuments 26 and 28) and a round altar (Monument 25) were also uncovered on Terrace 6. Although most of the five stelae had been mutilated, several were sufficiently intact to determine that their bas-relief carvings depict individual personages. This emphasis on displaying specific individuals, and later "decapitating" these monuments, is a major feature of Gulf Coast Olmec monumental art (e.g., Angulo 1987: 155; Grove 1981, 1987b: 423). Because these carvings deal with specific personages, probably the rulers of the site, I have classified the general theme of the monuments as "political" and "rulership" (Grove 1984: 49–68). The decapitated statue of a seated personage (Monument 16), found 60 years ago by Eulalia Guzmán

Fig. 4   Chalcatzingo Monument 9.

in a small gully that separates Terrace 6 and Terrace 15 (Guzmán 1934: fig. 10, no. 6), is consistent with the rulership theme of that site area.

The rulership theme is further reiterated on Terrace 25 by the presence of a large tabletop altar, Monument 22 (Fash 1987). Such altars are an important monument type at Gulf Coast centers and appear to have functioned symbolically as a ruler's "throne" or seat of power (Coe and Diehl 1980: 294; Grove 1973: 135; 1981: 64). Chalcatzingo's Monument 22 is the only tabletop altar ever discovered outside of a Gulf Coast Olmec center and is of further interest because it is situated within an unusual architectural feature, a large rectangular, stone-walled sunken patio (Fash 1987: figs. 7.1, 7.4).

Such sunken patios constitute a sacred space that symbolically represents an entrance or interface to the infraworld, and thus the Monument 22 altar sits within that interface. Symbolic infraworld interfaces frequently occur in the architecture of Mesoamerican sites in forms such as sunken or enclosed plaza areas and ballcourts (e.g., Gillespie 1991: 339; Schele and Freidel 1991: 291). A large sunken walled patio contemporaneous with Chalcatzingo's occurs at Teopantecuanitlán, Guerrero (Martínez Donjuan 1982, 1985, 1986). That center seems to have had significant ties with Chalcatzingo (Grove 1987b: 429; 1989: 142–145) and may have been its closest regional peer during the Middle Formative period. The present archaeological data suggest that such sunken patios may be an architectural form distinctive of Formative period Central Mexico (i.e., Teopantecuanitlán and Chalcatzingo).[4]

Chalcatzingo's Sacred Landscape

The sacred landscape at Chalcatzingo combines natural *sacred geography* (i.e., geographic features with sacred symbolism; e.g., Vogt 1981) with a constructed landscape. The Cerro Chalcatzingo, at the southern periphery of the settlement area, was clearly an integral part of the site's cosmological template, for it is the location of two groups of mythico-supernatural carvings. These two groups of carvings communicated different messages. Cloud and rain symbols predominate in the reliefs high on the hillside adjacent to a natural rainwater drainage channel. On the other hand, depictions of zoomorphic supernaturals dominating humans prevail in the reliefs on the talus at the base of the mountain.

The constructed landscape begins with Terrace 1 at the base of the talus slopes. This terrace was the location of an elite residence, and there is no evidence that monuments had ever been erected in this area. The site's massive earthen platform mound delimits the northern (downhill) edge of the terrace, and a large quatrefoil supernatural face (Monument 9), had apparently been erected atop the mound. The presence of two similar quatrefoil supernatural faces on the Cerro Chalcatzingo (Monuments 1 and 13), and the overall "mountain" symbolism of these quatrefoils (Angulo 1987: 140–142; Grove 1987b: 427), suggest that Monument 9's placement on the massive earthen platform may have identified that platform mound as a "sacred mountain" within the site's constructed landscape.

---

[4] Ann Cyphers (this volume) reports evidence of a wall behind San Lorenzo Monument 14, a large tabletop altar, and suggests the possibility that the wall is part of a sunken patio, a prospect that remains to be further tested archaeologically. Radiocarbon dates from the Teopantecuanitlán patio (Martínez Donjuan 1986: 77), suggest its earliest construction phase may date to ca. 1400 B.C.

To the north, on the three terraces immediately beyond the platform mound (Terraces 6, 15, 25), are low stone-faced platforms and monuments depicting personages. Terrace 25 is also the location of a sunken patio and tabletop altar. Rulership is the dominant theme in monuments in this site sector.

A definite north-south spatial dichotomy is manifested in the monument distribution and themes at Chalcatzingo, and the northern and southern sectors of the site's MMZ are physically separated by the great platform mound. Rulership monuments and stone-faced platforms occur in the sector north of that platform, and the mythico-supernatural carvings are in the sector to its south. In the far south, high on the natural sacred mountain, a "sky cave" entrance to the otherworld is depicted (Monument 1), while its complementary opposite, a sunken patio—an entrance to the earthly otherworld—is positioned in the far north. There is also a general symmetry to the north-south monument placements. In terms of actual measured linear distance, the earthen platform that separates the northern and southern sectors is positioned midway between the northernmost and southernmost carvings (Cerro Chalcatzingo Monuments 1 and 2–5, Terrace 25's Monument 23).

LA VENTA'S MONUMENTS AND THEIR DISTRIBUTIONS

The easternmost Gulf Coast Olmec center, La Venta, situated on the humid, tropical coastal plains of Tabasco, is notable for its abundance of both stone monuments and earthen mound architecture. La Venta's complex of mounds extends for more than a kilometer and is dominated near its north end by one of Middle Formative Mesoamerica's largest pyramid structures, the 30 m tall Mound C-1 (see González 1988: fig. 1; Adams 1991: map 3-2). Robert Heizer (1968: 15–21) was one of the first scholars to suggest that Mound C-1, built atop a raised basal platform, symbolized a sacred mountain. Most of La Venta's 80 known monuments occur in and around the mound-plaza groups designated as Complexes A and B, immediately to the north and south of Mound C-1 (Fig. 5).

Complex A extends northward from the foot of Mound C-1's basal platform. The enclosed plaza area of this architectural complex is renowned in the history of Olmec archaeology, for it has been the focus of nearly all the significant archaeological research conducted at La Venta prior to 1985. The 1942–43 excavations of Stirling and Drucker (Drucker 1952) and the 1955 research of Drucker, Heizer, and Squier (1959), both within Complex A, uncovered some of the most spectacular Olmec creations ever found. These included great buried mosaic pavements, massive offerings of serpentine blocks, caches of jade celts, and major tombs. The latter may be the graves of several of La Venta's

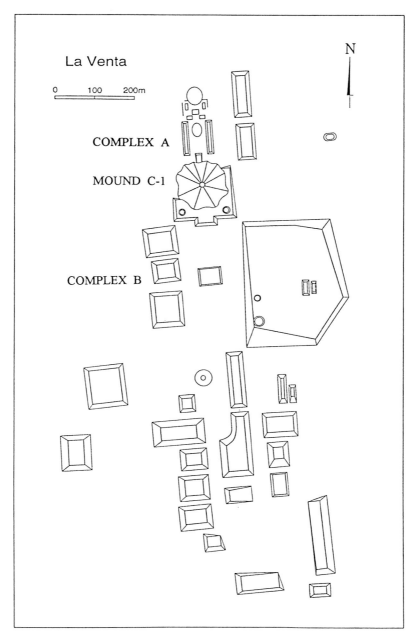

Fig. 5 La Venta, showing locations of Mound C-1 and Complexes A and B. Drawing by Marie J. Zeidler.

rulers. Many of these discoveries occurred along a north–south axis bisecting the complex. This axis can also be extended further south to bisect Mound C-1 and Complex B as well. In some instances the extended axis is relevant to the monument placements described below.

Until recently (González 1988; Heizer, Graham, and Napton 1968), Complex B had received comparatively little archaeological attention. The complex extends southward from Mound C-1's basal platform and includes a 7 ha plaza area ("Plaza B") whose perimeter is well defined by platform mound architecture, including the large raised "Stirling Acropolis" along the plaza's east side. Although the architecture of Complex B is not well dated, the visible mounds of both Complexes B and A appear to be Middle Formative period constructions. The monument distributions in both of these areas are most easily discussed in terms of their form categories.

Colossal Heads (Fig. 6)

The Olmec are perhaps best known to the public as the creators of colossal stone heads. These heads are "personage" carvings and seem to be portraits of individual Olmec rulers (Coe 1977: 186; Grove 1981: 65–67), either as living ruler or revered ancestor. Their placement within a site's sacred landscape must therefore be considered from the perspectives of both rulership and ancestors. Only 4 of the 17 known Olmec colossal heads occur at La Venta. Heads 2, 3, and 4 were found ca. 110 m beyond Complex A (Drucker 1952: 9) and constitute the northernmost monument grouping at La Venta. They had been arranged "facing north, forming an irregular line approximately 100 m. east to west" (1952: 9). In contrast, the fourth, Head 1, had been positioned south of Mound C-1, in Plaza B.

Altars (Fig. 7)

Several different monument forms at La Venta have been classified as "altars," sculptures that, as noted earlier, seem associated with rulership. Five of La Venta's nine altars are of the tabletop variety, large rectangular monuments distinguished by their projecting upper ledge and large frontal niche with a seated personage. Two subtypes of tabletop altars can be distinguished: Type A, which depict only the seated personage within the niche (La Venta Altars 3, 4, 6), and Type B, in which the niched personage holds a "baby" (La Venta Altars 2, 5). Non-tabletop altars are Altars 1, 7, and 8, and possibly also Monument 59.

Although the nine monuments listed above include several very different forms of altars, eight of these carvings are located in Plaza B south of Mound

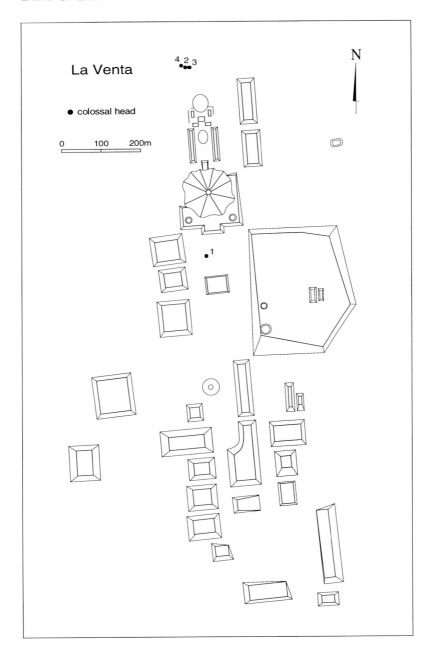

Fig. 6 La Venta, the distribution of colossal heads. Drawing by Marie J. Zeidler.

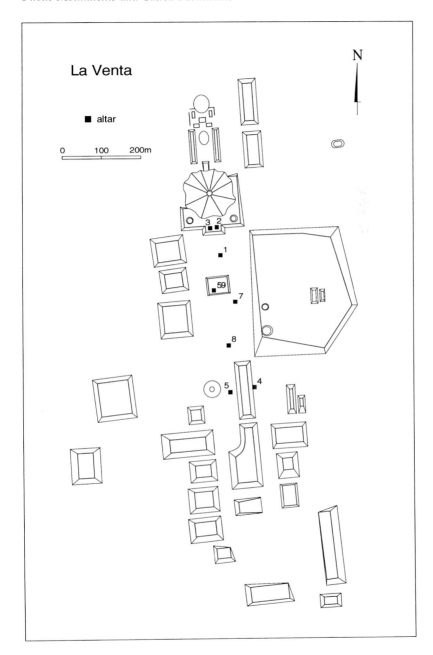

Fig. 7 La Venta, the distribution of altars. Drawing by Marie J. Zeidler.

C-1,[5] and they comprise the majority of the major monuments displayed in that large plaza area. Their distribution within the plaza is also informative. The tabletop altars occur only at the north and south extremities of Plaza B, and in both instances occur as Type A-and-B pairs. The southern pair, Altars 4 [Type A] and 5 [Type B], are arranged on opposite sides of a low range mound (Mound D-8), where they are positioned so that they create an east-west alignment with a conical mound, D-1, in the plaza. That alignment seems deliberate and may have demarcated the plaza's southern limit. More than 400 m north, at the upper edge of Mound C-1's basal platform, are Altars 2 [Type B] and 3 [Type A].

A special configuration also occurs in the altar pairs: the Type A and B altars were positioned to face in opposite directions. Although this might be considered as merely coincidental in the case of Altars 4 and 5, erected on opposite sides of Mound D-8, the same opposition occurs with Altars 2 and 3 on the basal platform below Mound C-1, and it is more convincing there. Altar 2 faces onto Plaza B, and thus its frontal scene would have been visible to viewers on the plaza. In contrast, Altar 3 was apparently positioned facing toward Mound C-1, and therefore its main imagery would not have been visible to those viewers. In both pairs, the Type B altars (personages holding babies) face toward the plaza, and Type A altars face away from that area.

Spaced nearly equidistantly across Plaza B, between altar pairs 2-3 and 4-5, are Altars 1, 7, and 8. All occur east of the site's north-south axis, except for smaller Monument 59 found on Mound B-4 (Clewlow and Corson 1968: end map). The wide (ca. 110 m) spacing between these various altars means that even if the plaza area was an entirely open vista, the monuments nevertheless could only have been viewed individually, suggesting that their positioning reflects a purposeful processional arrangement.

Stelae (Fig. 8)

Stelae are a monument form that appears to have gained importance only late in Olmec prehistory, at which time they became the medium for displaying low-relief images of personages and supernaturals. La Venta's three most famous stelae—Stelae 1, 2, and 3—all depict particular personages. Stelae 1 and 3 were both found in Complex A north of Pyramid C-1. Stela 1, in relatively high relief, depicts a personage standing within a rectangular niche that is marked

[5] La Venta Altar 6 occurs outside the MMZ in Complex F (the "Cerro Encantada"), ca. 700 m northwest of Complex A (González 1988: fig. 1; Adams 1991: map 3-2). Stylistically, it is a very late carving.

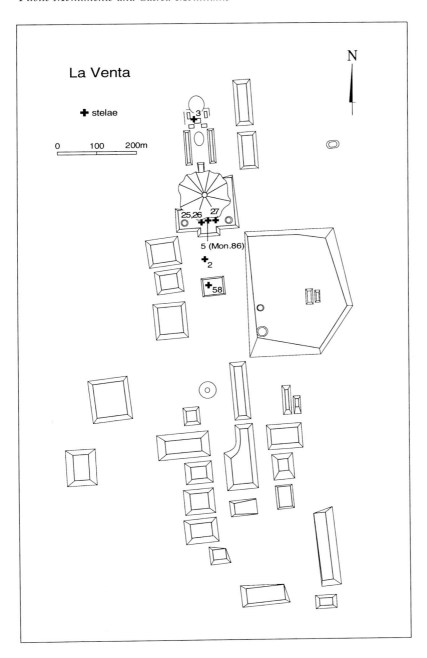

Fig. 8 La Venta, the distribution of stelae. Drawing by Marie J. Zeidler.

iconographically as the mouth of a supernatural creature, that is, an otherworld entrance. It is notable that the stela had been erected a few meters west of Tomb C in alignment with that tomb's large stone crypt grave (Drucker 1952: fig. 14). Stela 3, with a "narrative" scene showing two personages, was positioned in the area of Complex A referred to as the "Ceremonial Court" and hidden behind the columnar basalt wall that enclosed that area. In contrast, Stela 2 was erected on Plaza B south of Mound C-1. There it was situated adjacent to Colossal Head 1, and both monuments were openly displayed. All three stelae occur west of the site's north–south axis.

Although Stelae 1, 2, and 3 are among the best known of La Venta's monuments, several large green schist stelae have been found at the site but have not received the attention they deserve. These green schist stelae all occur in the Plaza B area, and all are carved with great supernatural faces (Fig. 9). One of these, Monument 58, had stood on Mound B-4 in Plaza B (Clewlow and Corson 1968: end map). The more important pair, Monuments 25/26 and 27, were erected at the southern base of great pyramid Mound C-1, where they are positioned so that they flank the mound's north–south axis. Monument 86 (Stela 5), a recently discovered stela with a mythico-supernatural scene depicting four personages, one of whom is descending from the sky, stands between Monuments 25/26 and 27 (González 1988: fig. 1; 1994).

Other Carvings (Fig. 10)

Unlike the massive altars, stelae, and colossal heads, which are essentially immobile, smaller carvings such as anthropomorphic statues were more readily portable. Several of these could have been used in rituals or moved from place to place, therefore the locations at which they were discovered are relevant in only the most general terms. Those carvings for which provenience data are available primarily cluster around the periphery of Plaza B, including east of the plaza on the Stirling Acropolis. The virtual absence of small monuments in Plaza B itself suggests that none had been permanently displayed there.

A few smaller monuments were found in Complex A, primarily within the enclosed Ceremonial Court. Three additional carvings—Monuments 19, 20, and 21—had been positioned north of Complex A near Colossal Heads 2, 3, and 4.

La Venta's Sacred Landscape

The northern limit of the Major Monument Zone at La Venta is defined by Colossal Heads 2, 3, and 4, and is separated from the southernmost monuments, Altars 4 and 5, by a distance of ca. 840 m. Mound C-1 is situated near the midpoint of that distribution, effectively separating the zone into a northern

Fig. 9 La Venta stela Monument 25/26.

and a southern sector. The majority of the principal monuments at the site—seven altars, a stela, and a colossal head—were positioned in the southern sector within Plaza B. They are all monuments which by their very size, and by their placement in a processional arrangement in that large open area, could visually communicate their iconographic messages to many viewers at one time. The north end of Plaza B is dominated by the wide elevated apron of Mound C-1's basal platform, and it is therefore notable that the other architecture surrounding the plaza is likewise comprised of platform mounds, that is, mounds that in many instances could have functioned as

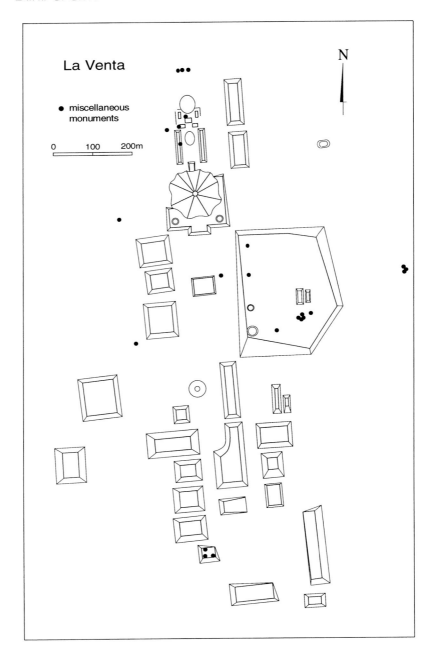

Fig. 10 La Venta, the distribution of miscellaneous monuments.
Drawing by Marie J. Zeidler.

elevated "stages" for rituals meant to be viewed by people gathered within the plaza. The southern sector of La Venta's MMZ seems to be accessible public space, an area in which rulership/personage monuments were displayed in a processional arrangement, and thus an area in which public ritual activities probably took place. Many of these rituals may have been related to the monuments. Even the vast majority of the site's smaller monuments for which there are provenience data are found on the east and west fringes of Complex B.

In contrast, in the northern sector, the major objects and offerings in Complex A were not meant to be accessed or viewed. Complex A is a restricted precinct partially enclosed by long range mounds. It is an area of major tombs, and the elaborate offerings found there were *buried* and thus were not meant to be viewed or accessed. Even the few monuments situated within Complex A, such as Stela 3, were not openly displayed but were hidden behind the large wall of columnar basalt pillars of the complex's Ceremonial Court.

The cosmological meaning of the sacred landscape represented in the northern sector can be inferred from the presence of major tombs there: north is the realm of the ancestors and the past and probably also a sky realm.[6] The placement of three colossal heads 110 m beyond Complex A, in the far north, is consistent with that cosmological referent, for in the Middle Formative sacred landscape represented at La Venta, these Early Formative period portrait carvings of Olmec rulers would indeed be the *ancestors*. The fact that these three heads were not buried, but visible and positioned to create "an irregular line approximately 100 m. east to west" (Drucker 1952: 9), implies that they too had been spaced in a processional arrangement and were meant to be viewed.

An interesting contrast is manifested in the positioning of the major monuments openly displayed within the northern and southern sectors. Those in the southern sector are spaced along the central area of the sector, while tombs and buried offerings occur in the central area of the northern sector and the displayed monuments occur at that sector's perimeter. That basic north-south dichotomy, and the separation of those two sectors by Mound C-1, the constructed "sacred mountain," was clearly a significant aspect of La Venta's template. However, the MMZ's center-line axis also

---

[6] A number of scholars have pointed out the association of north with the celestial/sky realm in Classic Maya cosmology, and Ashmore's (1989, 1992) analyses of Classic Maya sacred landscapes discuss that correlation very well. For a variety of reasons, aspects of Complex A (and particularly the Ceremonial Court area) also seem to have associations with a celestial otherworld. Susan Gillespie has called my attention to the association between "north" and "the past" in some other Mesoamerican cosmologies.

created an east and west division that produces a lesser pattern: altars are positioned east of the axis and colossal heads and stelae west of it.

SAN LORENZO'S MONUMENTS AND THEIR DISTRIBUTIONS

San Lorenzo is situated 60 km inland from the Gulf of Mexico, atop a long plateau that rises ca. 50 m above the floodplains of the Coatzacoalcos and Chiquito Rivers. The plateau area had been artificially built up in Olmec and pre-Olmec times to create a space more than 1,100 m long and up to 700 m wide (Coe 1968: 44–46; 1981: 119; Coe and Diehl 1980: 27–28, map 2). That remodeling of the hilltop required organization and planning, and was certainly carried out for reasons that transcended the mundane: it arguably created the basic sacred landscape at San Lorenzo. More than sixty monuments have been found on the plateau, and several smaller sites situated several kilometers from the plateau—Tenochtitlán, Potrero Nuevo, Los Treinta, and El Azuzul—also have a few monuments (see Fig. 14). The monuments of these peripheral sites are discussed in a separate section of this chapter.

The reconstructible pattern of monument distribution at San Lorenzo exhibits some distinct differences from that of La Venta. Some of the variation may be due to the fact that the sites are not completely contemporaneous. San Lorenzo has more Early Formative period monuments, such as colossal heads, while late Middle Formative period monuments, such as stelae, are rare there. Similarly, San Lorenzo lacks a major earthen mound comparable to La Venta's C-1, and mound-plaza groups dating to the site's Olmec occupation have not yet been distinguished there. Although the Group A mounds and the Mound C3-1 pyramid in the center of the San Lorenzo plateau have a layout reminiscent of La Venta's Complex A (see, e.g., Figs. 10–12), they seem to be Early Postclassic constructions (Coe and Diehl 1980: 29, 388, fig. 12). The possible exceptions are one or two small mounds, exposed in stratigraphic cuts, that may have been constructed in the late Middle Formative period Palangana phase (1980: 62–71, 200–201, figs. 44, 45). Finally, while the zones of monument distribution at La Venta and Chalcatzingo comprise one-third or less of the total site areas there, the major monuments at San Lorenzo occur across nearly the entire upper surface of the plateau, and the MMZ and main site area are essentially equivalent.[7]

---

[7] Ann Cyphers' current research at San Lorenzo (e.g., Cyphers, this volume; personal communication) indicates that the total site area is even greater, also encompassing the terraces and hillslopes below and beyond the upper surface of the plateau.

Colossal Heads (Fig. 11)

In 1994 San Lorenzo's tenth colossal head was discovered. Only about half of these heads occur in good archaeological contexts, however, and the remainder have been found in the *barrancas* that have eroded into the plateau over the centuries. Therefore, only general observations can be inferred from the positioning of the heads.

Three of the heads (2, 4, and 7) occur in the northeastern quarter of the San Lorenzo plateau, and the other seven have been found along the sides of the South-Central Ridge (1, 3, 5, 6, 8, 9, 10). Colossal heads are absent in the north-central area of the plateau, creating an interval of separation between the northern and southern heads of more than 300 m. In both areas the individual heads are spaced more than 100 m from each other, perhaps again representing a processional arrangement, particularly in the cases of heads 2, 4, and 7 (north) and heads 1, 6, 9, and 10 (south).

Altars (Fig. 12)

Only two unequivocal tabletop altars have been found at San Lorenzo. Monument 20 (Type B) was found in the far northwest area of the plateau. Monument 14 (Type A) is positioned in the west-central sector of the site. Although separated by more than 400 m, these two altars are in a virtual north-south alignment.[8]

Evidence suggests that several other tabletop altars had also been displayed on the plateau at some time. Monument 18, in the southeastern corner of the South-Central Ridge, is apparently the basal fragment of a tabletop altar. The stone's low-relief carving depicts a pair of dwarfs, each with one upraised arm, as if to "support" the missing tabletop. Monument 60, on the east side of the plateau near head 1—and nearly due north of Monument 18—may likewise be a basal fragment. The most interesting evidence, however, is the astute observation by James Porter (1989) that oddly sculpted areas on two of the site's colossal heads (2 and 7) indicate that these monuments had been altars before being recarved into their present form.

Four other carvings have also been classified as altars at San Lorenzo: two large rectangular stone slabs, Monuments 8 and 51, and two "circular altars,"

---

[8] It is also notable that while separated by almost one km, the northernmost and southernmost colossal heads, 4 (north) and 3 (south), are in a virtual north-south alignment, and heads 5 and 8 are positioned close to that alignment line. However, because of *barranca* erosion, the discovery location of head 3 may be only approximate to its original position on the plateau.

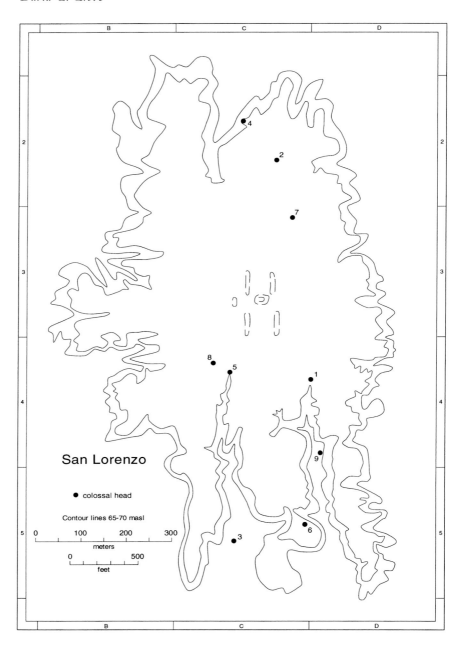

Fig. 11 San Lorenzo, the distribution of colossal heads. North is at top of map. Drawing by Marie J. Zeidler.

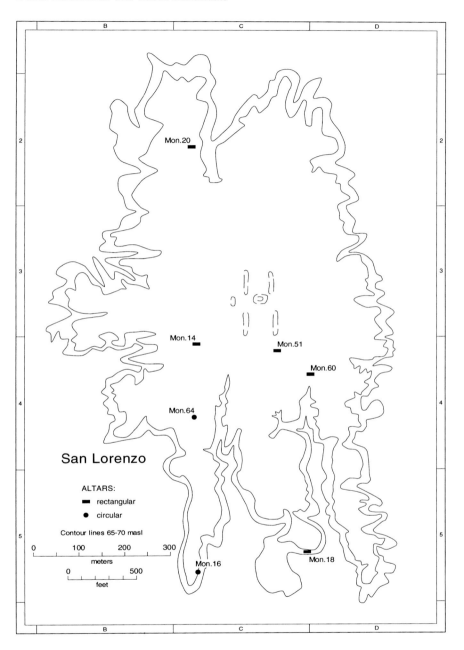

Fig. 12 San Lorenzo, the distribution of altars. North is at top of map. Drawing by Marie J. Zeidler.

279

Monuments 16 and 64. Both rectangular slabs are positioned in the same general east-west "latitude" of the plateau as the Monument 14 and 60 altars. On the other hand, the "circular altars" are located on the plateau's Southwest Ridge. There they appear to be positioned along an extension of the north-south alignment formed by Monuments 14 and 20.

Other Carvings (Fig. 13)

The majority of smaller monuments on the plateau occur along the Group C and D ridges, in the western-central sector of the site, away from most of the major monuments. These smaller carvings consist primarily of anthropomorphic and zoomorphic statues. Based upon her recent excavations of the Group D Ridge, Ann Cyphers (this volume) suggests that monument recycling and recarving took place in that site area, a function that may partly explain the large number of fragmentary and smaller monuments found there.

San Lorenzo's Sacred Landscape

Even though San Lorenzo lacks a major mound, the north-south dichotomy that is basic to the organizational template at Chalcatzingo and La Venta is nevertheless present. The majority of the large monuments occur in the southern half of the plateau. The southern sector begins with an east-to-west band of altars (Monuments 8, 14, 51, 60) located just below the site's midline. Seven colossal heads occur to the south of these altars. There they are widely spaced and could have been viewed only one at a time. That fact, and the possible linear positioning of heads 1, 6, 9, implies that they are arranged processionally. As at La Venta, this southern sector was the area in which rulership/personage monuments were displayed.

Only four major monuments are presently known in the entire northern sector, an altar (Monument 20; Type B) and three colossal heads. All these monuments were positioned near the outer limits of the northern sector. Only a few traces of possible Olmec period architecture occur in the extensive north-central area of the plateau, that is, the zone equivalent to the location of Mound C-1 and Complex A at La Venta,[9] and these seem to date to the Late Middle Formative period (Palangana phase) after San Lorenzo's "apogee." Whereas at La Venta the elaborate tombs of Complex A helped identify north as symbolically the realm of "ancestors," no such tombs have yet been discovered at San

---

[9] Interestingly, the site's modest Early Postclassic period Group A Mounds are positioned at the same equivalent template location as La Venta's Mound C-1 and Complex A. While perhaps coincidental, it is as if their placement was governed by a very long-lived template.

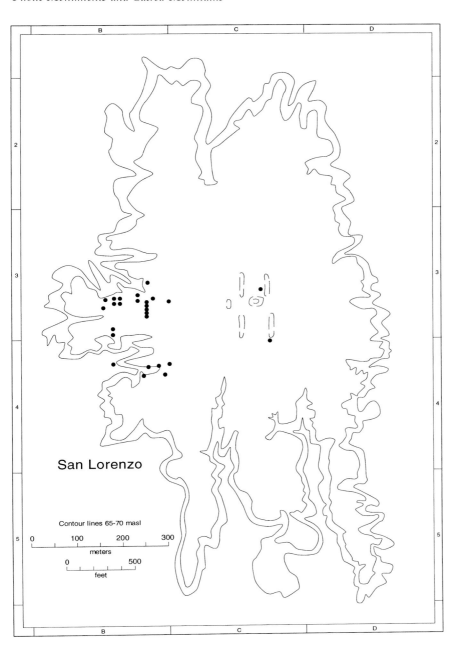

Fig. 13 San Lorenzo, the distribution of miscellaneous monuments. North is at top of map.
Drawing by Marie J. Zeidler.

Lorenzo. Therefore, attributing a similar cosmological significance to that site's northern sector is more problematical.

As noted above, James Porter (1989) has observed that two colossal heads at San Lorenzo had been recarved from their original monument form, altars. That physical transformation, from ruler's "thrones" to ruler's portrait heads, was a significant symbolic transformation as well. These conversions were presumably carried out following the death of the rulers, that is, when they themselves were transformed into ancestors. Therefore, it is perhaps meaningful that precisely these two heads, 2 and 7, were both positioned in the northern sector. Similarly, the heavily "mutilated" condition of the northern sector's tabletop altar (Monument 20) may perhaps reflect the initial stages of the recarving process intended to convert that altar into another ancestral colossal head for that sector.

Only generalized east-west differentiations appear in the monument patterns. In the western portion of the plateau a north-south line is created by the site's two tabletop altars, Monuments 14 and 20. If that line is used as a referent, almost all massive monuments—including all colossal heads—occur east of the line, while virtually all small monuments are found west of it.

THE SAN LORENZO PERIPHERY AND SACRED LANDSCAPE

The majority of the carvings at the sites peripheral to San Lorenzo—Tenochtitlán, Potrero Nuevo, El Azuzul, and Los Treinta (Fig. 14)—are thematically different from those on the plateau. The exact nature of these sites, and of the positioning of their monuments in relation to mound groups, plazas, or other features, remains to be determined. Nevertheless, even lacking such data, these monuments aid in understanding San Lorenzo's sacred landscape.

Seven of the twelve carvings at these sites depict felines, usually shown as snarling or in "dominating" positions over humans. For example, Matthew Stirling (1955: 8) described Tenochtitlán Monument 1 as "an anthropomorphic jaguar seated on a human figure" and Potrero Nuevo Monument 3 as possibly representing "copulation between a jaguar and a woman." However, as others have noted, these carvings more likely represent aggression and domination (Davis 1978: 454; Medellín 1960: 95). Furthermore, two of the four monuments recently discovered at El Azuzul are snarling felines. In contrast, the few feline carvings found at San Lorenzo (e.g., Monuments 7, 37, 77) do not display any aggressiveness.

Aggressive felines are clearly a major component of the peripheral monuments, but other carvings occur there as well. Potrero Nuevo Monument 2, one of the most frequently published of all Olmec monuments, is a tabletop

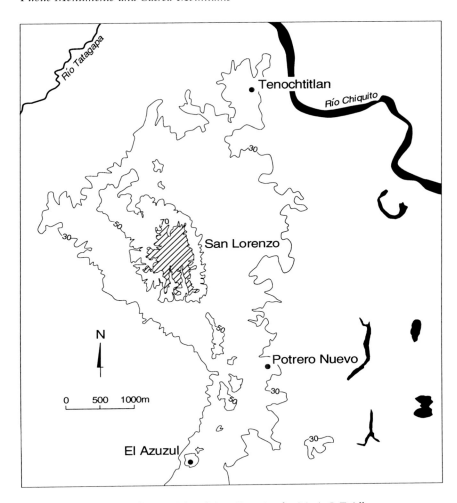

Fig. 14 San Lorenzo and its peripheral sites. Drawing by Marie J. Zeidler.

altar carved with the images of two supernatural dwarfs, their arms raised above their heads as if supporting the tabletop. Furthermore, a few personage/rulership statues also occur at the peripheral sites (e.g., Los Treinta, Monument 5; Xochiltepec ejido monument).

The contrasts between the monuments at the actual site of San Lorenzo and those on its periphery seem explainable by the general cosmology of Mesoamerican peoples, where an important distinction is made between center and periphery (see e.g., Hanks 1990: 306–307; Taggart 1983: 55–56). The

283

center symbolizes inhabited space, the village, while the periphery is a place of the supernatural and of danger. As Taggart (1983: 55) explains: "The center is represented with words standing for the human community. . . . The center represents the moral order. . . . It is juxtaposed against the periphery." The latter is identified with the word "forest." Encounters with the personified forces of nature take place more often in the periphery. Within that paradigm, therefore, the carvings involving dwarfs, or jaguars dominating humans, pertain to the periphery. Their locations—Tenochtitlán, Potrero Nuevo, and El Azuzul—likewise place them on the actual spatial periphery of the main center, San Lorenzo.

Taggart (1983: 56) also makes the important observation that "present is to the past as the center is to the periphery." Therefore, the center/town/inhabited space represent the present and socio-cosmic order, while the periphery/forest/mountains symbolize the mythological past and disorder, chaos. From that perspective, carvings depicting jaguars dominating humans—on both the Gulf Coast and at Chalcatzingo—are portraying events of the mythological past.

SUMMARIZING THE BASIC GULF COAST OLMEC TEMPLATE

This chapter has used a neutral etic category, the Major Monument Zone, to attempt to explore and elucidate the sacred landscapes at Chalcatzingo, La Venta, and San Lorenzo. The results suggest that the inhabitants of these three sites did position monuments purposely to segment space and that there is some emic reality to the MMZ and its component sectors.

At La Venta the MMZ is located at the north end of the site's extensive area of architecture, while at San Lorenzo the MMZ comprises almost the entire upper surface of the plateau. Mound C-1 stands near the midpoint of La Venta's zone, while at San Lorenzo there is no central pyramid mound.[10] Yet while the

---

[10] The north-south linear size of the MMZ (i.e., the distance from northernmost to southernmost monuments) is ca. 1,000 m at San Lorenzo, and ca. 840 m at La Venta. A mathematical "midpoint" of that linear distance can obviously be calculated. I discussed that mathematical midpoint in my presentation of this paper at Dumbarton Oaks, but to avoid overcomplicating the material I have not emphasized it in this chapter. Nevertheless, the results are intriguing, particularly for La Venta. Because the placement of La Venta's Heads 2, 3, and 4 was not precisely measured (see Drucker 1952: 9), the midpoint can only be approximated. Those calculations disclose that while Mound C-1 visually separates the northern and southern sectors, the mound is definitely not positioned at the linear midpoint. Instead, the midpoint (and the east-west midline it creates) more likely falls on the large basal platform at the southern foot of Mound C-1, where the midline may have been defined by the two small conical mounds that occur at the east and west corners of the basal platform or by the southern (upper) edge of the platform (Figs. 5–9; also González 1988:

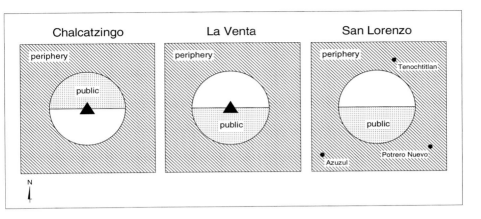

Fig. 15 The basic sacred landscape templates of Chalcatzingo, La Venta, and San Lorenzo. Drawing by Marie J. Zeidler and David Grove.

organization of La Venta and San Lorenzo may seem quite different, within the MMZ at both sites the patterns in the distribution of monument types, and in the iconographic themes those carvings display, indicate that these sites actually shared fundamental structural similarities in the placement of their monuments, that is, a similar template (Fig. 15).

The most evident structural principle is that the MMZ area has distinct northern and southern halves (sectors), and at both San Lorenzo and La Venta the majority of the monumental art was positioned in the southern sector. The images on these carvings relate to personages and rulership, and in the southern sectors they were openly displayed in processional arrangements in the sectors' central area. These carvings were unquestionably intended to be viewed. The predominance of displayed rulership monuments in this sector suggests that this site area was associated with public rituals related in some manner to that theme.

In contrast, the northern sectors at La Venta and San Lorenzo are nearly devoid of major displayed carvings; the few monuments erected in the north are positioned near those sectors' outer edges rather than their central areas. However, even these northern carvings are again laid out in a processional

---

fig. 1; Adams 1991: map 3-2). If the linear midpoint was at all culturally relevant to the north-south dichotomy expressed in the sacred landscape, then the constructed "sacred mountain" (Mound C-1) lies just within the "ancestral" (northern) sector. Similar measurements suggest that Chalcatzingo's main mound may also be positioned slightly asymmetrically and just within the "ancestral" sector.

arrangement. The presence of tombs and buried offerings and the restricted (nonpublic) nature of much of the northern sector of La Venta suggest that, in the Olmec template, north was cosmologically the region of the otherworld, ancestors, and the past.[11]

At present, an "ancestor" symbolism can be inferred only for San Lorenzo's northern sector, and such an attribution is complicated by the fact that the three colossal heads displayed in the northern sector, together with the seven displayed in the south, may *all* have represented past rulers (ancestors). Nevertheless, a mitigating factor may be that the San Lorenzo pattern reflects the distribution of Early Formative monuments within the cosmological template, while the La Venta pattern represents the distribution of both Middle Formative carvings and Early Formative colossal heads. Furthermore, the problem noted above does not negate the template's basic north-south dichotomy, nor the fact that within the template the principal display of monuments occurs in the southern sector.

At La Venta the primary mound, C-1, visually divides the northern and southern sectors. Large supernatural faces carved on stelae are displayed on the southern (public) side of the mound, where they are visible from Plaza B. These images may have visually designated that great mound as a symbolic "sacred mountain." Although San Lorenzo lacks a comparable Formative period constructed sacred mountain anywhere on the plateau,[12] the site's basic template—the sacred landscape—is nonetheless similar.

The La Venta data are valuable for revealing the fundamental structural template of the MMZ, while it is through the monuments at the small sites surrounding San Lorenzo that the nature of the periphery in the Olmec sacred

---

[11] It is worth noting that the main architectural components at La Venta extend beyond Complexes A and B to also include Complex D (see Adams 1991: map 3-2; González 1988: fig. 1). In fact, La Venta's three enigmatic sandstone monuments (52, 53, 54) occur at the south end of Complex D in a possible east-west alignment with Mounds D-17 and D-19. In terms of linear measurements, the three complexes are essentially of equal size, and, although this study has focused on Complexes A and B, the entire grouping can also be perceived as a north-central-south triadic arrangement. The reader may be reminded, as I am, of the somewhat similar triadic organization of Tikal's Great Plaza area a millennium later: the North Acropolis and the burials of ancestral rulers/the Great Plaza with publically displayed rulership monuments along its northern edge/the Central Acropolis elite residential-administrative complex of ruling dynasty (e.g., Ashmore 1992).

[12] Susan Gillespie has suggested to me that, in the sacred landscape of San Lorenzo, the entire plateau may have been regarded as a sacred mountain, thus perhaps obviating the need for a major mound. If that was the case, the supernatural and domination carvings found at peripheral sites below the plateau would have been positioned around the "base" of that sacred mountain, in the same relative position as the domination scenes on the talus slopes of the Cerro Chalcatzingo.

landscape becomes clear. The relatively benign monuments of the San Lorenzo plateau stand in contrast to the domination (and dwarf) carvings found at Tenochtitlán, Potrero Nuevo, and El Azuzul. These distributions seem to reflect the general Mesoamerican cosmological principle that the center symbolizes civilized space, whereas the periphery is the region of the supernatural, danger, and the mythological past.

CHALCATZINGO'S TEMPLATE: HOW OLMEC IS IT?

Beyond the obvious fact that Chalcatzingo's monuments are executed according to Gulf Coast canons, the site's organizational template also exhibits several strong correspondences with the basic templates of La Venta and San Lorenzo (Fig. 15). For example, Chalcatzingo's MMZ has distinct northern and southern sectors of approximately equal size. Also, as at La Venta, Chalcatzingo's sectors are physically separated by the site's major mound, and rulership monuments are displayed exclusively in one sector. Nevertheless, while Chalcatzingo follows many of the same structuring principles that operated at the Gulf Coast Olmec centers, it also executes those principles somewhat differently. The greatest and most explicit contrast is that directionality of the north-south dichotomy and the monument distribution pattern is reversed at Chalcatzingo. The site's rulership monuments are displayed in the northern sector, while it is the southern sector (Terrace 1 and others flanking the Cerro Chalcatzingo's talus slopes) that is nearly devoid of monuments.

The cosmological symbolism of the southern sector at Chalcatzingo is unclear. If it is "ancestral," then it is notable (yet perhaps coincidental) that the site's most richly endowed elite burials come from atop the massive platform mound and from the elite residence on Terrace 1 (Merry de Morales 1987a: 100–108; 1987b: 457–465). One such interment, Burial 3, found within a stone crypt beneath the latter structure, had been entombed with a stone head (Monument 17) severed from a "rulership" statue (1987a: 103–105), evidence suggesting that in life that person had served in a rulership capacity.

At La Venta and San Lorenzo, the few monuments in the "ancestral" sector occurred only along the margins of that sector. The talus carvings of the Cerro Chalcatzingo are situated in a somewhat analogous location, yet they are thematically different. They are not images of ancestral personages, but depict zoomorphic supernaturals dominating humans. As such, they are most comparable in both theme and positioning to the domination carvings that occur at Potrero Nuevo, El Azuzul, and Tenochtitlán on the periphery of San Lorenzo plateau. The domination carvings at Chalcatzingo are also situated on the periphery, at the base of the *cerro* (sacred mountain) and just beyond the constructed landscape (see note 10).

At the Gulf Coast Olmec centers there is no feature of sacred geography exactly equivalent to the Cerro Chalcatzingo, nor are there any carvings directly similar to "El Rey" (Monument 1) and the other rain-fertility carvings high on the hillside. Although the "El Rey" bas-relief shares important iconographic motifs with Altar 5 at La Venta (Grove 1989: 132–134), it exhibits an equally important dissimilarity. Monument 1 is characterized by a large quatrefoil supernatural face, as are Monuments 9 and 13. Significantly, such quatrefoils are *not* found in Gulf Coast Olmec monumental art. I have suggested above that the large supernatural faces of Chalcatzingo's Monument 9 and La Venta's Monuments 25/26 and 27 marked their respective massive central mounds as sacred mountains.[13] While these carvings are similar in where they were displayed and in their probable symbolic function, their supernatural images are completely different. The closest regional and temporal analogs to Chalcatzingo's three quatrefoil faces are found in the sectioned-quatrefoil "hill glyph"/place glyph motifs that begin to be manifested in Late Formative period monumental art in Oaxaca (e.g., Caso 1965: fig. 15).

A further contrast occurs with Chalcatzingo's tabletop altar, Monument 22. This Gulf Coast type monument is positioned near the far end of the rulership sector, just as are Altars 4 and 5 at La Venta. However, Monument 22 is situated within a sunken patio, an architectural form not yet shown to occur at Gulf Coast Olmec sites. In addition, unlike its monolithic Gulf Coast counterparts, the Chalcatzingo altar is constructed of 20 large stone blocks, even though suitable altar-sized boulders abound nearby (Fash 1987: 93). The altar's iconography also diverges from Gulf Coast canons. Whereas the upper ledge of Gulf Coast altars is usually carved with an earth band composed of inverted U-elements, Monument 22's upper ledge is decorated with a non-Olmec "elongated oblong" motif (Grove 1987b: 430, fig. 27.6).

The above examples help illustrate the eclectic nature of Chalcatzingo, its monumental art, and its sacred landscape. While the site's carvings clearly have their roots and canons in Gulf Coast Olmec monumental art, and there is also a strong Gulf Coast component to the themes of some carvings, at Chalcatzingo those elements are united with motifs and traits that seem more common to Central Mexico (Morelos, Guerrero, and Oaxaca; Grove 1989: 142–145), and together they are manifested within a template that is an inversion of the Gulf Coast template.

---

[13] It seems possible that the concept of erecting large supernatural faces on the public side of a site's main mound, as exemplified at La Venta and Chalcatzingo, may represent a Middle Formative period antecedent to the great supernatural masks that adorn Late Pre-Classic Maya pyramids, such as at Cerros and Uaxactun.

Does Chalcatzingo's template predate the appearance of the Gulf Coast elements? A point strongly favoring that possibility is that the earliest building stages of Chalcatzingo's massive platform mound—the construction separating the north and south sectors—date to the Early Formative period (Amate phase; Prindiville and Grove 1987: 63), centuries before the site's adoption of monumental art (ca. 700 B.C.) and/or other unequivocal evidence of interaction with the Gulf Coast Olmec sites. This implies that Chalcatzingo's basic organizational template (i.e., a northern and southern sector separated by a midpoint mound) was in place by ca. 1000 B.C. and that the Gulf Coast elements were later incorporated into that existing sacred landscape.

FORMATIVE PERIOD SACRED LANDSCAPES AND FUTURE RESEARCH

The analyses of monument distributions at Chalcatzingo, La Venta, and San Lorenzo demonstrate that, in spite of the great physical differences between these three centers, certain similar structuring principles nevertheless operated in the positioning of their monuments and major public architecture. Furthermore, the distinctive distribution of particular monument types and monument themes within these sites implies a cosmological foundation to those structuring principles. Thus, through their mounds and monuments, Chalcatzingo, La Venta, and San Lorenzo manifest sacred landscapes as an important component of their built environments. While this chapter has stressed the dichotomy present within the MMZ, nearly all the monuments of the MMZ deal in one way or another with rulership, past or present; they are thus essentially "historical." In contrast, the peripheral monuments are more related to cosmology and the mythological past, and the fact that such monuments *were* erected at sites on the periphery of San Lorenzo implies that a center's sacred landscapes extended out to the surrounding communities as well. That extension may also be reflected in the character of the monuments displayed at more distant secondary centers in the hinterlands of San Lorenzo, La Venta, and Laguna de los Cerros (for the latter, see Grove et al. 1993).

Because very little attention has been directed to the organizational principles of Formative period sites, it is presently difficult to ascertain which shared features of the three templates discussed above are perhaps pan-Mesoamerican or at least more common to a wide area of Mesoamerica and which might be inherently Gulf Coast Olmec. The dualistic organization of a site's Major Monument Zone area may be one of these more "pan-Mesoamerican" patterns.

Sacred landscapes seem to have been a significant characteristic of Mesoamerican sites from the Formative period on, although as noted at the beginning of this chapter, the principles underlying the organization of any site are seldom self-evident. Elucidating the templates of the vast majority of Formative period sites will be difficult, particularly in the absence of monumental art or other features that carry some interpretable cosmological significance. Nevertheless, the knowledge that sacred landscapes and organizational templates may have been fundamental to the way Mesoamerican societies conceived of and arranged space has exciting potential as an analytical approach for understanding more about these societies, their sites, and the distribution of activities within those sites.

Acknowledgments Over several years this study has benefited from discussions with many people, including Wendy Ashmore, Rosemary Joyce, Joyce Marcus, and Kent Reilly. Susan Gillespie tirelessly read many drafts of this chapter and contributed extremely valuable comments and insights. The students in my 1993 graduate Olmec seminar, and particularly Anthony Vega, deserve credit for the insight that Chalcatzingo Monument 9 marked that site's major platform mound as a sacred mountain.

BIBLIOGRAPHY

ADAMS, RICHARD E. W.
  1991   *Prehistoric Mesoamerica.* University of Oklahoma Press, Norman.

Angulo V., Jorge
  1987   The Chalcatzingo Reliefs: An Iconographic Analysis. In *Ancient Chalcatzingo* (David C. Grove, ed.): 132–158. University of Texas Press, Austin.

ASHMORE, WENDY
  1989   Construction and Cosmology: Politics and Ideology in Lowland Maya Settlement Patterns. In *Word and Image in Maya Culture* (W. Hanks and D. Rice, eds.): 272–286. University of Utah Press, Salt Lake City.
  1992   Deciphering Maya Architectural Plans. In *New Theories on the Ancient Maya* (Elin C. Danien and Robert J. Sharer, eds.): 173–184. University Museum Monograph 77. University Museum Symposium Series 3, University of Pennsylvania, Philadelphia.

BRODA, JOHANNA, DAVÍD CARRASCO, AND EDUARDO MATOS MOCTEZUMA
  1987   *The Great Temple of Tenochtitlan: Center and Periphery in the Aztec World.* University of California Press, Berkeley.

BRÜGGEMANN, JÜRGEN, AND MARIE-ARETI HERS
  1970   Exploraciones arqueológicas en San Lorenzo Tenochtitlán. *Boletín del Instituto Nacional de Antropología e Historia* 39: 18–23. Mexico.

CASO, ALFONSO
  1965   Zapotec Writing and Calendar. In *Handbook of Middle American Indians* (Robert Wauchope and Gordon R. Willey, eds.) 3: 931–947. University of Texas Press, Austin.

CLEWLOW, C. WILLIAM, JR., AND CHRISTOPHER R. CORSON
  1968   Appendix II: New Stone Monuments from La Venta, 1968. In *Papers on Mesoamerican Archaeology*: 171–203. Contributions of the University of California Archaeological Research Facility 5. Berkeley.

CLEWLOW, C. WILLIAM, JR., RICHARD A. COWAN, JAMES F. O'CONNELL, AND CARLOS BENEMANN
  1967   *Colossal Heads of the Olmec Culture.* Contributions of the University of California Archaeological Research Facility, 4. Berkeley.

COE, MICHAEL D.
  1968   San Lorenzo and the Olmec Civilization. In *Dumbarton Oaks Conference on the Olmec* (Elizabeth P. Benson, ed.): 41–71. Dumbarton Oaks, Washington, D.C.
  1977   Olmec and Maya: A Study in Relationships. In *The Origins of Maya Civilization* (Richard E. W. Adams, ed.): 183–195. School of American Research Advanced Seminar Series, University of New Mexico Press, Albuquerque.
  1981   San Lorenzo Tenochtitlán. In *Supplement to the Handbook of Middle American Indians,* vol. 1: *Archaeology* (Victoria R. Bricker and Jeremy A. Sabloff, eds.): 117–146. University of Texas Press, Austin.

COE, MICHAEL D., AND RICHARD A. DIEHL
  1980   In *the Land of the Olmec,* vol. 1: *The Archaeology of San Lorenzo Tenochtitlan.* University of Texas Press, Austin.

David C. Grove

COOK DE LEONARD, CARMEN
    1967   Sculptures and Rock Carvings at Chalcatzingo, Morelos. In *Studies in Olmec Archaeology*: 57–84. Contributions of the University of California Archaeological Research Facility 3. Berkeley.

CYPHERS GUILLÉN, ANN
    1992   Exploraciones arqueológicas en San Lorenzo Tenochtitlán, Veracruz: Temporada 1991. *Boletín del Consejo de Arqueología, 1991*: 65–66. Instituto Nacional de Antropología e Historia, Mexico.
    1993   Escenas escultóricas olmecas. *Antropológicas* 6: 47–52. Universidad Nacional Autónoma de México.
    1994a   Three New Olmec Sculptures from Southern Veracruz. *Mexicon* 16: 30–32.
    1994b   Olmec Sculpture and Architecture of the Azuzul Acropolis, Loma del Zapote, Veracruz, Mexico. Research and Exploration 10 (3): 294–305. National Geographic Society, Washington, D.C.
    1994c   San Lorenzo Tenochtitlán. In *Los olmecas en Mesoamérica* (John E. Clark, coord.): 43–67. Citibank, Mexico.

DAVIS, WHITNEY
    1978   So-Called Jaguar-Human Copulation Scenes in Olmec Art. *American Antiquity* 43: 453–457.

DE LA FUENTE, BEATRIZ
    1973   *Escultura monumental olmeca: catalogo.* Instituto de Investigaciones Estéticas, Universidad Nacional Autónoma de México.
    1992   *Cabezas colosales olmecas.* El Colegio Nacional, Mexico.

DRUCKER, PHILIP
    1952   *La Venta, Tabasco: A Study of Olmec Ceramics and Art.* Smithsonian Institution, Bureau of American Ethnology, Bulletin 153. Washington, D.C.

DRUCKER, PHILIP, ROBERT F. HEIZER, AND ROBERT J. SQUIER
    1959   *Excavations at La Venta, Tabasco, 1955.* Smithsonian Institution, Bureau of American Ethnology, Bulletin 170. Washington, D.C.

ELZEY, WAYNE
    1976   Some Remarks on the Space and Time of the "Center" in Aztec Religion. *Estudios de Cultura Náhuatl* 12: 315–334. Universidad Nacional Autónoma de México.

FASH, WILLIAM L., JR.
    1987   The Altar and Associated Features. In *Ancient Chalcatzingo* (David C. Grove, ed.): 82–94. University of Texas Press, Austin.

GAY, CARLO T. E.
    1972   *Chalcacingo.* International Scholarly Book Service, Portland.

GILLESPIE, SUSAN D.
    1991   Ballgames and Boundaries. In *The Mesoamerican Ballgame* (Vernon L. Scarborough and David R. Wilcox, eds.): 317–345. University of Arizona Press, Tucson.

GONZÁLEZ LAUCK, REBECA
    1988   Proyecto arqueológico La Venta. *Arqueología* 4: 121–165. Instituto Nacional de Antropología e Historia, Mexico.

1994   La antigua ciudad olmeca en La Venta, Tabasco. In *Los olmecas en Mesoamérica* (John E. Clark, coord.): 93–111. Citibank, Mexico.

GROVE, DAVID C.
1968   Chalcatzingo, Morelos, Mexico: A Re-Appraisal of the Olmec Rock Carvings. *American Antiquity* 33: 468–491.
1972   El Teocuicani: "Cantor Divino" en Jantetelco. *Boletin* (ser. 2) 3: 35–36. Instituto Nacional de Antropología e Historia, Mexico.
1973   Olmec Altars and Myths. *Archaeology* 26: 128–135.
1981   Olmec Monuments: Mutilation as a Clue to Meaning. In *The Olmec and Their Neighbors* (Elizabeth P. Benson, ed.): 49–68. Dumbarton Oaks, Washington, D.C.
1984   *Chalcatzingo: Excavations on the Olmec Frontier.* Thames and Hudson, London.
1987a   Chalcatzingo in a Broader Perspective. In *Ancient Chalcatzingo* (David C. Grove, ed.): 434–442. University of Texas Press, Austin.
1987b   Comments on the Site and Its Organization. In *Ancient Chalcatzingo* (David C. Grove, ed.): 420–433. University of Texas Press, Austin.
1989   Chalcatzingo and Its Olmec Connection. In *Regional Perspectives on the Olmec* (Robert J. Sharer and David C. Grove, eds.): 122–147. Cambridge University Press, Cambridge.

GROVE, DAVID C. (ED.)
1987c   *Ancient Chalcatzingo.* University of Texas Press, Austin.

GROVE, DAVID C., AND JORGE ANGULO V.
1987   A Catalog and Description of Chalcatzingo's Monuments. In *Ancient Chalcatzingo* (David C. Grove, ed.): 114–131. University of Texas Press, Austin.

GROVE, DAVID C., SUSAN D. GILLESPIE, PONCIANO ORTÍZ C., AND MICHAEL HAYTON
1993   Five Olmec Monuments from the Laguna de los Cerros Hinterland. *Mexicon* 15 (5): 91–95.

GUZMÁN, EULALIA
1934   Los relieves de las rocas del Cerro de la Cantera, Jonacatepec, Morelos. *Anales del Museo Nacional de Arqueología, Historia, y Etnografía* (ser. 5) 1 (2): 237–251. Mexico.

HANKS, WILLIAM F.
1990   *Referential Practice: Language and Lived Space among the Maya.* University of Chicago Press, Chicago.

HEIZER, ROBERT F.
1967   Analysis of Two Low Relief Sculptures from La Venta. In *Studies in Olmec Archaeology*: 25–55. Contributions of the University of California Archaeological Research Facility 3. Berkeley.
1968   New Observations on La Venta. In *Dumbarton Oaks Conference on the Olmec* (Elizabeth P. Benson, ed.): 9–36. Dumbarton Oaks, Washington, D.C.

HEIZER, ROBERT F., JOHN A. GRAHAM, AND LEWIS K. NAPTON
1968   The 1968 Investigations at La Venta. In *Papers on Mesoamerican Archaeology*: 127–154. Contributions of the University of California Archaeology Research Facility 5. Berkeley.

HOPKINS, NICHOLAS
1984   Otomanguean Linguistic Prehistory. In *Essays in Otomanguean Culture History* (J. Kathryn Josserand, Marcus Winter, and Nicholas Hopkins, eds.): 25–64. Vanderbilt University Publications in Anthropology 31. Nashville.

LEÓN PEREZ, IGNACIO, AND JUAN CARLOS SÁNCHEZ IBÁÑEZ
1991–1992   Las gemelas y el jaguar del sitio El Azuzul. *Horizonte* 5–6: 56–60. Instituto Veracruzano de Cultura, Veracruz, Mexico.

MANRIQUE CASTAÑEDA, LEONARDO
1975   Relaciones entre las áreas lingüísticas y las áreas culturales. In *Balance y perspectiva de la antropología de Mesoamerica y del Norte de México: antropología física, lingüística, códices*: 137–160. XIII Mesa Redonda, Sociedad Mexicana de Antropología, Mexico.

MARTÍNEZ DONJUAN, GUADALUPE
1982   Teopantecuanitlán, Guerrero: un sitio olmeca. *Revista Mexicana de Estudios Antropológicos* 28: 128–133. Sociedad Mexicana de Antropología, Mexico.
1985   El sitio olmeca de Teopantecuanitlán en Guerrero. *Anales de Antropología*: 215–226. Universidad Nacional Autónoma de México.
1986   Teopantecuanitlan. In *Primer Coloquio de Arqueología y Etnohistoria del Estado de Guerrero*: 55–80. Instituto Nacional de Antropología e Historia y Gobierno del Estado de Guerrero, Mexico.

MEDELLÍN ZENIL, ALFONSO
1960   Monolitos ineditos olmecas. *La Palabra y el Hombre* 16: 75–97. Universidad Veracruzana, Xalapa.

MERRY DE MORALES, MARCIA
1987a   Chalcatzingo Burials as Indicators of Social Ranking. In *Ancient Chalcatzingo* (David C. Grove, ed.): 95–113. University of Texas Press, Austin.
1987b   Appendix C: The Chalcatzingo Burials. In *Ancient Chalcatzingo* (David C. Grove, ed.): 343–367. University of Texas Press, Austin.

NATIONAL GEOGRAPHIC MAGAZINE
1994   Olmec Head Emerges from a Mexican Ravine. *National Geographic* 186 (4): xvii.

NICHOLSON, HENRY B.
1990   Late Pre-Hispanic Central Mexican ("Aztec") Sacred Architecture: The "Pyramid Temple." In *Circumpacífica: Festschrift für Thomas S. Barthel* (Bruno Illius and Matthias Laubscher, eds.): 303–324. Peter Lang, Frankfurt am Main.

PIÑA CHAN, ROMAN
1955   *Chalcatzingo, Morelos*. Instituto Nacional de Antropología e Historia, Informes 4. Mexico.

PORTER, JAMES B.
1989   Olmec Colossal Heads as Recarved Thrones: "Mutilation," Revolution, and Recarving. *Res* 17–18 (Spring–Autumn): 23–29.

PRINDIVILLE, MARY, AND DAVID C. GROVE
1987   The Settlement and Its Architecture. In *Ancient Chalcatzingo* (David C. Grove, ed.): 63–81. University of Texas Press, Austin.

SCHELE, LINDA, AND DAVID A. FREIDEL

1991   The Courts of Creation: Ballgames and Portals to the Maya Otherworld. In *The Mesoamerican Ballgame* (Vernon L. Scarborough and David R. Wilcox, eds.): 289–315. University of Arizona Press, Tucson.

STIRLING, MATTHEW W.

1943   *Stone Monuments of Southern Mexico.* Smithsonian Institution, Bureau of American Ethnology, Bulletin 138. Washington, D.C.

1955   *Stone Monuments of the Rio Chiquito, Veracruz.* Smithsonian Institution, Bureau of American Ethnology, Bulletin 157: 1–23. Washington, D.C.

1968   Three Sandstone Monuments from La Venta Island. In *Papers on Mesoamerican Archaeology*: 35–39. Contributions of the University of California Archaeology Research Facility 5. Berkeley.

SUGIYAMA, SABURO

1993   Worldview Materialized in Teotihuacan, Mexico. *Latin American Antiquity* 4 (2): 103–129.

TAGGART, JAMES M.

1983   *Nahuat Myth and Social Structure.* University of Texas Press, Austin.

TOWNSEND, RICHARD F.

1982   Pyramid and Sacred Mountain. In *Ethnoastronomy and Archaeoastronomy in the American Tropics* (Anthony F. Aveni and Gary Urton, eds.): 37–62. New York Academy of Sciences, Annals 385. New York.

VOGT, EVON Z.

1981   Some Aspects of the Sacred Geography of Highland Chiapas. In *Mesoamerican Sites and World Views* (Elizabeth P. Benson, ed.): 119–138. Dumbarton Oaks, Washington, D.C.

Appendix

Monument Illustrations: Primary Sources

CHALCATZINGO

Mon. 1   Angulo 1987: fig. 10.7, 10.8; Cook de Leonard 1967: fig. 2; Gay 1972: fig. 11; Grove 1968: fig. 1; Grove 1984: fig. 4, pl. iv; Grove and Angulo 1987: fig. 9.3; Guzmán 1934: fig. 3; Piña Chan 1955: photos 17, 18.

Mon. 2   Angulo 1987: fig. 10.13; Cook de Leonard 1967: fig. 1; Gay 1972: fig. 17; Grove 1968: fig. 3; Grove 1984: pls. ii, 9; Guzmán 1934: figs. 8, 9; Piña Chan 1955: fig. 19, photos 15, 16.

Mon. 3   Cook de Leonard 1967: fig. 5, pl. 6; Gay 1972: pl. 9; Grove 1968: fig. 4; Grove 1984: fig. 31, pl. v; Grove and Angulo 1987: fig. 9.10.

Mon. 4   Angulo 1987: figs. 10.16, 10.17; Cook de Leonard 1967: fig. 3, pls. 2–4; Gay 1972: fig. 24; Grove 1968: fig. 5; Grove 1984: fig. 30, pl. vi; Grove and Angulo 1987: fig. 9.11.

Mon. 5   Cook de Leonard 1967: fig. 4, pl. 5; Gay 1972: fig. 25; Grove 1968: fig. 6; Grove 1984: fig. 29; Grove and Angulo 1987: fig. 9.12.

Mon. 6/7   Angulo 1987: figs. 10.5, 10.6; Gay 1972: figs. 28, 30; Grove 1968: figs. 2a, 2b; Grove 1984: pl. 12; Grove and Angulo 1987: figs. 9.4, 9.5; Guzmán 1934: figs. 6a, 6b.

Mon. 8   Angulo 1987: fig. 10.2; Cook de Leonard 1967: pl. 7; Gay 1972: fig. 32; Grove 1968: fig. 2c; Grove and Angulo 1987: fig. 9.6; Guzmán 1934: figs. 7a, 7b.

Mon. 9   Grove 1968: fig. 7; Grove 1984: fig. 8; Grove and Angulo 1987: fig. 9.17.

Mon. 11   Angulo 1987: fig. 10.1; Gay 1972: fig. 37; Grove and Angulo 1987: fig. 9.6.

Mon. 13   Angulo 1987: fig. 10.12; Grove 1984: fig. 32; Grove and Angulo 1987: fig. 9.13.

Mon. 14   Angulo 1987: fig. 10.3; Grove 1984: pl. 15; Grove and Angulo 1987: fig. 9.7.

Mon. 15   Angulo 1987: fig. 10.4; Grove and Angulo 1987: fig. 9.8.

Mon. 16   Gay 1972: pl. 21; Grove 1984: pl. 19; Grove and Angulo 1987: fig. 9.18; Guzmán 1934: figs. 12, 13.

Mon. 17   Grove 1984: pls. 25, 27; Grove and Angulo 1987: fig. 9.19.

Mon. 21   Angulo 1987: fig. 10.21; Grove 1984: fig. 12; Grove and Angulo 1987: fig. 9.21.

Mon. 22   Fash 1987: fig. 7.4; Grove 1984: fig. 15, pls. vii, 23; 1987b: fig. 27.6.

Mon. 23	Fash 1987: fig. 7.24.
Mon. 25	Grove and Angulo 1987: fig. 9.23.
Mon. 26	Grove and Angulo 1987: fig. 9.24.
Mon. 27	Angulo 1987: fig. 10.22; Grove 1984: fig. 10; Grove and Angulo 1987: fig. 9.25.
Mon. 28	Angulo 1987: figs. 10.23, 10.24; Grove 1984: fig. 13.
Mon. 31	Unpublished.

LA VENTA

Head 1	(Mon. 1) Clewlow et al. 1967: figs. 2, 3, pls. 1, 2, 6a; Stirling 1943: pl. 42a.
Head 2	Clewlow et al. 1967: figs. 4, 5, pls. 3, 4, 5; Stirling 1943: pl. 43.
Head 3	Clewlow et al. 1967: figs. 6, 7, pls. 7, 8; Stirling 1943: pl. 42b.
Head 4	Clewlow et al. 1967: figs. 8, 9, pls. 6b, 9, 10; Stirling 1943: pl. 44.
Stela 1	Drucker, Heizer, and Squier 1959: pl. 56a; Stirling 1943: pl. 33a.
Stela 2	Drucker 1952: fig. 49; Heizer 1967: pl. 2, figs. 2, 3; Stirling 1943: pl. 34.
Stela 3	Drucker 1952: fig. 50; Drucker, Heizer, and Squier 1959: pl. 55; Heizer 1967: pl. 1, fig. 1; Stirling 1943: pl. 35.
Altar 1	Stirling 1943: pl. 36.
Altar 2	Stirling 1943: pl. 38c.
Altar 3	Stirling 1943: pl. 39.
Altar 4	Drucker, Heizer, and Squier 1959: pl. 56b; Stirling 1943: pls. 37, 38b.
Altar 5	Stirling 1943: pls. 40, 41.
Altar 6	Stirling 1943: pl. 38a.
Altar 7	De la Fuente 1973: 33.
Altar 8	González 1988: fig. 4.
Mon. 19	Drucker, Heizer, and Squier 1959: fig. 55, pl. 49.
Mon. 20	Drucker, Heizer, and Squier 1959: fig. 56, pl. 50.
Mon. 21	Drucker, Heizer, and Squier 1959: fig. 57, pl. 51a.
Mon. 25	Drucker, Heizer, and Squier 1959: fig. 59, pl. 53.
Mon. 26	Drucker, Heizer, and Squier 1959: fig. 60b, pl. 53.
Mon. 25/26	González 1988: 129.
Mon. 27	Drucker, Heizer, and Squier 1959: fig. 60a, pl. 54.

Appendix

Mon. 52	Stirling 1968: pl. 1.
Mon. 53	Stirling 1968: pl. 2.
Mon. 54	Stirling 1968: pl. 3.
Mon. 58	Clewlow and Corson 1968: pl. 13b.
Mon. 59	Clewlow and Corson 1968: pl. 13c.
Mon. 86	González 1994: figs. 6.9–6.11.

SAN LORENZO

Head 1	Clewlow et al. 1967: figs. 13–15, pls. 16–18; Coe and Diehl 1980: fig. 423; Stirling 1955: pl. 6.
Head 2	Clewlow et al. 1967: figs. 16–18, pls. 19–21; Coe and Diehl 1980: figs. 424, 425; Stirling 1955: pl. 7.
Head 3	Clewlow et al. 1967: figs. 19–21, pls. 22–24; Coe and Diehl 1980: fig. 426; Stirling 1955: pl. 8.
Head 4	Clewlow et al. 1967: fig. 22–24, pls. 25–27; Coe and Diehl 1980: fig. 427; Stirling 1955: pls. 9, 10, 11a.
Head 5	Clewlow et al. 1967: figs. 25–28, pls. 28–31; Coe and Diehl 1980: fig. 428; Stirling 1955: pls. 12, 13.
Head 6	(Mon. 17) Clewlow et al. 1967: fig. 29, pls. 32, 36; Coe 1968: fig. 11; Coe and Diehl 1980: figs. 443, 444.
Head 7	(Mon. 53) Brüggemann and Hers 1970: fig. 29; de la Fuente 1992: fig. 1, pls. 30–32.
Head 8	(Mon. 61) De la Fuente 1992: fig. 2, pls. 33, 34.
Head 9	(Mon. 67) De la Fuente 1992: pls. 35, 36.
Head 10	Cyphers 1994c: figs. 4, 14; National Geographic Magazine 1994: xvii.
Mon. 7	Coe and Diehl 1980: fig. 430.
Mon. 8	Coe and Diehl 1980: fig. 431.
Mon. 14	Coe and Diehl 1980: fig. 439.
Mon. 16	Coe and Diehl 1980: figs. 441, 442.
Mon. 18	Coe and Diehl 1980: figs. 446, 447.
Mon. 20	Coe and Diehl 1980: figs. 449, 451.
Mon. 37	Coe and Diehl 1980: figs. 471, 472.
Mon. 51	Coe and Diehl 1980: fig. 492.

Appendix

Mon. 60   Brüggemann and Hers 1970: fig. 22.

Mon. 64   Brüggemann and Hers 1970: fig. 28.

Mon. 77   Cyphers, this volume, fig. 2.

Mon. 3   Stirling 1955: pls. 25, 26a; Coe and Diehl 1980: fig. 497.

EL AZUZUL

Small feline   Cyphers 1994b: fig. 11; León and Sánchez 1991–92: 57.

Large feline   Cyphers 1993: figs. 8, 9; 1994a: fig. 1; 1994b: figs. 9, 12; this volume: fig. 7.

The three monument group

Cyphers 1993: fig. 7; 1994a: fig. 2; 1994b: fig. 5; this volume, fig. 6; León and Sánchez 1991–92: 59.

LOS TREINTA

Mon. 5   Cyphers 1992: fig. 6; this volume, fig. 8.

POTRERO NUEVO

Mon. 2   Coe and Diehl 1980: fig. 496; Stirling 1955: pl. 23.

TENOCHTITLÁN

Mon. 1   Stirling 1955: pl. 2; Coe and Diehl 1980: fig. 499.

Mon. 6   Coe and Diehl 1980: 374, fig. 502.

XOCHILTEPEC EJIDO

Cyphers 1993: fig. 2; 1994a: fig. 4.

Commentary: Ritual, Social Identity, and Cosmology: Hard Stones and Flowing Water

BARBARA L. STARK

ARIZONA STATE UNIVERSITY

WITH THE TOPICS OF RITUAL, SOCIAL identity, and cosmology that guided the symposium, broad cultural interpretations are at stake in our treatment of the archaeological record. While many layers or dimensions of meaning can be addressed among these topics, a tension exists among perspectives in this volume regarding the degree of emphasis on the social and more particularistic on the one hand and the cosmological and more general on the other. I will add to this tension, as it seems likely that it may have been recognized, even sought, in the past.

I selected two themes to explore, stone and water, that were highlighted in two of the papers presented Sunday morning when I served as a discussant. Ponciano Ortíz and María del Carmen Rodríguez' presentation on El Manatí and Ann Cyphers' contribution on San Lorenzo dealt with Olmec ritual practices or monumental sculpture and constructions. Papers by David Grove, Michael Love, and William Ringle are also concerned with the monumental and its implications.

SACRED STONES

... monuments of its own magnificence ...

William Butler Yeats, 1928, in Rosenthal 1986: 102

Cyphers' evidence at San Lorenzo leads her to comment that stone itself may have been sacred. This remark and the observations by Ringle about the functions of monumentality stimulated me to reconsider how we think about

Olmec sacred stones. By "sacred" I mean related to spiritual, transcendental, or supernatural properties and requiring or inspiring reverence or devotion.

Cyphers found an area devoted to recarving of stone monuments (see also Porter 1990) and offerings made to a monument set aside for recarving. If the stones were sacred, this suggests a general meaning, an element of the Olmec view of the essential character of the cosmos. But can we rule out alternatives? More particularistic social factors could be reflected as well. Rulership commemoration or the individual(s) commissioning monuments (including ones that conveyed sacred themes) may have led to lineage or social group offerings to monuments through memory and continued ritual observance.

With greater time lapse, ritual practices directed at carved monuments may still occur. For example, a colossal head at the later Pacific Coast site of El Baul is the object of recent ritual dissociated from its now-unknown ancient role(s). We cannot argue that the stone per se is sacred in this later context, as the scarcity of carved monuments and especially the representational quality of this carving are sufficient to account for its present selection for ritual. Without the carved visage, it is questionable that the boulder would be the object of special interest, as there are many large rocks in streams in the area. A parallel exists between the supra-ordinary context of ritual and the unusual character of the monument in the environment.

A few years ago the state of Veracruz was scoured for carved sculptures by a former governor for the inauguration of a new building for the state museum of anthropology. If the stone monuments were not sacred to the Gulf Olmec, they are partly so today—valued emblems of the past, representatives of social continuity, contributors to a modern cultural identity, yet claimed and utilized by people in selected localities and thus acquiring a new, specific social meaning and function. The intrinsic qualities of carved monuments and the particular social contexts in which they function continue in a dynamic relation.

For comparison, can we posit that the Manatí offerings of wooden busts and staffs, in addition to celts and other items, indicate that wood was sacralized? Do wooden carvings help us understand the case for sacred stones? Perhaps Olmec celt offerings elsewhere also had wooden materials included, and the use of wood was not unique to El Manatí. However, hard tropical woods would be a much less scarce material than stone for the Gulf Olmec, unless a particular rare species had properties that others lacked.

Helms (1987) has written about the role of polished, black, wooden artifacts in the Caribbean, providing an ethnohistoric parallel. A particular species of palm yielded desirable qualities, and certain artisans possessed the expertise to process and work it. She argues on the basis of widespread evidence among native societies, including Mesoamerica, that black and blue-black were associated with cosmological realms and supernaturals. In the case of Gulf Olmec carved stone, as well as the Manatí wood busts, sometimes paint or pigment was added. Ortíz and Rodríguez (1989: 37, 44) describe red-orange paint covering much of a wooden staff and part of the faces of some wooden busts, which suggests that dark color was not a critical, unvarying feature. Nor is the finish of the busts consistent, indicating that the degree of polish was not crucial.

The ancient Manatí wooden objects do not provide a close parallel with the Caribbean case, but one of the Manatí busts is oddly shaped, perhaps to accommodate the wood used, and shows an adjustment to the presence of a knot (Ortíz and Rodríguez 1989: 44). Thus, on occasion, pieces of wood may have been employed that limited the scope of the carver, which might indicate some limitation in supply. However, no species identifications are available yet, and it is not possible to argue that the wood selected was scarce.

The Gulf Olmec focus on stone as a scarce material for artifact offerings and carving would not in itself constitute a case for sacred stone without the suggestive evidence of offerings to San Lorenzo monuments undergoing recycling. Many exotic materials circulated in Pre-Classic Mesoamerica and were endowed with special significance through prestige associations, workmanship, and their roles in restricted ritual contexts; the treatment afforded them does not imply that the raw material itself was sacred, unless unworked and thoroughly broken pieces were offered the same treatment as finished, complete ones. The carved symbolism of Olmec monuments appears to be crucial in their treatment rather than the stone itself, as a recycled monument was provided with offerings, but chips and fragments from stoneworking were not.

Subsistence Stones

Mundane stone artifacts reveal other aspects of Olmec ritual and contribute to the idea that stone itself was not sacred, but that its worked form and symbolism in ritual could make it so. Petrography at San Lorenzo demonstrated that different outcrops were used preferentially for monuments versus metates, apparently for functional reasons (Coe and Diehl 1980: 397–404), although the basalt for both was imported from Cerro Cintepec in the Tuxtla Mountains. The distance involved in procurement is one link between subsistence implements and carved monuments.

In their presentation at Dumbarton Oaks, Ortíz and Rodríguez noted that scattered mortars and metates, celts, and beads were among the earliest offerings in the El Manatí spring-fed pool (see also Ortíz and Rodríguez 1989: 31–32); also, two natural blocks of stone bore grooves that might have been used for sharpening celts. Later offerings there consisted of groups of celts in more formal arrangements, but grinding tools no longer were included. Two radiocarbon dates are mentioned for the oldest Manatí deposits, at about 1600 B.C. (Ortíz 1993: 18).

Much later at La Venta, some celts in offerings bear evidence of use, possibly in agriculture (Drucker, Heizer, and Squier 1959: 137–139). Sometimes Olmec celts are made of rarer greenstone, and some bear astonishing, glassy polish, seemingly making them labor-intensive versions of mundane objects. Yet both workaday and elaborate examples were placed in ritual caches. At La Venta, some "pseudo-celts" were fabricated, perhaps as surrogates for actual implements (Drucker, Heizer, and Squier 1959: 135). The celt seems to be the crucial notion rather than the material.

If mortars and metates are assumed to have been tied mainly to women's social roles in grinding maize or other foods, and if celts are assumed to have been associated with men's roles, including clearing forest for horticulture, then ritual offerings of these subsistence artifacts, both made from imported materials, initially involved two genders at El Manatí. The choice of celts and metates as appropriate offerings may reflect both their historical agricultural importance in land use and in transforming plants and the necessity of obtaining the materials nonlocally in the Gulf lowlands. Regardless of whether early domesticates were crucial in lowland subsistence or, instead, in feasting and social aggrandizement (compare Clark and Blake 1994), the significance of the implements in transformations remains the same. However, a connection with leaders' activities, especially rituals, would help explain the tendency to favor special imported materials and high labor investment in celts. The roots of transformational meanings would extend back into the Archaic period as food production was developed and increased in importance. Here I am looking backward to derive significance from historical antecedents rather than forward to the Late Post-Classic period, which has supplied many of the meanings imputed to Pre-Classic remains.

At El Manatí it appears that a segregation of ritual activities led to the predominance of men's(?) implements among later ground stone offerings, although Ortíz and Rodríguez (1989) interpret some of the busts as representing women. Marcus (this volume) notes a segregation of what she assigns as male and female ritual activities in the early Oaxaca record. Details of dating for El Manatí are not yet published. Initiation of offerings in the Early Pre-Classic period is suggested by Ortíz and Rodríguez (this volume). If a degree of segregation of ritual contexts occurred early among the Gulf Olmec, it became a rather consistent structural feature in view of the continuation of celt offerings without metates in the Middle Pre-Classic period at La Venta.

Thus manos and metates, like celts and monuments, were acquired from distant banks of raw material, but grinding tools were not placed in public or sacred offerings except for the earliest and least formalized Manatí offerings. Yet both grinding stones and celts were crucial in the transformation of the "raw to the cooked." If this parallel is accepted, we have an indication of differential social valuation of subsistence stones. Rather than conforming to a general, cosmological notion of sacred stones, I suggest that celts and grinding tools had meanings that developed from their historical roles, specifically from the extraction of resources from nature, and initially both were selected as part of a narrow range of materials offered back, perhaps to the underworld. Grinding tools were eventually excluded from public ritual practices. We can view subsistence stones as conveying information about changing social relations as well as ritual.[1]

Massive Stones

Mass in carved stone has several potential implications. Monument size can be viewed in economic terms. The labor investment to quarry and move multi-ton blocks may have made recycling of stone attractive to Gulf Olmec leaders, as Cyphers (this volume) remarks. If we anticipate a reduction sequence of monuments that shrank steadily in size through recarving, it is striking that the largest—thrones (altars), heads, and some stelae—emphasize people and leadership themes, while medium and smaller-sized carvings also represent creatures, including supernaturals, with more strictly mythic or sacred themes (compare Grove, this volume). Massive stones seem to have been devoted first to key presentations about leadership, supporting Grove and Gillespie's (1992) characterization of the Gulf Olmec tradition as emphasizing a cult of the ruler.

However, massive stones are more than just "fuss and feathers," that is, the sacred-social appurtenances of the person and prestige of the ruler. Trigger's (1990) exposition of the rationale for monumentality stresses its flagrant viola-

---

[1]Graham (1992) traces possible later historical links among Olmec cached celts, those used in lowland Maya kingly regalia, and Costa Rican celts adapted as ornaments and grave goods. He notes that in Costa Rica ornately carved metates also developed as symbols of chiefly power and wealth. He interprets such objects as "a new language of power"; special labor invested in them represents wealth—"a concrete index of the devotion and direction of past human labor" (Graham 1992: 169). In comparison, I view the Manatí metates and celts as symbolic because of their transformational roles. However, their fabrication from imported stone is congruent with Graham's perspective. Graham (1992: 175) interprets later, special celts in Costa Rica as symbolic of agriculture, warfare, and sacrifice. The earliest examples at Manatí, however, cannot be directly tied to warfare and sacrifice, except that they, like other items and some human bone, are offerings in a sacred place.

tion of the "principle of least effort." Monumentality was conspicuous consumption that objectified the social power used to mobilize human labor. The monumental achieved a universal message by its violation of a universally understood principle. Trigger (1990) continues with a consideration of additional aspects of monumentality and elite legitimization, both across and within classes. Such messages about social power have many ramifications (e.g., Ringle, this volume, and Grove, this volume, for explorations of how settlement space was orchestrated symbolically with major monuments and architecture).

Another universal dimension is important for understanding Olmec carved monuments. In a calculus developed by Helms (1993), geographic, temporal, and spiritual distances occur along horizontal and vertical spatial dimensions and on a time scale (calibrated through events). The distant and less known is equated with the supernatural or sacred. These concepts can have expression at varied scales, with space divided along the same lines when domestic and community or settlement space is contrasted with natural surroundings.

In Mesoamerican schema, there was a vertical axis along which the underworld, the earthly plane, and the celestial world were closely articulated; the surrounding natural environment—its hills, springs, or caves—offered access to the underworld. For this reason, natural features of the landscape likely were seen as cosmologically significant. Massive stone monuments have the weight, solidity, and durability of immutable parts of the landscape. Massive stones brought to riverine sites on the coastal plain have a character different from that of tools. Their limited portability assimilates them to the landscape and nature, and, once they are carved, either their visible (or historically remembered) imagery or their embodiment of qualities of nature may affect their treatment. Perhaps this leads us back to "sacred stones," but only big ones. By sheer size they assimilate to the landscape and become part of the essential; any observer would have to mobilize a social effort to shift them. The same is true for massive architecture.

Trigger (1990) comments on the communication of power by physical scale that can be apprehended personally and thus universally, for example, by observers who walk across enormous architectural constructions. Love (this volume) comments on the fixity and obtrusiveness of monumental architecture. Surely physical scale is as important a universal message as conspicuous consumption. Gulf Olmec stone monuments at riverine sites fuse the qualities ascribed to the geographically distant with the fixity of the natural landscape where outcrops and hills do not change appreciably in the span of a human life. Alteration of the natural and sacred transforms it into part of the immediate social realm and requires mobilization of social action, a fitting display and confirmation of a ruler's power. Helms (1993) discusses the importance of transformation, travel, and the distant, dangerous, and dimly understood for the expression of a ruler's authority.

A recycling of stone monuments does not undermine these ideas until the stone is so decreased in size that it no longer is particularly difficult to move, although even small carvings retain their special qualities derived from importation. For centers located near stone sources, like Tres Zapotes, monumental stone presents a message derived from physical scale, not distance.

Cowgill (1993) asked whether we can elaborate a "middle range theory of mind" that identifies general cognitive principles shaping cultural particulars of the archaeological record. If there are universally accessible messages in massive stones and in the monumental in general, we can discern some elements of such a theory. Gulf Olmec monuments at riverine centers were obtained from deposits well removed spatially; their presence drew the horizontally distant, more mysterious, and sacred to the center in a violation of the principle of least effort. Monumental sculptures and constructions are material symbols in an accessible, universal language of physical size, weight, and durability. In a Mesoamerican context, at least, these monuments called attention to the vertical axis involving celestial and underground regions—both, like the stones, relatively inaccessible; monument size and relative immobility provided a link with features of the landscape that naturalized cultural and social messages in worked stone. Monumental stones, suitably manipulated, constituted a nexus of social and sacred statements. The sacred quality of massive worked stone, which required labor mobilization for its expression, became thoroughly entangled with its social messages.

FLOWING WATER

... where lies a coffer burly all of blocks ...
And the water warbles over into, filleted with glassy grassy quicksilvery shives ...

Gerald Manley Hopkins, in Gardner 1963: 86

As Sullivan notes (1991: 207), "water comes in different forms; its containers are essential structures of the cosmos. Waters inhabit the sky and fill its clouds, waters dwell in named mountains, spill out of mountain springs and caves, cascade down." The El Manatí spring analyzed by Ortíz and Rodríguez formed a natural shrine illustrating the same preoccupation with spring water suggested by Cyphers for the San Lorenzo drain system, which Krotser (1973) also viewed as ritually important. Cyphers' excavations indicate that one San Lorenzo pond postdates the Pre-Classic, making this aspect of water control question-able in the Olmec repertoire.

One perspective on water control emphasizes its practical functions. Water is not a scarce resource in Gulf Olmec country, although water quality is variable because of seasonal flooding and the sediment load of rivers. In some Veracruz locales today, such as in the Mixtequilla on the west side of the Lower Papaloapan basin, hand-dug wells tap the water table, providing domestic water and allow-ing pump or "pot" irrigation during the dry season. Whether this possibility existed in southern Veracruz and Tabasco is not clear. In a hot climate, high water consumption is important physiologically, and water is often used for more frequent bathing.

Do these functional considerations help us understand the San Lorenzo stone channels and the Manatí spring offerings? Not really. Rather than performing a unique practical function, natural springs probably embodied a dramatic emis-sion of water from the underworld and, symbolically, the dynamic quality of water in seasonal rains and floods that provided for agricultural success and regulated aspects of fishing and travel. At least at some sites, the Gulf Olmec were concerned with water and its control and integration into the layout of centers. This may have set in motion a continuing pattern of symbolic water manipulation that can be observed in the trans-Isthmian lowlands. As I indicate below, water was important as part of a simultaneously sacred and practical landscape. Water also figured in architectural planning.

Of Land and Water[2]

To consider the implications of a preoccupation with symbolic water con-trol, I briefly sketch the historical outline of a trans-Isthmian tradition that unfolds in post-Olmec times and contrast it with other parts of Mesoamerica. El Balsamo, a Middle or Late Pre-Classic center on the Pacific Coast of Guate-mala, had a shallow pool constructed on the top of one mound (Clewlow and Wells 1987: 31).[3] At the center of Izapa on the Pacific Coast of Chiapas, a subterranean stone-lined channel enters a boulder-faced, buried reservoir near the largest mound, Mound 60. A surface pond is positioned in front of this mound (Lowe, Lee, and Martínez 1982: 167–263). At Izapa small springs flow to the Río Izapa, and effigy and plain troughs and basins occur in some num-

---

[2] This adapts a phrase from Nietschmann's (1973) title.

[3] Shook (Shook and Hatch 1978) interpreted a low area immediately west of El Balsamo as a formal reservoir, but it is not integrated with central architecture and remains undated. Shook observed it in the rainy season and represents it as rectangular. In the dry season this form was not apparent to me.

bers, some placed to catch or direct spring water. Lowe, Lee, and Martínez (1982: 103) interpret the troughs and basins as evidence of concepts of sacred spring water. Pond construction is continued in some Classic period centers on the Pacific coast; Voorhies' (1989: 105) map of Acapetahua shows two such features near major mounds in the Classic portion of the site.

By the Late Pre-Classic to Classic period on the Gulf Coast, pond systems became a fixture of public space and site planning in the Mixtequilla region. Ponds, often squared off, are integrated with formal architecture. At Cerro de las Mesas, temple platforms and other public constructions ring a formal pond system (Stark and Heller 1991), while at Azuzules, another Classic center in the Mixtequilla, a pond surrounds the formal construction, making the center almost an island (Stark, unpublished field data). At centers along the Lower Río Cotaxtla, Daneels (1997) recorded architectural arrangements in which slope and connections to the river channel would have recharged ponds with water and fish during the rainy season. The geographic and temporal extent of these Classic period patterns in the Gulf lowlands deserves further study. In northern Veracruz at Tajín, probably in the Epi-Classic or Early Postclassic, stream diversion or runoff catchments from constructions at Tajín Chico fed an artificial cistern that may be depicted on low-relief carvings (Cortés 1989). The Tajín cistern and drains reflect a combination of practical and symbolic functions, improving drainage from built areas and establishing a body of water for rituals adjacent to public buildings. Generally in the trans-Isthmian lowlands, encirclement and horizontal axial proximity of water and sacred buildings were emphasized.

The symbolic importance of springs and other aquatic features is documented in the Mexican highlands as well, but with somewhat different expression. The Middle Pre-Classic center of Chalcatzingo, Morelos, was located adjacent to a spring, and there is water symbolism on bas-reliefs at the site. The dammed and partly channeled stream flow draining the hill behind the center is fed by a spring. The stream seems to have been directed into agricultural production below, but also to have fed a series of ponds, where it was stored for domestic use or pot irrigation on terraces (Angulo 1993: 195–208). Perhaps the closest parallel to trans-Isthmian features is ponds constructed inside caves and rockshelters on the hillside above the center, where the pools likely served in a ritual setting (Angulo 1993: 198; Grove and Cyphers 1987: 53–54).

At Teopantecuanitlán, Guerrero, also a center with Olmec-related art, a stone-lined channel probably drained an impoundment pond fed by runoff and a spring originating in the hill behind the site (Martínez Donjuan 1986: 64–65). At these two highland sites, practical functions of water control have overshadowed the symbolic qualities of spring water and pools in archaeological interpretations.

At Cholula, Puebla, construction of the Great Pyramid began as early as the Late Pre-Classic period; the pyramid is situated at a spring that still supplies water in wells at a shrine (McCafferty and McCafferty n.d.). Later in the Terminal Pre-Classic and Classic periods at Teotihuacan in the Basin of Mexico, river canalization played a symbolic role in the architectural layout of the city, as analyzed by Sugiyama (1993). Springs occur today, mainly within the southern portion of the city, but do not seem to have been a major focus of public architecture (Millon 1973: 38, 47). Stone drainpipes within the cave-tunnel under the Pyramid of the Sun suggested the presence of a spring to Hayden (1981: 3), but other supporting evidence of a spring is unavailable. Barba et al. (1990: 431, 435) argue that some other cave-tunnels below the city contained springs. Apart from the ambiguous case of the Pyramid of the Sun, springs do not seem to have been magnets for architectural effort, even though sacred springs (or water imagery) are portrayed in a Tepantitla residential mural (Kubler 1967: figs. 4, 5; Hayden 1981: 5). Millon, Drewitt, and Cowgill (1973: 9, 17, 18, 77) suggest four reservoirs occurred in the city; they are located among residential compounds rather than integrated into central precincts, but two are near major structures, the Ciudadela and the Pyramid of the Moon.

Still later in the Post-Classic period, the position of Tenochtitlán in the lake system of the Basin of Mexico and the aquatic symbolism of some offerings in the Templo Mayor have been suggested to signify a cosmogram (Broda 1987; Matos 1987). Thus a series of major centers in the central highlands demonstrates an interest both in sacred natural water sources and in the integration of architecture with them. Perhaps this tradition underlies the Nahuatl concept for "city-state," *altepetl*. "The word itself is a slightly altered form of the metaphorical doublet *in atl, in tepetl,* 'the water(s), the mountain(s),' and thus it refers in the first instance to territory, but what is meant is primarily an organization of people holding sway over a given territory" (Lockhart 1992: 14). However, with the possible exception of a pit or well within the Ciudadela at Teotihuacan (Sugiyama 1993: 121), these highland cases do not follow in detail the layout principles discernible in the trans-Isthmian lowlands, where the proximity of pools of water and sacred buildings was emphasized.

The integration of artificial water storage features with public architecture is not usually handled with such overt symbolism in the Maya Lowlands as in the trans-Isthmian lowlands. Practical functions of water storage are more obvious, and reservoirs are commonly placed near, but not formally integrated with, the layout of public architecture; instead, reservoirs are positioned to draw upon the catchment offered by formal complexes (Scarborough 1993). Edzna, Campeche, is an exception (Matheny et al. 1983: 67–82, 196, 200). Canals there may have had multiple functions, such as providing drainage, domestic water, transport, aquatic resources, and defense (by surrounding the "fortress" at Edzna). However, Matheny et al. (1983: 80–81) note that the Great Canal is aligned toward a major building complex, Cinco Pisos, for 3 (of 12) km, as are several other canals. It is likely that canal orientation (or building placement) was in part symbolic. Two symmetrically placed ponds within the "fortress" also suggest a combination of practical and symbolic functions (Matheny et al. 1983: map 9). In sum, natural sources of water had symbolic importance at many Maya centers, for example, the cenote at Chichén Itzá (Tozzer 1957: 199), but, Edzna excepted, major architecture was not geared to incorporate bodies of water. "Adjacency" and convenience seem to be featured.

To what should we ascribe a continued interest in and elaboration of aquatic features in public space in the trans-Isthmian lowlands? Ponds have numerous potential functions: borrow pits for fill, reservoirs in the dry season (uncontaminated by stock), fish tanks, defensive isolation of the center if they encircle it, but, above all, a cosmologically significant setting for centers. Ponds contributed to an integrated arrangement of constructed earthen space with its buildings, interments, and offerings positioned beside the watery realm on which the land may have been conceived to have rested. Centers as elaborated in the Classic period of south-central Veracruz juxtaposed land and water in a fashion calculated to override the varied practical conveniences that ponds also offered.

Despite the cosmological implications of centers built "of land and water," human intervention is obvious. Leaders organized or commanded the construction and thus inserted their presence into the order of the cosmos, despite the fact that these twin natural elements can be appreciated easily from the banks of rivers or along the Gulf coastline. As with monumental carving, architectural statements sculpted with earth and water sought to incorporate the essential qualities of the landscape and cosmos, yet they remain quintessentially social in their communications.

In sum, I have explored how the manipulation of stones in ritual and the design of public space sought to naturalize social actions and relations in terms of fundamental properties of the cosmos—the world both as conceived and experienced. A tension between the particular and the general was inevitable. Because architectural and carved stone monuments were so intimately linked to early Gulf Olmec leadership in social hierarchies (as well as in post-Olmec societies), it is reasonable to view the ritual control of stones and water sources as the outcome of strategies of legitimation, whether consciously undertaken or simply favored in the varied efforts of leaders to elaborate and hold power. I doubt that the tension between the particular, or social, and general, or cosmological, is simply the optional variation in perspectives that we, as archaeologists, can bring to bear in analyzing the material record. Connected to a strategy of legitimization, this tension is an inherent outcome of past actions.

STUDYING RITUAL, SOCIAL IDENTITY, AND COSMOLOGY

One problem with interpretative approaches that seek meaning in ritual, social identity, and cosmology is to decide which among many meanings are convincing. This introduces dilemmas raised explicitly by postprocessualist archaeology in recent years, although Mesoamericanist investigations of symbolism have a very long history.

From a postprocessual perspective, the material record is supercharged—not merely suited to analysis of economic or social information but suffused with culturally constituted meaning governing and negotiated by people, past and present. There are multiple meanings, and our own meanings intervene between us and the record from the past. From this perspective, there is a profusion of "voices" from and about the past. For example, regarding Gulf Olmec imagery, the jaguar, toad, rattlesnake, caiman, possibly shark, and fish have spoken to someone, at least (Coe 1989; Furst 1981; Grove 1987; Joyce et al. 1991; Luckert 1976; Stocker, Meltzoff, and Armsey 1980), yet it is impossible for all of these interpretations to be accurate about the same material objects unless, as sometimes suggested, Olmec representations blend attributes from this bestiary. Complementary distributions of motifs on different kinds of vessels imply that at least some of these interpretations apply to different representations (Joyce et al. 1991).

In contrast to this example of a degree of cacophony in "voices," recently Lounsbury (1991: 810) wrote in regard to Proskouriakoff's (1960) and Berlin's (1958) pivotal work on Maya writing, which had countered conventional wisdom: "Their papers embodied such elegant detective work, were so thoroughly researched and carefully crafted, and had their conclusions stated so cautiously, that no knowledgeable reader could fail to appreciate them and be persuaded." The symposium papers in this volume recognize both diversity and shared patterns in the Pre-Classic period and suggest that we can indeed discriminate among alternative accounts of past symbolism, ritual, social identity, and cosmology in terms of how much evidence is accounted for and how parsimoniously.

The new analyses and discoveries reported in this volume are particularly exciting with regard to the detail and variety that are recognized for social groups and ritual activities. Many new questions can be raised as a result. Does El Manatí reflect smaller-scale community ritual (people who did not haul in massive stones), different rituals at springs, or simply diversity in practices among communities? Does the recycling of San Lorenzo area monuments and the possibility of changing monument arrangements imply diversity and fluidity in Olmec ritual practices? Or does it mean that the instability of chiefdoms led later rulers to capitalize on the raw material of earlier monuments, reverently perhaps, but subverting them to their own sculptural programs?

Instability among Pre-Classic societies is a particularly crucial topic that I hope will be clarified with continuing research. Part of what is at stake are competing groups—some of the multiple "voices" in the past. Cohen (1978: 56–57) has argued that chiefdoms are unstable and fissiparous and that states are not, because they effectively combat such tendencies. Likely this contrast is overdrawn, but it is a significant issue. Although the lifespan of centers is not directly tied to the orderly succession of rulers, fragmentation of a chiefdom might be expected to "demote" a paramount center severely.

In apparent contradiction to the evidence of instability among historic chiefdoms, a number of early centers in the Mesoamerican Early and Middle Pre-Classic continued to be important during a fairly lengthy span of time and do not suggest the degree of instability predicted by some theories. Low population densities during the Early and Middle Pre-Classic periods point to favorable conditions for agriculturalists in respect of available land; these conditions argue for expectations concerning the stability of social hierarchies different from those exemplified during historic times. Perhaps dissident aspirants to high office more easily relocated, leaving centers and factions that continued their roles. These are among the questions that must be left for future research. In establishing new findings and demonstrating the importance of new questions, the studies in this volume highlight the importance of ritual, social identity, and cosmology in understanding the Mesoamerican Pre-Classic.

Acknowledgments I thank the contributors for the stimulus their papers provided, as well as David Grove, Rosemary Joyce, and Dumbarton Oaks for their invitation to participate in the symposium "Ritual, Social Identity, and Cosmology." John Chance, George Cowgill, David Grove, Joyce Marcus, Geoffrey McCafferty, Vernon Scarborough, Saburo Sugiyama, and Barbara Voorhies provided helpful comments or information, but they are not responsible for the content of this essay.

BIBLIOGRAPHY

ANGULO V., JORGE
    1993   Water Control and Communal Labor during the Formative and Classic Periods in Central Mexico (ca. 1000 B.C.–A.D. 650). In *Economic Aspects of Water Management in the Prehispanic New World, Research in Economic Anthropology,* suppl. 7 (Vernon L. Scarborough and Barry L. Isaac, eds.): 151–220. JAI Press, Greenwich, Conn.

BARBA P., L. A., LINDA MANZANILLA, R. CHAVEZ, LUIS FLORES, AND A. J. ARZATE
    1990   Caves and Tunnels at Teotihuacan, Mexico: A Geological Phenomenon of Archaeological Interest. In *Archaeological Geology of North America* (N. P. Lasca and J. Donahue, eds.): 431–438. Centennial Special Volume 4, Geological Society of America, Boulder, Colo.

BERLIN, HEINRICH
    1958   El glifo "emblema" en las inscripciones Mayas. *Journal de la Société des Américanistes,* n.s., 47: 111–119. Paris.

BRODA, JOHANNA
    1987   The Provenience of the Offerings: Tribute and *Cosmovision.* In *The Aztec Templo Mayor* (Elizabeth Hill Boone, ed.):185–209. Dumbarton Oaks, Washington, D.C.

CLARK, JOHN E., AND MICHAEL BLAKE
    1994   The Power of Prestige: Competitive Generosity and the Emergence of Rank Societies in Lowland Mesoamerica. In *Factional Competition and Political Development in the New World* (Elizabeth M. Brumfiel and John W. Fox, eds.): 17–30. Cambridge University Press, Cambridge.

CLEWLOW, C. WILLIAM, JR., AND HELEN FAIRMAN WELLS
    1987   El Balsamo: A Middle Preclassic Complex on the South Coast of Guatemala. In *The Periphery of the Southeastern Classic Maya Realm* (Gary W. Pahl, ed.): 27–40. UCLA Latin American Studies 61. University of California, Los Angeles.

COE, MICHAEL D.
    1989   The Olmec Heartland: Evolution of Ideology. In *Regional Perspectives on the Olmec* (Robert J. Sharer and David C. Grove, eds.): 68–82. Cambridge University Press, Cambridge.

COE, MICHAEL D., AND RICHARD A. DIEHL
    1980   *In the Land of the Olmec,* vol. 1: *The Archaeology of San Lorenzo Tenochtitlan.* University of Texas Press, Austin.

COHEN, RONALD
    1978   State Origins: A Reappraisal. In *The Early State* (Henri J. M. Claessen and Peter Skalnik, eds.): 31–75. Mouton, The Hague.

CORTÉS HERNANDEZ, JAIME
    1989   Elementos para un intento de interpretación del desarrollo hidráulico del Tajín. *Arqueología* 5: 175–190.

COWGILL, GEORGE L.
    1993   Distinguished Lecture in Archeology: Beyond Criticizing New Archeology. *American Anthropologist* 95 (3): 551–573.

DANEELS, ANNICK

1997   Settlement History in the Lower Cotaxtla Basin, Veracruz, Mexico. In *Olmec to Aztec: Settlement Patterns in the Ancient Gulf Lowlands* (Barbara L. Stark and Philip J. Arnold III, eds.): 206–252. University of Arizona Press, Tucson.

DRUCKER, PHILIP, ROBERT F. HEIZER, AND ROBERT J. SQUIER

1959   *Excavations at La Venta, Tabasco, 1955.* Smithsonian Institution, Bureau of American Ethnology, Bulletin 170. Washington, D.C.

FURST, PETER T.

1981   Jaguar Baby or Toad Mother: A New Look at an Old Problem in Olmec Iconography. In *The Olmec and Their Neighbors* (Elizabeth P. Benson, ed.): 149–162. Dumbarton Oaks, Washington, D.C.

GARDNER, W. H.

1963   *Poems and Prose of Gerard Manley Hopkins.* Penguin, Harmondsworth, England.

GRAHAM, MARK MILLER

1992   Art-Tools and the Language of Power in the Early Art of the Atlantic Watershed of Costa Rica. In *Wealth and Hierarchy in the Intermediate Area* (Frederick W. Lange, ed.): 165–206. Dumbarton Oaks, Washington, D.C.

GROVE, DAVID C.

1987   "Torches," "Knuckle Dusters," and the Legitimization of Formative Period Rulership. *Mexicon* 9 (3): 60–65.

GROVE, DAVID C., AND ANN CYPHERS GUILLÉN

1987   The Excavations. In *Ancient Chalcatzingo* (David C. Grove, ed.): 21–55. University of Texas Press, Austin.

GROVE, DAVID C., AND SUSAN D. GILLESPIE

1992   Ideology and Evolution at the Pre-State Level: Formative Period Mesoamerica. In *Ideology and Pre-Columbian Civilizations* (Arthur A. Demarest and Geoffrey W. Conrad, eds.): 15–36. School of American Research Press, Santa Fe.

HAYDEN, DORIS

1981   Caves, Gods, and Myths: World-View and Planning in Teotihuacan. In *Mesoamerican Sites and World-Views* (Elizabeth P. Benson, ed.): 1–39. Dumbarton Oaks, Washington, D.C.

HELMS, MARY W.

1987   Art Styles and Interaction Spheres in Central America and the Caribbean: Polished Black Wood in the Greater Antilles. In *Chiefdoms in the Americas* (Robert D. Drennan and Carlos A. Uribe, eds.): 67–84. University Press of America, Lanham.

1993   *Craft and the Kingly Ideal: Art, Trade, and Power.* University of Texas Press, Austin.

JOYCE, ROSEMARY A., RICHARD EDGING, KARL LORENZ, AND SUSAN D. GILLESPIE

1991   Olmec Bloodletting: An Iconographic Study. In *Sixth Palenque Round Table, 1986* (Merle Greene Robertson and Virginia M. Fields, eds.): 143–150. University of Oklahoma Press, Norman.

KROTSER, G. RAMÓN

1973   El Agua Ceremonial de los Olmecas. *Boletín* 6 (ser. 2): 43–48. Instituto Nacional de Antropología e Historia.

KUBLER, GEORGE
  1967   *The Iconography of the Art of Teotihuacan.* Studies in Pre-Columbian Art and
          Archaeology 4. Dumbarton Oaks, Washington, D.C.

LOCKHART, JAMES
  1992   *The Nahuas after the Conquest.* Stanford University Press, Stanford.

LOUNSBURY, FLOYD G.
  1991   Distinguished Lecture: Recent Work in the Decipherment of Palenque's
          Hieroglyphic Inscriptions. *American Anthropologist* 93 (4): 809–825.

LOWE, GARETH W., THOMAS A. LEE, JR., AND EDUARDO MARTÍNEZ ESPINOSA
  1982   *Izapa: An Introduction to the Ruins and Monuments.* Papers of the New World
          Archaeological Foundation 31. Brigham Young University, Provo.

LUCKERT, KARL V.
  1976   *Olmec Religion: A Key to Middle America and Beyond.* University of Oklahoma
          Press, Norman.

MARTÍNEZ DONJUAN, GUADALUPE
  1986   Teopantecuanitlán. In *Primer Coloquio de Arqueología e Etnohistoria del Estado
          de Guerrero* (Roberto Cervantes-Delgado, comp.): 55–80. Instituto Nacional
          de Antropología e Historia and Gobierno del Estado de Guerrero, México,
          D.F.

MATHENY, RAY T., DEANNE L. GURR, DONALD W. FORSYTH, AND F. RICHARD HAUCK
  1983   *Investigations at Edzna, Campeche. Mexico,* vol. 1, pt. 1: *The Hydraulic System.*
          Papers of the New World Archaeological Foundation 46. Brigham Young
          University, Provo.

MATOS MOCTEZUMA, EDUARDO
  1987   Symbolism of the Templo Mayor. In *The Aztec Templo Mayor* (Elizabeth Hill
          Boone, ed.): 185–209. Dumbarton Oaks, Washington, D.C.

MCCAFFERTY, SHARISSE D., AND GEOFFREY G. MCCAFFERTY
  n.d.   Tlachihualtepetl: The Great Pyramid at Cholula as Sacred Landscape. Paper
          presented at the 59th annual meeting of the Society for American Archaeology,
          Anaheim, 1994.

MILLON, RENÉ
  1973   *The Teotihuacan Map,* pt. 1: *Text.* University of Texas Press, Austin.

MILLON, RENE, R. BRUCE DREWITT, AND GEORGE L. COWGILL
  1973   *The Teotihuacan Map,* pt. 2: *Maps.* University of Texas Press, Austin.

NIETSCHMANN, BERNARD
  1973   *Between Land and Water: The Subsistence Ecology of the Miskito Indians, Eastern
          Nicaragua.* Seminar Press, New York.

ORTÍZ C., PONCIANO
  1993   Semblanza arqueológica de Veracruz. *Arqueología Mexicana* 1 (5): 16–23.

ORTÍZ C., PONCIANO, AND MARÍA DEL CARMEN RODRÍGUEZ
  1989   Proyecto Manatí 1989. *Arqueología* (ser. 2) 1: 23–52.

PORTER, JAMES B.
  1990   Las cabezas colosales Olmecas como altares reesculpidos: "mutilación,"
          revolución y reesculpido. *Arqueología* (ser. 2) 3: 91–97.

Proskouriakoff, Tatiana
    1960   Historical Implications of a Pattern of Dates at Piedras Negras. *American Antiquity* 25: 454–475.

Rosenthal, M. L. (ed.)
    1986   *Selected Poems and Three Plays of William Butler Yeats,* 3rd ed. Collier Books, New York.

Scarborough, Vernon L.
    1993   Water Management in the Southern Maya Lowlands: An Accretive Model for the Engineered Landscape. In *Economic Aspects of Water Management in the Prehispanic New World, Research in Economic Anthropology,* suppl. 7 (Vernon L. Scarborough and Barry L. Isaac, eds.): 17–69. JAI Press, Greenwich, Conn.

Shook, Edwin M., and Marion P. Hatch
    1978   The Ruins of El Basamo, Department of Escuintla, Guatemala. *Journal of New World Archaeology* 3 (1): 1–38.

Stark, Barbara L., and Lynette Heller
    1991   Cerro de las Mesas Revisited: Survey in 1984–1985. In *Settlement Archaeology of Cerro de las Mesas, Veracruz, Mexico* (Barbara L. Stark, ed.): 1–25. University of California, Institute of Archaeology Monograph 34. Los Angeles.

Stocker, Terry, Sarah Meltzoff, and Steve Armsey
    1980   Crocodilians and Olmecs: Further Interpretations in Formative Period Iconography. *American Antiquity* 45: 740–758.

Sugiyama, Saburo
    1993   Worldview Materialized in Teotihuacan, Mexico. *Latin American Antiquity* 4 (2): 103–129.

Sullivan, Lawrence E.
    1991   Reflections on the Miraculous Waters of Tenochtitlan. In *To Change Place: Aztec Ceremonial Landscapes* (Davíd Carrasco, ed.): 205–211. University Press of Colorado, Niwot.

Tozzer, Alfred M.
    1957   *Chichen Itza and Its Cenote of Sacrifice: A Comparative Study of Contemporaneous Maya and Toltec.* Harvard University, Memoirs of the Peabody Museum of Archaeology and Ethnology 11. Cambridge, Mass.

Trigger, Bruce G.
    1990   Monumental Architecture: A Thermodynamic Explanation of Symbolic Behaviour. *World Archaeology* 22 (2): 119–132.

Voorhies, Barbara
    1989   A Model of the Pre-Aztec Political System of the Soconusco. In *Ancient Trade and Tribute: Economies of the Soconusco Region of Mesoamerica* (Barbara Voorhies, ed.): 95–129. University of Utah Press, Salt Lake City.

Index